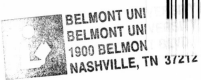

Donne, Castiglione,
and the Poetry of Courtliness

Donne, Castiglione,

and the

Poetry of Courtliness

Peter DeSa Wiggins

*Indiana
University
Press*

BLOOMINGTON & INDIANAPOLIS

This book is a publication of
Indiana University Press
601 North Morton Street
Bloomington, Indiana 47404-3797 USA

www.indiana.edu/~iupress

Telephone orders 800-842-6796
Fax orders 812-855-7931
Orders by email iuporder@indiana.edu

Library of Congress Cataloging-in-Publication Data

Wiggins, Peter DeSa.
Donne, Castiglione, and the poetry of courtliness / Peter DeSa Wiggins.
p.   cm.
Includes bibliographical references and index.
ISBN 0-253-33814-X (alk. paper)
1. Donne, John, 1572–1631—Political and social views. 2. Politics and literature—Great Britain—History—17th century. 3. Castiglione, Baldassarre, conte, 1478–1529. Libro del cortegiano. 4. Castiglione, Baldassarre, conte, 1478–1529—Influence. 5. Donne, John, 1572–1631—Knowledge—Literature. 6. Political poetry, English—History and criticism. 7. English poetry—Italian influences. 8. Courts and courtiers in literature. 9. Courtesy in literature.   I. Title.

PR2248 .W48 2000
821'.3—dc21
00-040743

1 2 3 4 5   05 04 03 02 01 00

CONTENTS

To the memory of two great teachers,
Frederick Dupee and Maurice Valency

ACKNOWLEDGMENTS

Most of my debts are to the College of William and Mary, which has allowed me to develop as a scholar at my own pace and has subsidized the writing of this book with two Faculty Research Assignments. Generations of alert, inquisitive students in English 324 peer out from these pages. Without them I could not have pursued this study for so many years nor would it have any merit. My colleagues—Terry Meyers, Robert P. Maccubbin, Chris Bongie, and Adam Potkay—offered advice and encouragement when it was most needed, and, although it is customary in this place to attribute the felicities of one's work to a long list of generous persons and shoulder sole responsibility oneself for the defects, Adam Potkay's assistance in sorting out matters historical was so pervasive as to defeat my powers of discrimination. To attempt to credit everyone who vitally contributed to my thinking about John Donne would involve dredging up decades-old memories of incidents such as the debate (which I stumbled into at the mailboxes in the English office and which got louder and louder) with my colleague of that era, Margie Westerman, over the mental powers of the female addressees of certain Donne poems. Thanks, Margie, belatedly something clicked, and thanks to everyone else. My thanks also go out to Dave Morrill, Bonnie Chandler, Amy Scherdin, and Michael B. Holt for their patient support in my long struggle with word-processing technology (and for keeping a straight face).

A Newberry Library National Endowment for the Humanities Fellowship during the 1989–90 academic year and a Huntington Library Research Grant during the summer of 1990 enabled me to produce a first draft, which Elizabeth S. Donno submitted to the same scrutiny received once upon a time by my M. A. thesis when I was her student at Columbia University. If this book has any appeal outside its area of subspecialization, the multidisciplinary Fellows Seminar at the Newberry Library, where I first presented my various rough ideas, deserves most of the credit. In the spring of 1990, an invitation, arranged by Jane Tylus, to lecture at the University of Wisconsin enabled me to refine some of those ideas. It was John Bender, during his NEH Summer Seminar at Stanford University in 1980, who first directed my attention to English portrait miniatures. I owe my abiding interest in comparison of the arts to him, to my fellow seminar participants, and to James V. Mirollo, who brought Mannerism and the Baroque to Columbia University's Department of English and Comparative Literature in time for me to choose it as a field in my doctoral exams.

Substantially revised versions of the following articles form parts of chapters 2, 3, and 4: "The Love Quadrangle: Tibullus 1.6 and Donne's 'Lay Ideot,'" *Papers on Language and Literature* 16, 2 (Spring 1980): 142–150; "Aire and Angels: Incarnations of Love," *English Literary Renaissance* 12, 1 (Winter 1982): 87–101; "G. P. Lomazzo's *Trattato dell'arte della pittura, scultura, et architettura* and John Donne's Poetics: 'The Flea' and 'Aire and Angels' as Portrait Miniatures in the Style of Hilliard," *Studies in Iconography* 7–8 (1981–82): 269–288; "Preparing Towards Lucy: 'A Nocturnall' as Palinode," *Studies in Philology* 84: 4 (Fall 1987): 483–493. Listing these reminds me of how long I have struggled with the enigma of John Donne, how long it took me to see even a glimmer of light, how crude my early efforts were to coax that light into visibility to anyone but myself, and how much I owe to the brilliant publications of predecessors too numerous to mention here but whose labors I am now for the first time able to appreciate. If books can be friends, then Dwight Cathcart's *The Doubting Conscience* and Donald Guss's *John Donne, Petrarchist* have been very good ones to me over the years.

Lastly, were it not for the serenity afforded me by a teaching exchange at Leiden University in the spring of 1998, the inspiration I received from my students there, the friendly welcome from colleagues in the English faculty, I might not have had the fortitude to produce yet another, and a final, draft of this study. A cozy apartment on Vreewijkstraat, the canals and gardens of Leiden, and a little coffee shop off the Rapenburg made it possible.

Donne, Castiglione,
and the Poetry of Courtliness

Introduction

Poetry, in this latter age, hath proved but a mean mistress to such
as have wholly addicted themselves to her family. They who have
but saluted her on the by, and now and then tendered their visits,
she hath done much for, and advanced in the way of their own
professions (both the law and the gospel) beyond all they could
have hoped or done for themselves without her favor.

—Ben Jonson[1]

To write about John Donne almost four centuries after his death is to get
caught in something like a holy war (*polemic* seems too tame a word), and
I am aware that the following pages are unlikely to please either camp.
The field is divided between those for whom Donne was an alienated
radical aloof to profane matters and those who insist that he was quite
the opposite, an ambitious conformist using poetry, as Jonson suggests,
in order to crash the establishment. Champions of the radical Donne
include Earl Miner, Arnold Stein, Anthony Low, and Richard Strier; of
the conformist Donne, John Carey, Arthur F. Marotti, and Jonathan
Goldberg.[2] The radicals are strengthened by the subtlety of their readings, weakened by their selective use of historical evidence. Conversely,
by embracing every detail of Donne's social background, the conformists have unearthed new knowledge and shed new light on the old, but
their readings are often so reductionist as to provoke embarrassing comments of this sort:

> When the magic word "power" appears in Donne studies we almost
> always find a cruelly emptied out, vitiated Donne—the Donne of
> Carey, or the Donne of Marotti—who has nothing in him except sim-
> plistic ambitions and an immense appetite for exhibiting his wretched
> plight before a coterie of self-pitying no-accounts . . . or the Donne of
> Goldberg, cringing self-interestedly before the absolutist pretensions
> of James.[3]

One should be able—along with Jonson—to read Donne's secular poetry as expressing social concerns and even as having agency in a bid for
political influence without diminishing it beyond recognition and call-

ing down scorn on oneself. However, in the present state of Donne studies, Donne's mind and art appear to be unsafe in the neighborhood of his
life, and the life at risk of being consumed by the fictions that Donne
produced. Donne fits rather well Jonson's description of the poetic amateur whose verse could give a boost to a career in church or state; however, to Jonson, Donne was also "longer a-knowing than most wits do
live" and a judge whose approval could seal one's title to be regarded as
a poet. Clearly Jonson admired Donne as a poet and yet was able at the
same time—as vexing to him as it may now and then have been—to contemplate Donne as having used his poetry to find a standpoint *inside* the
social establishment from which to view it in a detached, critical way. I
hope to demonstrate in the following pages how Donne might have
achieved that standpoint.

The purpose of this study is to show that Donne's quest for a political career in the late Elizabethan and early Jacobean regimes could produce poetic performances of subtlety and originality. The regimes to
which Donne sought membership were spacious, subtle, and daring.
They embraced exceptional individuals and found outlets for them. Drake
and Shakespeare were well served by the world Donne shared with them
and were loyal subjects without being drained of subjective autonomy.
As David Norbrook has demonstrated, a dialectical movement toward
power was available to Donne and his contemporaries.[4] Donne criticism
in both camps seems to have forgotten this, just as it has also forgotten
that the social practices of the Elizabethan period were codified in texts
like *The Courtier* of Castiglione, notable for a dialectical complexity and
elusiveness equal to Donne's own. In the following pages, I shall demonstrate that *The Courtier* constituted a paradigm structure within which
Donne could retain his critical detachment, maintain the highest standards of poetic excellence, and at the same time write a poetry of ambition designed to advance his political interests. I shall treat *The Courtier*
as a langue subtle and flexible enough to give rise to paroles of such force
and grace as Donne's best secular poems. While my study is indebted
throughout to the findings of scholars in the conformist camp, it abandons their methodology, which too often leaves one blinking away confusion as to whether one is reading about John Donne or John Dean.

With the studies of Marotti and Carey in play for well over a decade, there is a compelling need for a less positivist approach than
theirs—one that places their historical findings in perspective with a
poetic achievement of greater complexity than their readings suggest.
Marotti claims that Donne's poems speak "the language of social life at
a particular historical moment,"[5] and hence readers must become ac-
quainted with the special audiences, often the specific individuals, at the
Inns of Court, at York House, at the court itself, and elsewhere in public

life, among whom Donne circulated his poems. However, as this process unfolds in Marotti's study and many useful facts of early modern manuscript culture come to light, the conception of a "language" falls into abeyance, with the consequence that the facts are granted sole explanatory power and we begin to wonder if we are not experiencing a revival of Edmund Gosse. The illocutionary force of Donne's poems—their role in his social gambit—is not to be captured by biographical particularization no matter how minute. While Marotti's study does an excellent job of providing the pieces in the game of poetic self-assertion played by Donne's society, it does not tell us how Donne moved them.

However, even if one is undisturbed by Marotti's methods and one believes that a literary text can be treated as a reflection of its author's biography, one still cannot match the "reflections" in Donne's case with the biographical "realities." The *Songs and Sonnets* contain no internal evidence for dating, and the external evidence, as Carey points out, tells us merely that Donne wrote many of these poems by the time he was forty.[6] There is, of course, Jonson's statement (made, one suspects, in a defensive moment) that Donne wrote his best poems before he was twenty-five,[7] but then we are left wondering which poems Jonson considered Donne's best. The attempt to postulate circumstances of composition for Donne's poems is doomed, and yet the poems continue to show up in positivist criticism categorized as having to do with Donne's marriage or his wife's death or his dismissal from Egerton's service. The better to support a claim that Donne was reinventing love, one study claims that Donne wrote certain undatable poems after his wife died.[8] In another study, the passing reference to a "plaguy bill" in that sardonic roll call of calamities in "The Canonization's" second stanza conjures up the specific 1603–4 plague and hence serves as evidence that the poem is among "The Love Lyrics of the Married Man" written after Donne married Ann More.[9] One effort of the present study will be to avoid the misfeasance which has become almost a trope of Donne studies: to concede in one's notes that a poem is undatable and then to proceed in one's text as if one had not heard oneself. If we are to understand what Donne was doing in writing his poems—if we are to grasp any of his "moves" in the social game—a more discourse-oriented approach to his life, mind, and art is essential.

What "we are typically in search of," says J. G. A. Pocock in his introduction to *Virtue, Commerce, and History*, are "modes of discourse stable enough to be available for the use of more than one discussant and to present the character of games defined by a structure of rules for more than one player."[10] *The Courtier*, whose dialogue Castiglione cast as a game, was the approved repository in Donne's society of the rules of political advancement, of the codes to be observed and the moves to make in that society, and there is much evidence that Donne's contemporaries regarded themselves as "discussants" in a discourse branching out of Castiglione's idealized Urbino into their own London, whose growing corruption intensified their need for an idealized self-conception. *The Courtier*, it is my contention, provides at least some of the important moves for which Marotti's and Carey's studies, and R. C. Bald's biography, have given us the tantalizing pieces. In the absence of these moves, we are left authoring our own past, substituting our own moves for Donne's, and presuming that he was "up to" whatever we would have been "up to" in his circumstances. Not always a bad procedure—if one has the wit and imagination of a Stoppard.

The facts of Donne's life that we have recently been given are indeed tantalizing and absorbing, and as such make urgent the need for controlling paradigms. In *John Donne: Life, Mind, and Art*, John Carey depicts a lurid, post-Watergate Donne, a man of blind ambition, scrambling for a career in government until in his early forties he was forced to accept ordination. Carey hammers on the unsettling truth with which R. C. Bald confronted Donne scholarship: that the great Church of England preacher—the "brave Soule" whose flame "shot such heat and light as burnt" his congregation's "earth" and made their "darkness bright," who "committed holy Rapes" upon their will—would never have come into being if the ambassadorship to Venice had not eluded him. More recently, Paul R. Sellin has argued that Donne exercised diplomatic skills after his ordination. Accompanying Viscount Doncaster to Germany in 1619, he may, when Doncaster was absent, have served as the mission's second in authority.[11] However, even if we had only Bald's biography, we would have plenty of evidence that for about twenty-five years at the close of the sixteenth century and beginning of the seventeenth Donne was ambitiously seeking a place in the political establishment. During roughly the first half of this period, he rose from residency at Oxford and then at Lincoln's Inn to political prominence as Sir Thomas Egerton's secretary and as a member of Elizabeth's last parliament, not without risking his neck in hazardous military adventures in Cadiz and the Azores. Then for almost a dozen years he suffered the consequences of his clandestine marriage to Ann More, never giving up hope of recouping his prospects for civil office until clobbered by royal fiat. Even if at various points during this quarter century Donne had not written his elegies, satires, and lyric poems, his would be a life ripe for novelization. As it is, the stunning dramatic immediacy of his poems sweeps us into his world, and we forget that it is not our own.

Cultural codes governing ambitious behavior in late-sixteenth-century England differed from today's, and yet, in reading historical criticism whose premise is that Donne was a social climber, one scarcely ever meets with consciousness of this problem. The indexes, for instance, of Marotti's and Carey's books contain no entry for Castiglione, and yet, during the quarter century of Donne's most ambitious writing, *The Courtier* was the major, and the *approved*, repository of codes governing ambitious behavior—of codes to be deciphered and enacted by aspiring statesmen. That Thomas Hoby and his printer thought so is indicated by the full title page of the English translation:

THE COURTYER / OF / COUNT BALDESSAR CASTILIO / DIVIDED INTO FOURE BOOKES. / VERY NECESSARY AND PROFIT- / ABLE FOR YONGE GENTILMEN / AND GENTIL-WOMEN ABIDING / IN COURT, PALAICE, OR PLACE, / DONE INTO ENGLYSHE BY / THOMAS HOBY / 1561.

In his prefatory epistle to Lord Hastings, Hoby refers to *The Courtier* as "a storehouse of most necessarie implements for the conversation, use, and trayning up of mans life with Courtly demeanors."[12] That readers agreed, viewing Castiglione as a guide for getting ahead in the late Elizabethan and early Stuart political world, is indicated by reprints of Hoby's translation in 1577, 1588 (with parallel texts in French and Italian), and 1603, and more importantly by Thomas Sackville's commissioning of the Latin translation (*Balthasaris Castilionis Comitis, de curiali sive aulico, libri quatuor*), which was first published in 1571 and reprinted during Donne's lifetime in 1577, 1584, 1585, 1593, 1603, 1612, and 1619. The combined number of printings in English and Latin suggests that *The Courtier* was the most popular of all courtesy texts in England and that Roger Ascham's favorable judgment of Castiglione remained the norm until at least the end of Elizabeth's reign.[13] Donne's reference to Castiglione in his fifth satire—to be treated in the next chapter—indicates that Donne was familiar with *The Courtier* and, in fact, shared Sackville's opinion that the book taught "what in Court a Courtier ought to be." Sackville's appreciation of *The Courtier* is captured in his commendatory verses published with Hoby's translation (p. 1):

> The prince he raiseth huge and mightie walles,
> Castilio frames a wight of noble fame:
> The king with gorgeous Tissue clads his halles,
> The Count with golden vertue deckes the same. . . .

Donne's appreciation, I hope to show, was considerably subtler than this, but no less enthusiastic. For the moment, I would only suggest that Donne found an issue of absorbing concern in the slippery relations of "golden vertue" with "gorgeous Tissue."

Hence, it is surprising that seekers after the language of social life spoken by Donne and his contemporaries should never have consulted

Castiglione, whose text was not buried in obscurity during the late Elizabethan period nor violently polemical. *The Courtier* was endorsed and
promoted by the power elite of Donne's time and is still respected for
literary merits which could easily have won Donne's respect. Moreover,
its status in Donne's time and place far overshadowing other courtesy
texts makes it possible to avoid the potentially totalizing and anachronistic consequences of an attempt to piece together a composite language of social life out of a selection of courtesy texts most of which
Donne would have despised and which in any case we have no evidence
that he read—except for *The Courtier*. One can read *The Courtier* in
confidence that Donne read it and that it voiced a language of social life
specific to late Elizabethan England which was respected by Donne's
potential employers, including the Queen herself. Of course, certain
scornful references to courtiers scattered throughout Donne's secular
poems—and concentrated in Satyre IV—may have induced some readers to conclude that Donne scorned the court, when, in fact, he only
scorned the "untowardly Asseheades" (p. 29)—as Hoby in his colorful
way renders the Italian, "sciocchi"—the maladroit, would-be courtiers
to be found there, and was only establishing his own superior credentials
for a role at court by censuring the inexpert.[14] Thanks to studies like
Marotti's and Carey's, readers will in the future greet Donne's dismissive remarks about courtiers with a healthy skepticism.

The clearest indication of what *The Courtier* meant to Elizabethans
on the make—clearer even than its full title in the Hoby translation—is
afforded by the prefatory material of the more popular Latin version.[15]
Bartholomew Clerke's 1571 translation of all four books into Latin at the
behest of Thomas Sackville, Lord Buckhurst, completed Hoby's natu-
ralization of *The Courtier* as an English cultural product and at the same
time conferred universality on the text by casting it in the international
language of the learned. Serving as Buckhurst's secretary at the time of
Buckhurst's ascendancy at court, Clerke occupied the kind of post that
Donne, a generation later, was to risk his life in storms at sea and battles
on land to obtain under Egerton. So we are fortunate to possess, published along with the translation, Clerke's letters to the Queen and to
Buckhurst and Buckhurst's reply. They situate Castiglione's text within
the social milieu to which Donne sought entrance. They measure the
value attached to *The Courtier* by an Elizabethan Privy Councillor and
by his secretary—by an arbiter of social conduct and by an aspirant
to social acceptance. They also shed light on the Queen's appraisal of
The Courtier, since Buckhurst announces in his letter to Clerke that the
Queen approved Clerke's translation of Book I when he, Buckhurst,
himself presented it to her in person.[16]

Clerke's letter to the Queen, probably written at the time of Buckhurst's presentation, deserves close reading. It has not, to my knowledge, received attention, and yet it situates within an atmosphere of profound anxiety that language of social life adopted by secretaries (like Donne and Clerke) and statesmen (like Buckhurst and Egerton), and it represents Castiglione's text as therapeutic.

Not long ago (Illustrious Prince) that most distinguished nobleman, Lord Buckhurst, urged me to write an account of your Royal Court and (what is much more difficult) of Your Majesty. Although I owe him as much as it is decent for one person to confess that he owes another, yet when I considered your extraordinary virtues, first of the mind, then of the body, when I remembered you to be superior to your sex, superior to mortality itself, then—since no sound, no word, as I hear, can escape your lips even by chance, but that it seems deserving of adornment with lasting memorials in writing—I was thrown into a violent fright, lest, in desiring to serve your excellency and to satisfy a man most renowned and deserving of my best efforts, I should rashly and unadvisedly assume a burden heavier than Aetna. And thus (as the proverb goes) I had the wolf by the ears. For, on the one hand, I considered it the part of a fool and a coward to fear overmuch, but, on the other hand, the part of a man of little judgment to dare to attempt such great matters with greater equanimity. This solemn deliberation had kept me in a state of agitation and anxiety for a considerable stretch of time when it came to me that a certain Italian by the name of Castiglione had brought to pass a work of great distinction on a similar subject. And if that work could be translated not inharmoniously by me into the Latin tongue, I thought that it might be no mean test, so to speak, of my style, and signs, as well as even the strongest arguments, might be drawn therefrom as to whether I could somehow satisfy the demands of such high endeavors. For, if I wrote less well in Latin than he in Italian (which, in truth, I fear is the case) all our labor would be in vain, all effort foolish, since the English court is in no way inferior to that of Urbino, and your Serene Highness surpasses by many degrees all of those Gonzagas and other Italian gentry. And yet now I have set foot in I know not what labyrinth. In order the more honestly to set myself free from it, I have submitted this little work, whatever its worth, to the penetrating judgment of your divine nature, so that you may either doubt not that I have powers sufficient for a narrative of such great importance, or else so that you may (if it so pleases you) discern the contrary. . . . Wherefore, if to your majesty (in all your candor and clemency) our faculties seem not unworthy of such undertakings (though to me they are wont to seem unworthy by far), I, for my part, will devote myself to those most difficult of all labors, while your dignity, whatever may befall, will always be most like unto itself.[17]

Caught between fear of seeming pusillanimous in his hesitancy to act on Buckhurst's request and fear of offending the Queen by presuming to attempt an original work on her court, Clerke exhibits a consuming anxiety of the more ambitious among the Elizabethan lower gentry—among Donne's own class, that is. How to strike a balance between cringing and strutting in the presence of superiors was the question, and Castiglione (with the seal of approval given him by the Queen's tutor) came to these ambitious place seekers as the healing inspiration that Clerke found him to be. There was, however, a test to pass.

Clerke's (perhaps nervous) confusion of categories—verbal skill with social status—lays bare ambitious motives which his rhetoric would as soon conceal, but more importantly it brings certain assumptions to light which are so irrational that it is hard to believe that Clerke could ever have scrutinized them. If, says Clerke, his text of *The Courtier* does not meet the stylistic standard set by the Italian one, he is disqualified as a maker of original texts about Elizabeth's regime because her regime ranks higher than the Italian ones inscribed within *The Courtier.* According to this line of thought, the text representing a regime must rank as high among other texts of its kind as the regime ranks among other regimes. It looks as if Clerke has proposed himself a task heavier than Aetna indeed, since he would never be able to admit that there is a regime ranking higher than the one that he serves, and hence he would have to be a better writer of social history than anyone outside England in order to do it justice. That Clerke seems untroubled by this consequence of his thinking suggests that he regards his social status as a member of the Elizabethan regime a qualification in itself for writing about it with the requisite skill. Then a competent translation of *The Courtier* since it is endorsed by the regime would, to his way of thinking, confirm his social status as well as his linguistic and rhetorical skills. One naturally wonders if then, in Clerke's view, the best practitioners of a regime's social codes—that is, those in social authority—would not also be the most skillful composers of the texts within which that regime announced itself to be inscribed and if, conversely, the skillful composition of a text within which a regime acknowledged its social codes to be inscribed would not be an effective way to ascribe to oneself a social authority not previously evident. Clerke appears to believe rather literally in "the historicity of texts and the textuality of history."[18]

In Thomas Hoby's case, one does not have to wonder long. In his epistle to Hastings, Hoby declares that he hesitated a long time before undertaking his translation "to see if any . . . better practised in the matter of the booke (of whom we want not a number in this realme) would take the matter in hand" (p. 5). Hoby fears that his authorship of *The Courtier*, if only through translation, will be regarded by aristocratic readers as presumptuous—as a claim to social authority. Both Hoby and Clerke exhibit implicit belief in an affinity between rhetorical competency and social hierarchy so radical in the peculiar case of their project as to qualify the successful in one category for success in the other. For them, *The Courtier* is a text woven deeply into the social fabric of the regime in which they write, and translating it is a risky social performance. Why else would Clerke feel compelled to exempt the Queen from contamination by any text which he might happen to compose about her regime as a result of his having passed the test of translating *The Courtier*? For both her protection and his—but mainly his—he must declare her to be immune to contamination from the textuality to which her endorsement of *The Courtier* might expose her regime. For Hoby and Clerke, *The Courtier* represents a site of dangerous (and intriguing) porousness in their culture's conceptual diaphragm separating written composition and social practice, rhetorical expertise and social authority, proficiency in the realm of the aesthetic and prerogative in the world of politics.

The Courtier enjoyed a unique social status in late Elizabethan England. If through translating its text into English and Latin one could be regarded as laying claim to social authority, then certainly one could lay claim to such authority through translating oneself into a courtier by means of those social codes of which its text was the approved repository. *The Courtier* was a thread leading out of the labyrinth of morbid, crippling self-consciousness for aspirants to political power and a challenging test of their capacities to succeed at Elizabeth's court, just such a test as translation of its actual text represented for Clerke before attempting an original account of Elizabeth's court. For Clerke as aspiring author and his fellow members of the lower gentry as aspiring statesmen, *The Courtier* was a guide, and it was an imposing, but secure, threshold to be crossed before they graduated into the circle of the politically active and the intellectually protected in the Elizabethan regime. Clerke's letter to the Queen, by expressing the anxieties and hopes of these men, gives a clear indication that their need of Castiglione's text was deeply felt. Implicit in the following chapters is the contention that Donne's poetry was admired by his contemporaries largely because it recognized this need and represented a peculiarly brilliant performance of that language of social life of which Castiglione's text was the approved articulation.

Donne felt the same hopes and anxieties as other place seekers of his time and found *The Courtier* to be a compelling text. His reference to it in his fifth satire is evidence that he had read at least two books. He also had before his eyes the flesh-and-blood texts furnished by Elizabeth's great courtiers—Hatton, Sackville, and Ralegh—embodiments of everything that his culture approved in Castiglione. However, the real difficulty of reading Donne's satires, elegies, and lyric poems as products of social codes inscribed in *The Courtier* has to do with Donne's independence, his originality, and his skepticism, and not with establishing what should be obvious—that *The Courtier* was a bible for ambitious young men like Donne. Donne was the most innovative poet of his generation reading *The Courtier*, not just any ambitious Oswald or Osric.[19] Hence, Hoby's digest of do's and don't's ("A Breef Rehersall of the Chiefe Conditions and Qualities in a Courtier") appended like an ass's tail to his otherwise fluent, sensitive English translation is of no use in understanding how Donne read the text. Donne would have scorned this attempt to turn Castiglione's dialogue into a handbook. His "True Character of a Dunce" ridicules the type of person who depended on rule books and proverbs to get through the day. To understand Donne reading Castiglione, I have, therefore, gone directly to Castiglione's text and have sought those codes or moves which Donne perceived there and which generated, not only approved courtly behavior among actual courtiers, but also *The Courtier* itself as a compelling text. My thesis is that Donne enacted those codes in some of his most esteemed secular poems—among others, Satyre III, Elegy XIX, "Aire and Angels," "The Flea," "The Canonization," and "A Nocturnall upon S. Lucies Day." The poems to which we return as if mesmerized by their appeal keep us coming back because they exhibit the allure of accomplished Elizabethan courtiers, beguiling diplomats, bewitching conversationalists, graceful, intelligent masters of repartee. They possess the allure of human beings whose profession it was to make themselves attractive. Hence, they remain attractive to those of us who still enjoy this game— and vexing to those who do not. Donne experienced the same anxieties as did other members of his class, but he resolved them, I shall argue, with a subtler and more innovative understanding of the courtly aesthetic than any other poet of his generation. David Norbrook's cautionary statement could serve (as well as Jonson's) as the epigraph of this study: "To speak of the discourse of power as something one had either to accept or to subvert *en bloc* is to overlook the degree to which that discourse could be refashioned by individual choices."[20]

At this point, it should be noted that the courtly aesthetic deriving from Castiglione came down to English poets of Donne's generation mediated by texts like Sidney's *Apology for Poetry* and Puttenham's *Arte of English Poesie*. Daniel Javitch's pioneering study of the poetry of courtliness concerns itself with this process and with the advantages won for English poetry by the existence of stylistic features shared by poetry and courtliness.[21] One would suppose Donne, as poet, to have been influenced at least as much by mediating texts dealing in a direct way with poetic composition as by *The Courtier* itself, which has little to say on the subject. One would have a right to such a supposition, however, only if there were evidence that Donne regarded himself primarily as a poet and that he was interested in the major literary theoretical texts of his day. All the evidence (which I shall treat in the next chapter in connection with Satyre II), whether in his early correspondence or in his poetry itself, points in the opposite direction. Donne was a brilliant poet who shunned the name of poet. He wrote fascinating poems but did not acknowledge them to be his principal activity. In this, he belongs in the company of Wyatt, Sidney, Sackville, Ralegh, and Greville, and not in that of the "professional" poets, Shakespeare, Spenser, Jonson, and Drayton.[22] Moreover, he is unlike Sidney in that he never allowed himself to be drawn into literary debates or defenses of poetry, and he differs from the other major poets in his category, except Ralegh, in social rank. Like Ralegh, he was a gentleman amateur in poetry, but a gentleman of low rank who could not count on his status (as certainly Sackville could) to lend him charisma. Like Ralegh, he had to strain every nerve to give the impression that there was something more to him than his accomplishments, something of as much consequence as hereditary rank, and yet he had only his accomplishments with which to create the impression.

Since his talent was for poetry, Donne used poetry toward this end. He was a member of the lower gentry using a poetic talent to make himself seem as qualified as higher ranking aristocrats for sensitive posts in government. He was not a poet reading *The Courtier* and its mediating texts for the benefits to be gained for poetry from its resemblances to courtliness. Hence, those social codes which he discovered in Castiglione's text and carried over into the composition of his best poems were not necessarily the ones already discovered by Sidney and Puttenham to be "mutual stylistic features" of poetry and courtliness;[23] instead, they were the very codes by which Castiglione could author a text like *The Courtier* and by which persons could raise themselves to the greatest heights of power and rank at Elizabeth's court. Whether they were suitable for writing the kind of poetry that Donne saw all around him, compatible or not with conventional poetic composition, Donne carried them over in his project of using poetry to create the impression of an aristocratic self, and, in the process, he revolutionized poetic composition. He reduced stale Petrarchan conventions to the small change in a new kind of transaction, while lending Petrarch's deep seriousness in defense of the personal and the intimate a new immediacy and dramatic intensity.

Because of the romantic story of his elopement with Ann More and the disastrous consequences for his career, it is too often forgotten that Donne was an immense success as a young place seeker in late Elizabethan London. An immense success at a time when the competition was at its severest. In his classic essay "Place and Patronage in Elizabethan Politics," Wallace T. MacCaffrey lists the types to be found in the monarch's service during Donne's early years: "The established magnate for whom politics is a secondary but essential part of life; the daring aspirant, soaring for the greatest prizes; the plodding placeman seeking a secure living; the zealot, the dedicated agent of the Divine Will—all join the cast on the political stage."[24] There can be no doubt that Donne was among the "daring aspirants" and that his talents—especially his poetic talent—created the right impression and brought him to the attention of the right people. At the age of twenty-six he became Sir Thomas Egerton's secretary, obtaining thereby a post which, as Bald points out, could easily have led to great things.[25] Moreover, there was time enough before the clandestine marriage for Donne's secretaryship to lead to at least one great thing: selection to serve in the 1601 parliament. Even though we possess no evidence to support Walton's contention that Donne was Egerton's principal secretary, we can be certain that he succeeded in his post, because it is inconceivable that Egerton would have selected any but the most accomplished in his employ to represent him in Parliament. At a time when Englishmen, as MacCaffrey puts it, "were turning away from their bad old habits of conspiracy and treason—of resort to force as the final arbiter in politics" and mastering "the subtler arts of persuasion and manipulation,"[26] Donne managed to convince the most powerful lawyer in the realm that he was a suitable spokesman for his interests. As a patron of poets, Egerton could not but have been influenced by Donne's poetry—among, of course, Donne's other personal attributes now lost to us.[27]

In *Parliamentary Selection*, Mark A. Kishlansky makes an important point for students of Donne's mind and art, for students especially of Donne's elusive and provocative secular poems. Kishlansky defines eligibility for selection to Parliament in terms which link Donne's poetry, Castiglione's text, and service with Egerton:

> Of course, in one sense politics pervades all social relations. Categories such as sexual politics or politics of the family remind us that no human relations are devoid of political meaning. But they also remind us that we cannot confuse generic and specific meanings of what is essentially an amorphous analytic category. The problem is complicated by the fact that in the early modern world there was no separation between the social and the political. Authority was integrated. Personal

attributes, prestige, standing, godliness—were all implicit in office-holding. Their presence qualified individuals for place, their absence disqualified them. Individuals represented communities by virtue of the possession of these qualities, not by reflecting the special interests or ideals of particular groups of constituents.[28]

This carefully worded statement does not, of course, deny that in the 1601 parliament Donne represented Egerton's special interests and ideals. However, it does make clear that the qualifications Donne had to exhibit in order to be selected by Egerton were social before they were political. Donne's politics Egerton could take for granted; his social skills he could not. Donne had to demonstrate them, beyond his poetry, in his demeanor, but the poetry could be used to alert an employer of Egerton's intellect to his secretary's social moves, to focus his attention on the more important ones, and to overcome their evanescence and preserve them in a form in which they became objects of contemplation while remaining agents in a social mission. Just as Castiglione depicted the conversation of his friends in the Urbino drawing room as embodying the principles of conduct which they discuss, Donne encoded his secular poems with rules of social intercourse refashioned from *The Courtier* and sent the poems forth as "discussants" (to use Pocock's term) in the social discourse influenced by Castiglione of such places as York House (Egerton's residence in London) where they exhibited their author's qualification for appointments like membership in Parliament. Like Clerke, the translator of *The Courtier*, Donne conceived of his writing as risky social performance, which either qualified or disqualified him for a place among the political elect, but unlike Clerke and more like Castiglione himself, Donne could also conceive of his writing as testing the establishment's qualifications to receive the services of individuals like himself. Did the establishment have the acuity to decode his performances?

Donne's chief problem in using poetry for ambitious purposes was that the ruling class regarded poetry as, at best, an avocation or pastime, at worst, a waste of time. In his letter to Clerke prefacing the Latin Castiglione, Sackville (himself a gifted poet) sets the tone to be used of professional literary types:

> When that Illustrious Prince, with her supreme judgment, her supreme knowledge of letters, gave her approval so openly to the first book [of your translation] which I myself presented to her Majesty in January, do you fear that literary homunculi will dare to cavil?[29]

Fear not, says Sackville, the criticism of midgets—mere literary professionals who might find Clerke's Latin awkward. Real authority, in all matters of taste, resides in the Queen and in men of hereditary rank like himself. (And the many printings of Clerke's translation indicate that that authority was real indeed.) The evidence of his second satire and his early correspondence makes it quite clear that Donne was in agreement with Sackville on the subject of literary homunculi. Poetry, as his second satire bears (perhaps anguished) witness, was the profession, in Donne's opinion, of innocuous, vulnerable, rather pathetic—but cheerfully deluded—individuals with never enough money in their pockets, and yet he, Donne, was left with it as his principal personal attribute (as Kishlansky puts it), his principal means of demonstrating his social qualification for noble employment like membership in parliament. He was, alas, a literary homunculus. That he succeeded as a poet, and not ultimately as a statesman, caused him sorrow, and perhaps never more than on the eve of ordination, when he felt obliged to issue confidential apologies for some of his poems. However, his early social successes led to overconfidence,[30] and, as I shall argue in the next chapter, contradictions inherent in his secretarial post may also have confounded him.

Donne's dilemma—of having to use a talent considered minor in order to prove major social aptitudes—turned out to be a formula for originality, as his poetry attests. Intensifying the dilemma and increasing the urgency of Donne's need to produce an original version of the poetry of courtliness was the fact that his social status could, at best, be considered precarious. He had to use a potentially discreditable pursuit to compensate for severe social deficiencies. In Kishlansky's list, "godliness" is a qualification for a seat in Parliament, and here Donne, the descendant of Sir Thomas More and nephew of Jasper Heywood (head of the Jesuit mission in England from 1581 to 1583) could only have seemed suspect, despite his military service against Spain.[31] It is likely that his suspect "godliness" was what made the wrath of Ann More's father implacable. Then there is "standing" in Kishlansky's list, and Donne, as the son of an ironmonger, was far beneath the higher gentry, to say nothing of the nobility. "Standing" he did not have. In fact, his claim to ancient lineage in the mists of Arthurian Wales might have struck contemporaries as a case of protesting too much, and especially since some of his father's questionable activities as a businessman shone too clearly in the recent past. John Ferne, Donne's contemporary and an expert on heraldry, paints a picture of the disadvantage of such paternity for a young man aspiring to noble service. According to Ferne, merchants, not only do not qualify by virtue of their calling for membership in the gentry, but are not even first among commoners, because their "practise . . . consisteth of most ungentle parts, as doublenes of toong, violation of faith, with the rest of their tromperies and disceites . . . ," and "their trade is neither of that honestie, ne yet ministring the like necessities to mans life, as doth the plowman." Later, Ferne admits that gentry have sprung "from the warehouse of a Merchaunt," but he adds that "time winneth much" and noble service through many generations is necessary to confirm them in gentle status.[32] Although Ferne concedes that merchants may be deserving of a coat of arms if they have performed notable service to the state, we have no evidence that John Donne, Senior, the papist ironmonger, had ever met that requirement. Instead, we have evidence that he may have been the unscrupulous dealer typical (in Ferne's opinion) of his class.[33]

However, even if what little we know of Donne's father did not suggest unsavory practices, Donne would still have been living in the shadow of the warehouse while he was at Lincoln's Inn, a companion of those "frolique Patricians" whom he mentions in his "Epithalamion Made at Lincolnes Inne." Ferne again paints a vivid picture of the type of prejudice which Donne might have encountered there and would have been forced to overcome. Ferne explains that a decrease in church livings made the Inns of Court essential in Donne's time to the younger sons of the aristocracy. However, access to the Inns by members of the yeomanry and merchant classes left less and less room for these younger sons and prevented them from obtaining the legal credentials and the income needed to serve their families and preserve the patrimony. According to Ferne,

> . . . the youthe, and manye florishing impes, of gentle stocke, are many
> of them cut off by untimely, nay shamefull deathes, into which the
> pungitive pricke of necessity, hath driven them, and others to abandon
> their countrye, and to gette their livinge with straungers, and all this
> for want of maintenance at home. Whereas the churles sonne, ietteth
> in his long robe, faced and fenced with gardes and ruffleth in his ruffe,
> and is cleped of eche one, a Rabbie, and man of worshippe which com-
> eth to passe, by usurping that facultye and vocation, at the first desti-
> nated as peculier, to gentlemen.[34]

The Lothian portrait comes to mind (in which Donne must have seen himself as the stylishly melancholy intellectual, but which to the modern undergraduate always suggests a pimp). Donne might easily have been regarded by some as a usurper. Everything about him, his religion, his class, and even his great poetic talent, must have seemed suspect, and yet it was with his suspect talent—one which he never gives evidence of valuing at even a fraction of the worth that posterity has discovered in it—that he set out to make up for his other deficiencies. The social pressure under which Donne wrote his secular lyrics was certainly great enough to produce, in this most ingenious of poets, a new and compelling performance of that language of social life to which his culture ascribed. Inscribing himself within the social system of the Elizabethan elite was, in Donne's case, a job for a mallet and chisel.

At the risk of casting Donne as the fool in a comedy, I shall conclude my discussion of his social position with a quotation from the second Parnassus play, whose topical satire attacks issues relevant to Donne's biography—among them the incompatibility of a conventional humanist education in poetry with the actual requirements of the London job market. Gullio, who fancies himself a more "compleat gentleman" than any on earth, is reviling Ingenioso, a university graduate trying to make his living in the London of Donne's youth. It seems that Gullio paid Ingenioso to ghostwrite a love poem for him, but the young woman to whom it was sent spurned it. Whereupon Gullio expresses astonishment, because he himself had deigned to adorn Ingenioso's "seely Invention with a prettie wittie Latinn sentence" of his own. Complaining that Ingenioso's dunceries only dishonored the "generous spirit" of his own contribution and disgraced him with his mistress, Gullio dismisses Ingenioso and promises that he will never again "norishe any such unlearned Pedantes—these universities send not foorth a good witt in an age." However, Ingenioso replies that the young woman was quite aware that nothing in the composition was actually Gullio's—nothing except "a sentence of Latinn" which she knew to be his because it contained a solecism. Gullio's retaliation constitutes a broad satiric attack (by the anonymous author or authors of the Parnassus plays) on aristocratic pretensions to a knowledge of letters, but it also captures in a humorous way Donne's attitude toward poetry.

> Peace youe impecunious peasant, as I am a soldier, I was never soe abusd since I firste bore arms. What you vassall, if a Lunaticke bawdie trull, a pocketinge queane detracte from my vertues, will thy audacious selfe dare to repeate them in the presence of this blade? Were it not that I will not file my handes upon such a contemptible rascalde, and that I will not have my name in the time to come, where my selfe shall be cronicled, disgraced with the base victorie of such an earth worme, I woulde prove it upon that carrion of thy witt, that my Lattin was pure Lattin, and such as they speake in Rhems and Padua. Why, it is not the custome in Padua to observe such base ruls as Lilie, Priscian, and such base companions have sett downe; wee of the better sorte have a priveledge to create Lattin, like knightes, and to saye, Rise upp Sr phrase.[35]

At first glance, the target of this tirade, Ingenioso, would seem to be Donne's counterpart, but—disturbingly—the "compleat gentleman," Gullio, voices the high-handed contempt of writers which the young John Donne—he of the Marshall engraving with sword hilt in hand and coat armor in prominent display—expresses in his letters to Henry

Wotton and in his second satire. Certainly, Donne would have sided with the Earl of Southampton (in Gullio, lampooned as a Renaissance Dan Quail) against Thomas Nashe (toasted as Ingenioso) in any popularity contest between the two. With Southampton, Donne shared both a fondness for plays and a history of involvement with the Essex faction, while Nashe represented a literary professionalism which Donne rejected.

While Gullio's outburst recalls the old Renaissance joke about Alexander the Great, who needed Aristotle to tell him that he could not create grammar rules the way he made laws in his conquered states, Gullio's attitude toward letters, if it were directed, not toward Latin grammar, but Elizabethan poetic convention, would parody Donne's own magisterial attitude. It was not for nothing that Donne's best critic in his own century declared him a monarch of wit. He did make poems rise up like knights, as if he had a sovereign privilege to abrogate the rules by which mere poets, the "base companions" who shared his talent, conducted their business. In a real way, Donne imposed a monarch's sense of style (Elizabeth's sense of style, as well as that of her prominent courtiers) on poetic composition in his time. Despite his social deficiencies and the aristocracy's obligatory disdain of poetry, he used his poems to prove himself an aristocrat, even if he had to transform poetry to do so. He brought himself to the attention of men like Egerton and entered the Queen's service, her dance at court, just as a respected Lord Chancellor, Sir Christopher Hatton, had done with his actual dancing skills. Then he soared for the highest prizes.

If it is true that human subjectivity is itself textual, then a large part of Donne's inner life could be said to be the text of which Gullio and Ingenioso are parodies. He contained the conflict which they enact, and which the Elizabethan regime made problematic, between achieved social acceptance and ascribed social authority, between merit and rank, learning and birth. The regime's peculiar canonization of *The Courtier* was one of its many hesitant moves toward the breakdown of these binary oppositions. By authorizing a codification of social practices specific to its elite (in a secular, modern text at that), the regime at once opened its mysteries to the achievers like Donne and clung to its prerogative of selecting them for admission. However, it also raised the possibility that it was itself authorized in the same way as its own text—that there was no prediscursive or extratextual "reality" ascribable to it, but that it was inscribed in the text of its own choosing. So it chose a difficult text in *The Courtier*, but not one beyond the reach of an achiever like Donne and certainly not beyond his acuity as a producer and an interpreter of texts. Donne perceived the opening represented by Castiglione's text and soared straight through it, but not without anguish and lingering doubts. To be disabused is not to have achieved tranquillity. Donne used *The Courtier* as a test of himself, no doubt, but also as a standard for measuring the regime's capacity to comprehend and appreciate individuals like himself. Nowhere is this latter process more evident than in poems like his third satire and "A Nocturnall upon S. Lucies Day." That Donne worried about whether or not he were understood is indicated by his choice of a motto to inscribe in the books that he owned. It comes from a poem ("S'i'l dissi," 206 in Petrarch's *Rime sparse*) which is precisely a complaint about being misunderstood.

Each of the four central chapters of this study focuses on a pattern in the dance at court—on a code or "move" emerging from that social discourse which came to Donne authorized in the text of *The Courtier* by the regime which he sought to enter. What are the codes by which Castiglione produced his elegant dialogue, by which Elizabethan courtiers sought to achieve "the styled identity specific to the governing class,"[36] by which Donne wrote poems whose "imperious wit" purged the Muses' garden and planted seeds of fresh invention? My answer to this question proposes no especially innovative reading of *The Courtier*, which would be an unlikely development even if it were my purpose. *The Courtier* is one of those barn doors by which Renaissance scholars have always measured what is big. It has been brilliantly read by generations of students. My purpose is only to map its encounter with John Donne. The following four codes linking Donne and Castiglione are the concerns of this book:

1. Distinguishing Castiglione's dialogue is its participants' tolerance of the dissonant in crucial areas of their experience, to the point where their tolerance becomes the mark of a disabused mentality. Castiglione's courtiers have the discretion to recognize that their exchanges sometimes reach a point of impasse where to attempt even provisory resolutions would be to engage in self-deception. Donne's *Satyres*, which are autobiographical in the tradition of Horace and Ariosto, depict Donne himself confronting impasses, resisting self-deception, becoming disabused. This movement accounts for their difference from all other English formal satire of the period and, more importantly, organizes all five into a unified account of the social life of an aspirant to political prominence in late Elizabethan London. With good reason, Donne referred to his *Satyres* as a "book."

2. Peculiar to Castiglione's courtiers is their preference (over serious debate) for provocative play that lures an interlocutor into drawing, not his own conclusions, but those which the courtiers have implanted in the course of a casual exchange. "Flickering provocations" is Hoby's percipient translation of the Italian, *illecebre*, for this move in the social chess game. Donne's poems engage their readers in the same way, provoking them to complete the aesthetic experience by supplying settings,

scenarios, and silent characters according to hints which the poems themselves implant. This "imaginative expansion" or "open form" accounts for the dramatic immediacy of Donne's best-known secular poems and leads, in Donne's adaptation of Castiglione, to a version of the literary Baroque.

3. By concealing the difficulty of their achievements and nonchalantly disparaging them, Castiglione's courtiers hope to produce the illusion of transcending their human limitations. This is the notorious *sprezzatura* by which the adept evokes wonderment (*meraviglia*) in his superiors in order to obtain grace (*grazia*). Because of his low status and his society's prejudices against poetry, Donne had to write excellent poetry and conceal, not only its difficulty, but the seriousness of his commitment to it in the first place. His effort to produce the impression of a transcendent reality (of an ascriptive being akin to hereditary rank) beneath the veil of his poetic achievement led to self-parody ("To his Mistris Going to Bed") and palinode ("A Nocturnall upon S. Lucies Day" and "A Valediction: of the Booke") and to performances like "The Canonization."

4. At risk of being taken for Iago's or Bosola's, Castiglione's courtiers make casuistry their business, dedicating much time (especially in Book III) to demonstrations that artifice in their case, whether in cultivating provocative repartee or a nonchalant demeanor, is the exception to the rule that dissimulation is evil. They (along with Donne and his speakers) demonstrate their sincerity by openly conceding that others might be at risk in dealing with them and that their talent for prevarication is dangerous. They acknowledge and describe in detail the worst that can be expected of their calculated detachment—their *disinvoltura*. This accounts for contrasting pairings *among* the speakers of Donne's lyrics, as with "Aire and Angels" and "The Flea," or "The Exstasie" and Elegy VI ("Recusancy"), where the cynical seducer appears in one poem, the principled lover in another. It also accounts for that apparent dissonance *within* individual poems which has caused such celebrated critical controversies as those between David Novarr and John Freccero over "A Valediction: Forbidding Mourning" and between William Empson and Rosemond Tuve over "A Valediction: Of Weeping"—controversies which sever the two parts of a courtly demonstration of sincerity by splitting the idealistic assertion of principle from the simultaneous acknowledgment of depressing possibilities.

These four moves or codes are capable, individually or taken together, of endless elaboration. They are seeds of social and verbal performances of great complexity—performances of seduction and persuasion, self-scrutiny and self-promotion—but they do not generate utopian social discourse or action. They are not subversive. Rather they generate ideological performances which idealize the status quo by enveloping it in an absorbing subtlety, by formulating a conscience for it, and by making it the object of nostalgia. They promote poetic innovation and marshal it in the service of a conservative social impulse.

One of these courtly codes by itself would be insufficient to link Castiglione with Donne, with the possible exception of the third one involving *sprezzatura*. However, I hope, by demonstrating all four to be constitutive of *The Courtier* and Donne's poems, to reveal a resemblance between Donne and Castiglione which is more than casual. Although the analytical process requires division and each following chapter focuses on a single code, implicit in all my readings is the contention that all four codes are at work in combination in every poem under consideration. The concluding chapter offers an integrated reading of a poem which has not received much attention in Donne criticism and also speculates about Donne and the political unconscious of late Elizabethan London. Finally, if these codes seem to belong as much to the aesthetic and rhetorical realms as to the social, I would argue that this is a reflection of Elizabethan culture's calculated absorption of the social into the aesthetic and its consecration of *The Courtier* as a principal locus of such activity.

I wish that I could measure all the ways in which this study is implicated in my own historical situation, but I can think of only one worth mentioning. Persons of my age in my culture have witnessed the steady concentration of enormous wealth and power in the hands of a very small group. We have witnessed a growth of the disproportion between the wealthy and the merely middle class to a point—when one considers the energy placed at the disposal of the wealthy by technology—where it can be said to equal the disproportion between nobles and commoners in the Elizabethan period. And we are deceiving ourselves if we suppose that the arts are not as much at the mercy of the powerful now as they were then. Hence, there is value—even if limited by changed historical conditions—in getting down to the details of a famous instance in Western history when a powerful aristocracy canonized a text for voicing a certain style of social intercourse which it thought to be its own and when a brilliant artist seized this opportunity, turned it to his advantage, built one political career out of it (which he lost), then built another, and in the process revolutionized his art form. Donne's poems and sermons are still alive for us, possibly because they are so frankly compromised by his ingenious opportunism, are so much the product of it, and exhibit so much tormented consciousness of the fact. We will always need more products of their kind.

1

The Satirical Art of the Disabused

The Art of Impasse

In an essay which is required reading for students of the Renaissance, Thomas M. Greene notes the propensity of Castiglione's courtiers to drift into embarrassing impasses over questions concerning the norms and ideals by which they live. They are unable to arrive at a convincing argument that their perfect courtier should be of noble birth, they have trouble distinguishing him from a common flatterer, they doubt whether ignorant tyrants can be educated even if the courtier retains his integrity in a corrupt court. For Greene, Castiglione's "dilettante of the drawing room" never quite succeeds in becoming "the advisor of the council chamber," because the Urbinese state lacks the freedom of the Greek polis. Castiglione's courtiers play together, but cannot act together to influence policy in a Renaissance despotism. Hence, their game of forming the perfect courtier might, at any moment, demystify the political authority in whose palace they are protected and reveal the futility of their aspirations to civic virtue—reveal their game to be nothing but a game. For Greene, their exchanges exhibit, at best, a "power of containment" and their frequent laughter marks moments of escape from the vortices within which their own discourse threatens to swallow them. In the Urbino of Greene's essay, the courtier's grace lies in the adroitness with which he glosses over his absurdity.[1]

No one would deny that a pervasive tension between the ideal and the real lends pathos and nostalgia to Castiglione's account of Urbino. However, this is also the reason that interpretations of *The Courtier* like Greene's, which treat the text as if it were a subtle form of satire, are unconvincing. Castiglione's nostalgia for those evenings in Urbino comes through too strongly. The ideal is never so subverted in *The Courtier* that the author must rush in with a containment strategy in order to rescue it; the ideal and the real qualify each other in Castiglione's text, and their incongruities are what lie behind the laughter of Castiglione's courtiers—not escapist relief. On the one hand, Greene's perception that the narrative force of *The Courtier* depends on a movement toward impasse demands respect. On the other hand, Greene's conclusions make it impossible to understand why *The Courtier* found so much favor in its own century with the very despots whose regimes would, according to Greene, have rendered its discourse nugatory. Furthermore, his essay forces us to ask why Castiglione would represent his courtiers (who were in life his personal friends) as confronting themselves with disruptive truths only to exhibit (to the obtrusive reader) their talent for retreat from full lucidity—only to exhibit the resiliency of their powers of self-deception. Surely, though Castiglione's narrative has its ironies, they are not so corrosive as to devour his courtiers in the manner of Swift's Irish children. The courtly laughter may at times be nervous, but it is not the laughter of the willfully self-deluded. To recognize and to be able to laugh at the incongruity of the real with the ideal, of social practice with social norms, is, instead, one of the foremost qualifications, according to Castiglione, of persons who would attempt to improve social conditions, or at least retard their decline. If Castiglione advocates recognition of impasse, of stalemate, of the disjunctive in human affairs, as the first prerequisite of statesmanship, then the laughter of his courtiers is the laughter of the disabused—not of the self-deceived. It is the laughter of people who do not deceive themselves into supposing that vexing questions are not vexing, or that stalemates are not stalemates, or that solutions to social ills are not, to a high degree, expedient. As writers of poetry, they would exhibit, like John Donne, a taste for oxymoron.

Elisabetta Gonzaga exercises authority over the courtly game in her Urbinese drawing room—actually authors it—by means of her silence. Her refusal to intervene in the dialogue, as a higher moral or political authority, insures that the male speakers will get stuck and that a share of the reader's amusement will derive from suspense over how these ingenious courtiers are to extricate themselves from their own debates. Power exercises itself by means of a calculated omission, which leaves surrogates to broach insoluble, even dangerous, questions, and thereby to act, on the one hand, as consciences of the regime and to demonstrate, on the other, with their confused efforts, the inevitability—even the desirability—of recourse to arbitration in social affairs. The impasse, for instance, over noble birth in Book I of *The Courtier* cries out for arbitration. Neither side of the debate adequately embraces the complexity of the issue, nor is either side ever on common ground with the other, and the expedient with which the courtiers escape their dilemma emphasizes the need for a better compromise. The importance of first impressions is not a strong enough argument to justify hereditary rights to office and precedence. Instead, with its cynicism, it weakens that side of the debate which it was supposed to support, and does so despite the various reasonable arguments in behalf of noble birth. Here Elisabetta's courtiers, left to their own devices, act out a comedy of impotence. They demonstrate what can be expected in the absence of authority sufficient to impose a compromise.

English readers of this episode in Donne's time would have been reminded of their own Elizabeth's arbitration of the issue. The eldest sons of noble officeholders in her regime inherited some—not all—of their fathers' offices and had to compete for the rest with contenders of lower origin, commoners or low ranking gentlemen, who—like Donne—had worked their way up the ladder of achievement at the Inns of Court and the universities and had exhibited exceptional aptitudes and personal qualities. English readers would have viewed Castiglione's Elisabetta as teaching her courtiers, by granting them freedom of speech, how impossible it would be for them to achieve on their own the advantages of a benevolent despotism like the English Elizabeth's. This response would have accorded well with Castiglione's avowed intentions, which were to represent an ideal case of despotism with a despot who possessed a conscience along with governing skills. Moreover, *The Courtier*'s popularity in England may have rested in large part on a tacit—and rather complacent—comparison of Elizabeths, in which the Italian Elizabeth demonstrated how much might have been lost to England if the English Elizabeth had married, as the Italian one did, and sidelined herself to parlor games.

If Castiglione's insistence on Elisabetta's reserve casts her most of the time as a subtle apologist for despotism, his representation of her as possessing authorizing power within her drawing room (and hence, within his dialogue, authorial force) casts her also as a patroness of the conscience of her class. Her reticence, therefore, often leads the courtiers into dangerous impasses—ones caused by absolutism and not easily resolved by arbitration. Greene cites a good example in Book IV when the Duchess asks Ottaviano Fregoso to reveal what he would tell the prince in case "that you have throughly gotten his favour, so as it may be lawful for you to tell him frankly what ever commeth in your minde." Here Ottaviano replies with laughter, "If I had the favour of some Prince that I know, and should tell franckly mine opinion (I doubt me) I shoulde soone loose it" (p. 279). When Greene states that this breezy rejoinder undercuts much of Ottaviano's subsequent discourse, he ignores the emphasis on "frankly" ("liberamente," in the original), which implies that there are other—indirect—ways of making one's opinion known. Far from being a "Freudian slip," as Greene describes it, it is a clear-sighted, conscious concession—on Ottaviano's part—of circumstances adverse to his argument and an acknowledgment—on Castiglione's part—that absolute power in the wrong hands can nullify the best in a courtier and turn courtiership into a corrupt and corrupting profession. Ottaviano's laughter signals an awareness which Castiglione shares with his admired Duchess that absolute power in the right hands, that is, in her hands and her husband's, must sanction critical discourse, even if it threatens, in Greene's words, to "destroy the delicate fabric of their social equilibrium."[2] Absolute power must look into the gulf which it creates or else devour itself. Apart from its demonstration of an important code of social discourse, this passage of Castiglione's book must have intrigued Donne and contributed to his lifelong sense—which he shared with the majority of persons in his time—that public service could be meaningful in despotic regimes. Certainly, it would have encouraged him to hope that his own gift of eloquence could be used with integrity and certainly without a devastating loss to his subjective autonomy.

What most lends *The Courtier* its air of idealism is not so much the brilliance of the model courtier fashioned in the Urbinese word game as Castiglione's depiction of the players themselves knit together in a society courageous enough to face its own contradictions. The unflattering glass that Elisabetta authorizes her courtiers to hold up—consciously, it must be emphasized—to themselves and to her husband's regime reflects a civilization's discontents as distinctly as Freud's mirror of modern society, and Castiglione might even be said to be a founder of the genre to which Freud's text belongs. Book III of *The Courtier*, with its agonizing over the difficulty of discerning sincerity, casts the Urbinese court in a spectral light. Here, the various deceptions endorsed earlier in the dialogue as means for the courtier to attract his employer's attention and tell him the truth are looked at from the point of view of the vulnerable female (and, by extension, from the point of view of the courtier's vulnerable male colleagues) as disqualifying him as a truth teller. With his *sprezzatura*, with his studied spontaneity, with his vigilant eye always fixed on his appearance in someone else's eye, can the courtier be said to have much more substance than a ghost? His mode of being may be a mode of nonbeing, his acting merely acting in the histrionic sense. Book III sharply reduces the distance between Urbino and Elsinore, that other land of ghosts, and contains the self-consciously destabilizing gesture, the courageous look into the void (on the part of Castiglione himself, as well as the courtiers in his dialogue) without which we would be unable to recognize Urbino as having a conscience.

The English Secretary

Donne's *Satyres* look into that same void—the torrent with which Satyre III closes is Donne's image of it—and attempt to forge thereby the conscience of that relatively small, exclusive club of the politically active at the close of Elizabeth's reign. Though at first these poems lack the authorization of an Elisabetta Gonzaga, the dramatic climax of their development occurs with the acquisition and triumphant declaration of that authority in Satyre V in the figure of Sir Thomas Egerton, the Lord Keeper. Apart from John T. Shawcross's argument that Donne composed the *Satyres* in 1597 and 1598, just as he was entering Egerton's service,[3] the focus on the Inns of Court and the legal profession in Satyres I and II and the concentration in Satyre III on the problem of secular power and its relation to religious freedom foreshadow Egerton's entrance—the entrance of England's most powerful lawyer, the most distinguished living alumnus of Lincoln's Inn, the prosecutor of Mary Stuart and Edmund Campion, and himself a former papist known to have undergone a long, arduous conversion to the Elizabethan Settlement before becoming one of its most ardent defenders. When Egerton is finally identified in Satyre V, the reader feels a mingled sense of wonder at the eminence of this historical figure who has condescended to enter Donne's satirical discourse and retrospective illumination as to the coherence of that discourse itself, as if Egerton crystallized it and brought it to a point. If the "wise man" at the close of Satyre IV who will, Donne hopes, "esteeme my writs Canonical" is Egerton, as Satyre V leads one to believe, then Egerton could be said to be referred to or else strongly suggested in all the satires and to be specifically designated as their legitimating authority. Certainly, in the context of Satyre V, the "grave man" of Satyre I (79), ignored by the speaker's superficial companion in favor of more fashionable passersby, suggests Egerton. Moreover, the use of the appellation "Sir" to designate Egerton in line 31 of Satyre V links Egerton to the "Sir" addressed in Satyre II. And even if the textual and historical evidence is inconclusive as to whether Egerton is the wise man alluded to in Satyre IV, I shall demonstrate that it makes no difference, because we would have to imagine an Egerton anyway in order to understand the conscience that Donne forges in his "book" of *Satyres*.[4] As much as any other single feature, this presence behind the written word of an Egerton fuses the five satires together as five parts of the one coherent book that Donne considered himself to have created.

We would also have to imagine an Egerton in order to describe the voice of Donne's satirist, which differs greatly from the many voices we hear in his *Songs and Sonnets* and *Elegies* and resembles in one important respect the voice of his *Holy Sonnets*. "Nothing in the classical and native precedents," says Arnold Stein, "quite corresponds to Donne's use of satiric spokesmen,"[5] and Alvin Kernan makes Donne the great exception to his argument that English satire in the 1590s adopted the persona of the rugged satyr. "There are no open revelations," in Donne's satiric voice, "of a twisted, complex character venting its own disappointment and mental sickness," according to Kernan; instead, Donne's satires are the least savage of the period and also the most consistent and coherent.[6] When we read Donne's *Satyres*, we are in much the same position as readers of his *Holy Sonnets*, in that the concept of the persona, so useful to understanding the dramatic set pieces comprising the *Elegies* and the *Songs and Sonnets*, loses its value.[7] In the *Satyres*, Donne describes a room much like the one he must have inhabited at Lincoln's Inn (I), he mentions his French servant (IV), whose existence R. C. Bald confirms for us in the standard modern biography, and he informs us of his appointment as Egerton's secretary and of Egerton's commission from Elizabeth to clean up corruption in the courts (V). More importantly, he raises issues—religious, aesthetic, and social—in satire after satire so woven into what is known of his life in the 1590s that it is useless for us, with our limited knowledge, to pretend that the *Satyres* are not an autobiographical text.[8] For all practical purposes, the voice of Donne's satirist is that of Egerton's secretary, or at least the voice of a young man who was seeking the opportunity to fashion himself as the confidant and spokesman of a great man like Egerton.[9] Readers must, of course, observe the caveat of all autobiography, which is that Donne, in reflecting on himself in the *Satyres*, is developing his self-image in a detached, purposeful manner, and along lines laid out, if not by conventional satire, certainly by conventions available to his culture and relevant to the circumstances of young office seekers in his time. The contention of this chapter (and this book) is that Castiglione shaped Donne's conception of the conventions by which one could engage in self-revelation. Finally, I do not wish to imply that the autobiographical voice or content of the *Satyres* enables us to date their composition, as their text could easily represent the reflections of a writer working ten years after the events he describes and just as ambitious as ever.

After surveying the *Letters to Severall Persons of Honour* and calling special attention to the famous letter to Sir Henry Goodyer in which Donne declares that "to be no part of any body, is to be nothing," Jonathan Goldberg speaks of Donne's dependence on his friends during the years immediately following his dismissal from Egerton's service as "self-constitutive": "This mode of self-creation through self-abandonment, placing oneself entirely in the hand of another, registers Donne's response to his sense that being a part of the world means allowing the world to work its will upon the self." Goldberg goes on, by way of the *Devotions* and the funeral sermon on King James, to demonstrate that Donne conceived his utterances to be "authorized acts of explication" voiced by a self constituting itself in subjection to King James's will.[10] In effect, according to Goldberg, but in the language of Satyre IV, Donne conceived his writs—in this case, his devotional prose—as esteemed canonical by the king. Goldberg's account of Donne's self-fashioning applies to the Elizabethan Donne as well as the Jacobean, except that it is Egerton during part of this early period whom Donne represents (possibly long after the fact) as authorizing those acts of explication which have come down to us as Donne's *Satyres*. Donne's continued revisions of the *Satyres* and his presentation of them to the Countess of Bedford as late as 1608 confirm that he regarded them as a serious, coherent work presenting him in a favorable light and setting forth his qualifications to act as the voice of a powerful patron. In fact, manuscript evidence leads Wesley Milgate to conjecture that Donne actually prepared a presentation copy of his *Satyres* for the Lord Keeper.[11] Donne did more, however, than to let his world and his employer work their will upon him. The "body" of which he conceives himself to be a part in the *Satyres* is greater than that represented by any single politician or political regime. It is the body of civil discourse formed by Castiglione, and the figure of Egerton is subsumed by it and idealized, just as Elisabetta Gonzaga undergoes apotheosis in *The Courtier.* This would explain how Donne could go on revising his satires long after dismissal from Egerton's service and feel no qualms about presenting them to the Countess of Bedford even though they constituted a reminder of his misconduct a scant six years earlier in marrying Ann More.

The position of secretary to Egerton gave Donne an opportunity to articulate courtly codes of discourse which were more subtle and more elegant than his actual office of state warranted, and it did so paradoxically by giving Donne occasion to style himself as subject to the voice of an absent authority, for that was what a secretary was supposed to do. Angel Day's *The English Secretary* was first published in 1586, but reissued (prior to and during Donne's employment with Egerton) in 1592, 1595, and 1599. Popular throughout the early seventeenth century as well, it provides our best contemporary account of a secretary's qualifications and duties. Day's treatise reads in many places as if it were the prototype of Goldberg's description of Donne's self-fashioning, and therefore should be regarded more as describing occasions for Donne's practice than as laying down prescriptions. In fact, readers of *The English Secretary* might be reminded of Donne's "True Character of a Dunce," and especially during the long, dreary passages devoted to rules for letter writing. Still, it is well also to remember that Day was describing the activities of an intellectual elite (whose membership included Francis Bacon) and to remember that the position of secretary to a Privy Councillor carried with it license to aspire to the highest posts in the Elizabethan regime. One need only read the famous letter of William Strachey, secretary to Sir Thomas Gates, governor in 1608 of the Virginia colony, which describes the shipwreck of the colonists in Bermuda and the starving time in Jamestown, in order to appreciate the skills of this class of functionaries. Shakespeare appreciated those skills in Strachey's case, as *The Tempest* proves, and Donne would have been only too glad to have Strachey's job, as his unsuccessful application for it indicates. So the occasions which we find in Day for Donne's courtly discourse are strong ones.

After explaining that the secretary is, according to the etymology of his title, "*quasi custos,* or *conservator secreti sibi commissi,*" Day compares him to the most private room in his master's house:

> By this reason, we do call the most secrete place in the house, appropriate unto our owne private studies, and wherein wee repose and deliberate by deepe consideration of all our waightiest affaires, a *Closet,* in true intendment and meaning, a place where our dealings of importance are shut up, a roome proper and peculiar to our selves. And whereas into each other place of the house, it is ordinarie for every neere attendant aboute us to have accesse: in this place we doe solitarie and alone shut up our selves, of this we keepe the key our selves, and the use thereof alone doe onelie apropriate unto our selves.

Like a "closet," the secretary possesses the qualities of covertness, safety, and assurance; he keeps his employer's secrets "closelie," away from the eyes, ears, and understandings of others; he retains them "securelie" in memory with the respect owing to matters of consequence; finally, he guards against negligence and mistakes that might render them damaging to his employer.[12] The secretary, to continue the architectural metaphor, constructs himself as the sanctum sanctorum of his employer's political world. It is easy to see how this noble conception of the secretary's role as the great man's confidant might have suggested to Donne an opportunity to create, as Egerton's secretary, an idealized picture of the court kept at York House, a picture rivaling Castiglione's of Urbino.

Flowing from this secrecy of the confidant (and friend, one is tempted to say, since Day's text in this place reminds one of nothing so much as Elizabethan friendship literature), the other principal requirement of a great man's secretary is sympathy, or what Day calls "chary affection":

> Much is the felicitie that the maister or Lord receiveth evermore of such a servant, in the chary affection and regard of whom affying

himselfe assuredlie, he findeth he is not alone a commander of his outward actions, but the disposer of his verie thoughts, yea he is the Soveraigne of all his desires, in whose bosome hee holdeth the repose of his safety to be far more precious, then either estate, living, or advancement, whereof men earthly minded are for the most part desirous.[13]

The ambiguous pronouns of this passage enact the exclusivity and intimacy of the relationship between the employer and his secretary, who here achieves the proportions of an alter ego. I shall argue that Donne writes his *Satyres* as if Egerton, or an idealized Egerton, a grave man and a wise man, were "the disposer of his verie thoughts, yea . . . the Soveraigne of all his desires," and that Donne records the success of the endeavor when he has the historical Egerton actually enter the poems to hire him as his spokesman.

On the practical, everyday level of the secretary's job, apart from its more exalted mission, sympathy was called for in writing his employer's correspondence:

Hereof is he exceedinglie to becom studious, and a zealous imitator in all thinges, to the intent that knowing the effects of his Lord, with what ends and purposes they are caried, & unto what forme and maner of writing he is speciallie addicted, he may the more easilie and with better contentment discharge that part of his service, wherein by continuall occurrents he shall have occasion daily to be imploied.[14]

This is, of course the sympathy, not of the confidant, but the employee and servant, and in fact a reader's interest in *The English Secretary* derives largely from its author's efforts to bridge the gulf between confidant and servant, which grows wider and wider the more Day writes. Almost two-thirds of Day's book consists of an anthology of model letters—hortatory, laudatory, monitory, and so on—for the novice secretary's zealous imitation in case his intuition of the great man's style and temperament flagged. The latter third of the book contains the discourse I have been quoting, a discourse which attempts to restore the secretary's dignity and to compensate for the servility implied by a collection of letters to be copied. Still, even this craven counsel to impersonate the master is, I shall argue later, used by Donne and transformed into a strategy for producing—in Satyre III—one of the most subtle and daring statements about religion in a Renaissance despotism that comes down to us from the Elizabethan period.

It is arguable that the impasse with which Day struggles was the one that defeated the young John Donne despite his mastery in his *Satyres* of Castiglione's art of impasse. Day's struggle to ennoble his discourse may mirror Donne's struggle to cope with life at York House. "Zealous imitator" and confidant, servant and friend, the figure of the secretary, in Day's description, embodies contradictions which go a long way toward explaining how the brilliant young soldier and politician who served Egerton could so forget himself as to steal his bride from the home of a gentleman much wealthier than himself and higher in rank. Styling himself as a great man's intimate, allowing his thoughts to be ordered by such a man, Donne may have forgotten, for a critical moment, that he was not actually such a man, or at least not yet such a man. He may have forgotten that he was still only a servant. Moreover, Egerton's cryptic remark, at the time that he was forced to dismiss Donne, that Donne was fit for a king's service, may have registered an uneasy awareness that his secretary was using his post as a platform for a higher type of discourse than was warranted in a strictly professional sense. If Milgate is correct that Donne prepared a presentation copy of the *Satyres* for Egerton, Donne may have misjudged his employer. Possibly the *Satyres* were proof to Egerton (either at the time of Donne's employment or years later) that his secretary was "overqualified" for the job.

The figure of the secretary destroyed by being caught unconsciously in the type of impasse concerning which he had to exhibit consciousness in order to qualify for his post is tantalizing. The reference to Castiglione in the introduction to Satyre V as the maker of good courtiers, but not necessarily as making courtiers good, brings the author of *The Courtier*, the master of the art of impasse, together with Egerton at the moment of Egerton's definitive entrance into Donne's poetic universe.

> Thou shalt not laugh in this leafe, Muse, nor they
> Whom any pitty warmes; He which did lay
> Rules to make Courtiers, (hee being understood
> May make good Courtiers, but who Courtiers good?)
> Frees from the sting of jests all who'in extreme
> Are wrech'd or wicked: of these two a theame
> Charity and liberty give me. (1–7)

We discover very shortly that the "liberty" to which Donne refers here was granted to him by Egerton, in whose service he now finds himself, and we learn that Egerton is in the Queen's service delegated to "weed out" the courtly sins enumerated in Satyre IV, which are so great that the Queen must, in one breath, be exempted from all knowledge of them and yet, in the next breath, be said to have authorized Egerton to weed them out.

> Greatest and fairest Empresse, know you this?
> Alas, no more then Thames calme head doth know

Whose meades her armes drowne, or whose corne o'rflow:
You Sir, whose righteousnes she loves, whom I
By having leave to serve, am most richly
For service paid, authoriz'd, now beginne
To know and weed out this enormous sinne. (28–34)

It is difficult to imagine how anyone can read these lines and still consider Donne to have been an alienated radical. The ambiguous positioning of the word "authoriz'd" momentarily claims for Donne himself
Elizabeth's delegated authority. Egerton enters the *Satyres* as, of course,
the grave man who will make courtiers good—who will take up where
Castiglione left off, that is—but the reference to Castiglione is anything
but dismissive or derogatory. He is invoked as a moral authority prohibiting laughter at the extremes of wickedness and wretchedness represented by the officers and suitors—the courtiers—whose practices Egerton must reform. Furthermore, in leaving who will make courtiers good
an open question before Egerton enters, Donne demonstrates as much
respect for its difficulty as Castiglione does. Apart from his respect for
The Courtier, Donne recognizes that to diminish Castiglione's moral
judgment would be to detract from the imposing difficulty of Egerton's
commission and hence to detract from the dignity of the man. Indeed,
the vicious circle described in Satyre V, in which officers and suitors
provoke each other to new heights of corruption, is the central impasse
to which Castiglione's text sensitizes its readers. If Egerton is to deliver
the arbitrating word that breaks impasses, they must be real impasses,
truly vexing dilemmas, or Egerton would be not Elizabeth's surrogate
but her exalted flunky, and Donne himself as Egerton's secretary would
exhibit a queasy resemblance to Day's description of the secretary in his
meanest capacity, or else to the pestering "Makeron" of his own fourth
satire. Hence, Donne places Castiglione, whose text is the consummate
representation of impasse in the life of public officials, at the threshold
of the satire introducing Egerton, and he actually introduces Egerton in
the context of that formidable ethical impasse which bedevils not only
Book III of *The Courtier* but virtually every exchange that the book pretends to record. How to be an officer and a suitor, and hence a courtier,
and retain one's integrity in the game? Donne's principal concern in the
Satyres is identical to Castiglione's throughout *The Courtier*.

Donne acknowledges Castiglione to be Elizabethan society's authority on the subject of enlightened, disabused discourse on the contradictions of public life. *The Courtier* stands at the threshold of honest
statesmanship, for Donne, as it did for Bartholomew Clerke, its Latin
translator, and for Clerke's employer, Thomas Sackville, Lord Buckhurst, and finally, as it did for Buckhurst's royal mistress, Elizabeth her

self. In Satyre V, the Queen, the Privy Councillor, and the secretary are fused within a discourse whose rules are laid down by Castiglione. The task of the English secretary, the spokesman and confidant, the other self, of an Egerton, is, then, in Donne's conception, to develop in himself Castiglione's disabused intelligence, and this is what Donne depicts himself as accomplishing in the *Satyres.* The mode of depiction, moreover, is an exceptionally complex dialogue like that which one experiences in *The Courtier.* In the *Satyres,* Donne becomes involved in exchanges, not only with contemptible figures in London life culminating in the "Makeron" of Satyre IV, but with an implied Egerton, in Satyres II and III, whose role we must reconstruct from hints scattered throughout the poems themselves. (This process of reconstruction essential to reading most of Donne's poems will be the subject of the next chapter). Most importantly, Donne engages in a dialogue with himself throughout the *Satyres,* a dialogue which seeps into his correspondence of the 1590s, which has everything to do with the encroachments of public service on private, subjective autonomy, and which is critical for understanding the mind of the John Donne who sought self-definition in public service. All these dialogues, as I shall attempt to demonstrate, swirl about vortices at their centers, impasses which have the same significance as those toward which Castiglione's courtiers are so powerfully drawn.

Poets and Lawyers

Satyre II emerges as a profound revision of his thinking on the part of that solemn youth who narrates Satyre I and who does not recognize that he is only the other half of one of those strange hermaphrodites made of "study and play"—inhabitants, according to Donne's "Epithalamion Made at Lincolnes Inne," of the Inns of Court. While that studious, priggish, self-deceived youth is as ridiculous as the frisky companion whom he deplores, the narrator of Satyre II has discovered a crisis which makes him not the butt of our laughter but a colleague and mentor in the discipline of self-scrutiny. The narrator of Satyre II is the same person who narrated Satyre I, but he has matured so much and so suddenly (as youths often do) that it takes a reader's breath away. In Satyre I, Donne gives a portrait of himself as a callow, if clever, youth—a portrait preparatory to the metamorphosis he will record himself as experiencing under the influence of a grave man's questions. The narrator of Satyre I is a clever observer of everyone but himself. So he creates a scene which is worthy of one of Castiglione's interlocutors, but he fails to recognize himself in it. A scene in Book II of *The Courtier* deserves quotation in full, because it could as easily be a source of Satyre I as Horace's *Sermones*, I.ix.[15]

> ... there be some fond persons that being in company with the greatest friende they had in the world, if they meete with one better apparrelled, by and by they cleave unto him: and if an other come in place better than he, they doe the like altogether unto him.
>
> And againe, when the prince passeth through the market place, through Churches or other haunted places, they make all men give them roome with their elbowes, till they come to their heeles, and though they have nothing to say to him, yet will they talk with him, and keepe him with a long tale, laugh, clappe the handes, and nod the heade, to seeme to have waightie businesse, that the people may see they are in favour. (p. 115)

This describes the "fondling motley humorist" to perfection and also, I shall argue, explains his behavior in a way that implicates the narrator of Satyre I in it.

Bringing the list of authors, that "constant company," with whom he communes in his "standing woodden chest" to a close on a comic anticlimax with the "giddie fantastique Poets of each land," the narrator of Satyre I fails to recognize his resemblance to the "headlong, wild uncertaine" companion who lures him into the street against his better judgment (10–12). That this, moreover, is Donne (the Donne perhaps of Satyre V who has learned to know himself) reflecting on himself in an earlier incarnation and laughing at himself, that this is Donne pointedly implicating an earlier self in the self-deceived discourse of Satyre I's narrator, is indicated by the oath which he makes his companion swear. If the "humorist" wishes to enjoy his fellowship, he must not prepare any speeches to court the "beautious sonne and heire" of some "velvet Justice" met along the way "with a long / Great traine of blew coats, twelve, or fourteen strong" (21–24). However, Donne owed, in large part, his introduction into the Lord Keeper's service to his friendship with Thomas Egerton, Junior, with whom he sailed to Cadiz and went on the Islands Expedition. Surely, Thomas Egerton, Senior, and other members of Donne's coterie reading Satyre I would have enjoyed a laugh at Donne's expense (a laugh allowed them by Donne, of course) and recognized the poem as depicting the secretary at a stage of development preceding his achievement of that disabused self-awareness which was an essential qualification for his post—which was one of those "personal attributes," in Kishlansky's phrase, which would later qualify him for selection to Parliament. It was not for the Donne they knew to adopt a holier-than-thou posture about courting the sons of powerful officeholders.

The narrator of Satyre II, on the other hand, leaves us no room to see around him, to ironize him. He knows—and is wrestling with the fact—that he himself can be counted a giddy, fantastic poet and that this character may accord no better with the gravity which he so admires than his former companion's infatuation with stylish clothes. When the narrator of Satyre I refers to "our dull Comedians" (99), he is completely unaware that his own poetic discourse resembles nothing so much as stage comedy and, in fact, derives its strength from the resemblance. The narrator of Satyre II has, however, been jolted into a new awareness of himself. The "Sir" whom he addresses, as if his satire were an epistle or a spontaneous rejoinder, is *an* Egerton, or the grave man of Satyre I, who has tugged his sleeve and asked him if his own constancy—since constancy seems to be his theme—stands up to scrutiny any better than his companion's. Does not your poetry (the grave man might have asked) resemble rather closely the dancing that your companion admires in that well-favored youth (83–85)? Do not you yourself (he might have asked) dance, as it were, "for company" (86), inasmuch as you write poetry—like this very satire—for your coterie of inner barristers, the ones whom you mention in your "Epithalamion Made at Lincolnes Inne"—"frolique Patricians, / Sonnes of these Senators wealths deep oceans"—whose favor it could do you no harm to win? Is not your po-etry only your manner of elbowing your way into the Prince's company and making believe that you have weighty business to discuss with him? In Satyre II, the narrator is no longer addressing an Osric who will let him get away with sanctimonious posturing. Instead, the tables have been turned, and he is being forced, by someone whom he respects, to look at himself as the "fondling motley humorist" and to consider his own involvement in the scramble to make connections and get ahead at the Inns of Court. Look at your own soiled hands, the grave man seems to have said. Moderate your Christian zeal enough to face your own con-tradictions.[16]

As Donne's only extended disquisition on poetry and on its social uses, Satyre II demands attention. However, its pessimism is chilling, coming, as it does, from one of the best poets of the era. Not for Donne the exalted claims of Sidney's *Apology for Poetry* or Jonson's aspirations to political influence through laureateship. Donne begins by conceding to his examiner that poetry—his poetry, along with everyone else's—is to be classed among "all ill things" (3). However, poetry is pitiable, not hateful. It has no power to injure others. Poets are innocuous—self-indulgent for the most part, self-destructive at worst. Donne admits that as a poet he may be someone "who write[s] to Lords, rewards to get" and hence may resemble "singers at doores for meat" (21–22), but he insists that this corruption of language is nothing to Coscus's tyranny over

words in the writing of contracts. Coscus can impoverish another man's
family down through generations, while poets only seek a livelihood,
and, most of the time, with scant success. Donne's unrelieved stress on
the futility of poetry is only one more way in which he differs from his
fellow satirists of the 1590s. Their attacks on poetry, on critics, on readers, and finally on each other make it only too clear that they regarded
poetry as a force to be reckoned with and took their own efforts seriously. Marston's "In Lectores" makes it "disconcertingly obvious," according to Roma Gill, "that he is more interested in flaunting his literary style than in edifying his readers,"[17] and Hall's lamentations over the
rape of the Muses only repeat the puritan charge that poetry is a danger
to the state—that it "brings dearths, and Spaniards in" (6), as Donne so
wryly puts it. In contrast with his fellow satirists, Donne never boasts of
his own poetic achievement, never criticizes his fellow poets or engages
in literary feuding with them, never complains about envious detractors,
never sets himself up as an arbiter of literary taste, as a critic of the critics, engages in no ostentatious displays of learning, and could not care
less about his reception by anything as vague and inconsequential as a
reading public.[18] Poetry is, for him, simply not a serious enough subject
to warrant so much concern, and, of course, the obverse of his argument
involving poetry and Coscus—poetry and bad lawyers—is that good
lawyers represent a much greater force for the good than do good poets.
Can it be doubted that Egerton would have agreed?

In the following lines, perhaps the most memorable of Satyre II, the
image of the convict reciting his neck verse crystallizes Donne's view of
the relation of poets and lawyers, of poetry and power:

> One, (like a wretch, which at Barre judg'd as dead,
> Yet prompts him which stands next, and cannot reade,
> And saves his life) gives ideot actors meanes
> (Starving himselfe) to live by'his labor'd sceanes;
> As in some Organ, Puppits dance above
> And bellows pant below, which them do move.

So much for Shakespeare and Jonson! Although Milgate argues that
Donne probably wrote these lines in 1594,[19] four years before Jonson
recited his neck verse to escape execution for the murder of the actor
Gabriel Spencer, it is impossible to read them and not think of Jonson
struggling to put behind him the degradation of the theatrical trade. If
David Riggs is correct, Jonson in murdering Spencer was murdering the
actor and playwright in himself, he was obliterating his past self as an
employee of the theatre owners, and at just the moment when he set out
to seek a place of influence in the political regime as an Horatian man of
letters—an advisor to kings.[20] Jonson may have thought of his duel with

Spencer as his rite of initiation as a gentleman, but Donne could not have regarded it as anything more than another proof of the impotence of the literary life. It is the lawyer, after all, who passes judgment on the neck verse, who decrees life or death for the poet, and it is the poet who must cope with the legal system, not the lawyer who must adjust himself to poetic fictions. Lawyers have access to power and use it, while professional poets, like Jonson, who regard poetry as having an independent status and its own kind of authority, are self-deceived and only suffer at the hands of the truly powerful.

The ambiguous concluding words of Satyre II, no matter how they are read, stress the impotence of poetry. The immediately preceding twenty-five lines of the poem, which describe Coscus seizing estates by twisting the language of contracts, suggest rather strongly that "drawes" is singular only in form and by contact with "none," and that "words" is its actual subject. Donne would then be saying that his words as a poet endanger no one, in the way that Coscus's legal jargon does; they subject no one to crushing penalties inscribed in statute books. He remains the innocuous poet, but at least no devourer of his fellow Englishmen, no destroyer of lands and ancient customs (103–109). He does not, like Coscus, contribute to unemployment while denying the poor charity (105). This is the reading most consistent with all that has preceded in Satyre II. Another possible interpretation (not requiring that the singular "drawes" not really be singular) would have Donne saying that no one—like Coscus's scribe or clerk—sets down Donne's words or draws them out, at his behest, in such a way as to place those of whom he writes within the jeopardy of vaguely written, and hence far-reaching, laws. Those, it is implied, who find themselves parties in Coscus's contracts, as opposed to figures in satirical poems, had better watch out for those laws. Again poets, even satirists, are harmless by comparison with lawyers. Finally, the reading that has Donne declaring than no one has brought libel charges against him because of his satires, though not consistent with the rest of the poem, only reinforces, in its way, the other readings. The reason that no one charges him with libel does not have to be, as some suggest,[21] that he has told the truth and is, therefore, exempt from the law, but simply that no one cares enough about what poets say to bother charging them. Just as "pistolets" are better artillery for moving love than love poems (17–20), money will sooner induce people to go to court than insults couched in rhyming satires. The burden, in any case, of Satyre II's closing lines is damnation of poets with negative praise. Poets are less dangerous than lawyers. Their words have no binding power.

This is a rather mild ending, though, considering the disparagement of poetry preceding it. For Donne, the literary profession is not only ineffectual but degrading. It could no more make a man a member of the gentry than, in John Ferne's opinion, commerce could, per se, with no outstanding service to the state. A poet emulating another poet is competing, according to Donne, in the doing of a discreditable thing, as if he were trying to out-fornicate a dildo (32), and poetic imitation amounts to eating someone else's meat in order to produce one's own excrement (25–30). The condemnation of poetic imitation occurs, not only in Satyre II, but in an early document, a letter, whose reference to Dante's *Inferno* indicates a focus on poetic authorities, not those in other branches of learning.

> S^r I am no great voyager in other mens works: no swallower nor de-
> vourer of volumes nor pursuant of authors. perchaunce it is because I
> find borne in my self knowledg or ap^{r}hension enough for (wthout for-
> feiture or impeachment of modesty I think I am bond to god thank-
> fully to acknowledg it) to consyder him & my self: as when I have at
> home a convenient garden I covet not to walk in others broad medows
> or woods especially because it falls not wthin that short reach wch my
> foresight embraceth to see how I should employ that wch I already
> know to travayle for inquiry of more were to labor to gett a stomach
> & then find no meat at home. To know how to live by the booke is a
> pedantery, & to do it is a bondage. For both hearers & players are more
> delighted wth voluntary then wth sett musike. And he that will live by
> p^{r}cept shalbe long wthout habite of honesty: as he that would every day
> gather one or two feathers might become brawne wth hard lying before
> he make a feather bed of his gettings. That Erle of Arundell y^t last
> dyed (that tennis ball whome fortune after tossing & banding brik-
> wald into the hazard) in his impriso[n]ment used more then much
> reading, & to him y^t asked him why he did so he answerd he read so
> much lest he should remember something. I am as far from following
> his counsell as hee was from petruccios: but I find it true that after
> long reading I can only tell y^o how many leaves I have read. I do ther-
> fore more willingly blow & keep awake y^t smale coole wch god hath
> pleased to kindle in mee then farr off to gather a faggot of greene
> sticks wch consume wthout flame or heat in a black smother: yet I read
> something. but indeed not so much to avoyd as to enjoy idlenes.

In the next breath, Donne tells us that he "flung away Dant the Italian a man pert enough to be beloved & to much to be beeleeved." In relegat-ing Pope Celestine V to hell simply for retiring from public office, Dante proves Donne's point that literary authorities are to be taken lightly. "If he will needs punish retyrednes thus what hell," Donne asks, "can his witt devise for ambitio?" If Donne had read further in the *Inferno* he might have developed more respect for Dante's wit, but it is unlikely that he would have changed his mind about imitating authors. Imitation is a bondage, stifling to one's genius, distracting to one's memory, pedantic, plodding, illiberal, graceless. Steeping oneself in literary art is, at best, a form of idleness; at worst, the escapist obsession of a beaten man like the Earl of Arundel, a recusant and a suspected traitor, who spent the last ten years of his life in the Tower.

The proper gentlemanly attitude toward authorities in things, like poetry, subject to one's own judgment is exhibited, according to Donne, by Christopher Hatton, a remarkably successful man, and one of Egerton's predecessors as Lord Keeper:

> . . . as ye chancell: Hatton being told after a decree made y^t his p^rdeces-
> sors was of another opinion he answered hee had his genius & I had
> myne: So say I of authors that they thinke & I thinke both reasonably
> yet posibly both erroniously; that is manly. . . . [22]

In both this letter and Satyre II, Donne concedes that real power rests with Lord Chancellors, not with poets, and since it is to their authority that one must submit despite one's own judgment, one should not add false authorities. Submission to literary authority only fosters self-deception as to the real powers holding sway over one's life. In the opening of Satyre II, a chastened speaker concedes all this to his sage examiner. However, he is not prepared to concede that freedom and enlightenment are to be obtained from a volte-face such as Coscus made when he turned from poetry to the legal profession.

Coscus is not a Hatton. He did not obtain his power through everything from personal charm great enough to make him the Queen's dancing partner to diplomatic skills refined enough to secure him the confidence of a divided Privy Council. He plodded on at the Inns of Court until "time (which . . . must make a calfe an oxe)" (41–42) made him a lawyer. Nor can the vast majority of lawyers ever hope to rise as high as Hatton or to exercise their own genius freely. The average lawyer puts in hours and hours "like an owlelike watchman" writing briefs and bearing his clients' burdens like an ass; for months on end he lies to everyone, inventing generous motives for his business in the courts where, despite his clients, he serves only his own avarice; "like a wedge in a blocke," he pushes and shoves his way to the front of the courtroom only to lie to "the grave Judge," to the Hatton or the Egerton, after having lied profusely to his own clients; he is "more shamelesse farre / Then carted whores." Submitting to the legal profession, fashioning oneself along lines laid down by real powers, may exhibit common sense, but it also in most cases results in an exchange of the "fondling, motley humorist," the "giddie, fantastique Poet," for a prostitute (64). Wesley Milgate cites a passage in translation from a medieval manuscript, *Liber de similitudinibus et exemplis*, to explain precisely why Donne could re-

gard Coscus as "more" shameless than a prostitute: "So many hire lawyers to defend their property, but they consume it. Also note that lawyers are worse than whores, since whores sell the viler and worse parts
of their body, but lawyers the nobler and better, forsooth, the mouth
and tongue."[23] I may be a poet, says the speaker of Satyre II to his
own "grave Judge," and you may have forced me to acknowledge what I
am, but tell me which is worse, the self-indulgent impotence of the self-
deceived poet that I showed myself to be in my last satire—that "giddy,
fantastique" poem to which you took exception—or the cynical materialism of a Coscus, of a clear-sighted, avaricious lawyer? As a poet, I may
have used words to attract powerful patrons, "wealths deep oceans,"
but, as a lawyer, what has Coscus done with words, if not crush the vulnerable? My words may be impure, tainted with self-interest, inconstant
with respect to higher truths, but no one has to listen to them in the way
that Coscus's words must be attended to, even though each constitutes
a rape.

Power corrupts language, along with everything else, insists the
speaker of Satyre II, and there is no escape from the impasse except the
partial one that comes with candidly acknowledging it. Political and
economic power may turn poetry into neck verse, but in the mouths of
lawyers it makes language a murderous weapon. When poets sing at rich
men's doors, they do so to eat like everyone else and stay out of jail. However, when Coscus sings "the language of the Pleas, and Bench," it is not
to beg at rich men's doors, but to break them down and confiscate estates. If poets choose to deceive themselves into thinking that literary
authorities are more powerful than magistrates and wealthy magnates,
they are merely pathetic, and their illusions represent a threat to no one
but themselves. However, those "words, words, which would teare / The
tender labyrinth of a soft maids eare" (57–58), which Coscus uses to seduce his mistress, sound sinister. In a precise, systematic way, they turn
the mistress into a commodity, into a piece of land to be seized by the
shrewdest, richest lawyer.[24] They do not attempt to persuade or entertain. They threaten and coerce, they prostitute her, by reminding her of
her price on the market and of her status as a thing subject to legal
authority, and hence to Coscus's manipulations. On the one hand, poets,
who ground their language on fictive authority, preserve the subject,
but—quixotically—at the cost of debilitating illusions. On the other
hand, Coscus, himself a prostitute, has only the language of the market-
place and the courts, a language that reifies the subject, both himself
as subject and whomever he desires. Which is worse, asks Donne in
Satyre II, the language of rampant materialism or the language of make-
believe?

Apart from preparing the reader for Satyre III and offering a suggestion as to Donne's religious position in the mid-1590s, the compari-

son of poets to papists (10) and Coscus to Luther (87–96) deepens the impasse with which Donne confronts his judge. Poets are "poore, disarm'd, like Papists, not worth hate" (10), but, for Coscus, entering the legal profession has been what leaving the monastery was for Luther. Having become a lawyer, Coscus is no longer subject to the law, just as Luther was no longer required to tell his beads when he ceased to be a friar. Now that he is the master of texts and makes them do his bidding, now that he no longer humbly submits to them as a monk does to the words of his prayers, Coscus, like Luther, adds the "power and glory clause" in the form of the many provisos he attaches to his titles and assurances. And since good works are out of fashion, no one scrutinizes Coscus's doings anymore than one would rummage through an old wardrobe (110–111). He is freer, in Protestant England, to make the words of the law serve his greed than he would be in a poetic land of misdevotion. Poet-papists, still restrained by the monastic rules of literary form and convention, still subject to the word as law—both civil and literary—are more likely than lawyers to scrutinize works. For them, works must measure up to words. For Coscus, words can always be found to justify one's works. In an address to Parliament in 1585, the Queen herself drew a comparison identical to Donne's: "I see many over-bold with God Almighty, making too many subtle scannings of his blessed will, as lawyers do with human testaments."[25] Papistical poets are less likely than legal Lutherans to substitute themselves for the text in the act of interpretation, to tyrannize over it. However, as idolaters of the text, they are also its deluded slaves. It is their fate always to be trying to live by truths which are to others, like Coscus, only matters of interpretation.

In Satyre II, Donne asks which is worse, the legal demystification of texts, or illusions of literary authority. If, on the evidence of this satire, Donne's religious leanings in the mid-1590s can be said to be more toward the Roman than the Reformed Church, the poem also forces one to conclude that he was no more satisfied with these leanings than he was with being a "scarce Poet" (44). Under the pressure of his grave judge's interrogation, Donne confesses his involvement with the rest of society, sheds a false sense of self-importance and aloofness, and begins to exhibit a taste for vexing questions of the sort that Castiglione made central to his discourse on statesmanship.

The Future of an Illusion

The step from poetry in Satyre II to religion in Satyre III is less abrupt than at first it seems. The metaphor of religion used to contrast poets and lawyers in Satyre II forms a link with Satyre III so firm as to constitute one piece of evidence that Donne considered his "book of satires" to be a coherent single work in five parts. The corruption of poetry by wealthy patrons, its reduction to panegyric and apologetics, is of limited consequence, because poetry deals in nothing but illusions anyway. On the other hand, religion—for Donne and his contemporaries—was no illusion, and yet "mens unjust / power from God claym'd" threatened in his day to reduce it, in practice, to the status of an illusion. Satyre III confronts the dilemma of retaining integrity and freedom of conscience, just as Satyre II does, but the stakes are infinitely higher. Facing the impact of civil authority on artistic creativity, Satyre II deflates its author's ego, but at least it does not place his immortal soul in question. In Satyre III, however, the disabused apprentice statesman summons all his courage to make a truly destabilizing gesture, one which could as easily convict his class of cynicism as create its conscience. He dares to open the question of a state religion's influence on individual conscience.[26] He acknowledges that salvation depends on freedom in the choice of a religion, and at the same time dares to ask how such freedom can exist in a state legislating only one religion. Donne voices this question in an equally daring way. He discards the dramatic, multivocal quality of Satyre I and abandons the dialogue structure of Satyre II, with its addressee in the form of the grave "Sir." Instead of projecting himself into characters like the "fondling, motley humorist," or Coscus, or his own deluded former self, Donne takes the step, in Satyre III, necessary to Angel Day's English secretary and projects himself directly into the mind of a powerful superior.

In Satyre III, Donne no longer stands outside, pressed by the grave man to acknowledge his own ulterior motives and hidden agendas. Instead, he moves inside the grave man's mind and speaks for, not to, him.[27] Donne adopts the "chary affection" of the secretary and represents himself as permitting the enlightened, disabused enforcer of the Elizabethan religious settlement to become "the disposer of his verie thoughts" and to speak through him to young men like himself. Donne, as poet, temporarily solves the problem of poetic imitation posed in Satyre II by representing himself as the "zealous imitator in all things," not of a Horace or a Juvenal, not of a literary authority, but of the workings of an Elizabethan Privy Councillor's mind. Donne impersonates an Egerton. Hence, the voice we hear in Satyre III seems, as Donne intends it to be, much older than that of the preceding satires, more stern and austere, and the poem as a whole seems to be the product of a much later period in Donne's life. However, scholars who argue that Satyre III was written long after the other satires may only be paying tribute to the success of a young John Donne's impersonation. Whether the historical

Egerton or anyone else in his position could ever have experienced the thought processes attributed to him by Donne, we cannot know. The authority figure represented in Satyre III is idealized, and yet—due to Donne's courageous rendering of the historical moment in its most challenging particulars—his words are credible. Donne threatens the ideal with the real at its corrosive worst, and consequently readers of Satyre III feel either as if Donne was a daring radical or as if this satire has opened a window into the heart of the Elizabethan regime at its best.[28] Persuasion by concession of adversative fact (of which this satire is an excellent example) is the subject of chapter 5.

Satyre III culminates in those lines which pass judgment on Mirreus and his cohorts, all lured by "lecherous humors" (53) in their choice of a religion, not guided by a free conscience. Here the voice of the Privy Councillor, speaking to Englishmen out of the whirlwind of the council chamber, comes through at its sternest: "but unmoved thou / Of force must one, and forc'd but one allow; / And the right . . . " (69–71). Satyre III achieves its dramatic impact from this dangerous confrontation of the issue of force. These lines represent the most concise statement in Elizabethan literature of the vexing dilemma posed by the doctrine of *cuius regio eius religio*, the doctrine that the regime dictates and is coterminous with its church. On the one hand, in Donne's time most of the English agreed with Elizabeth's Lord Treasurer, William Cecil (Baron Burghley),

> that there could be no government where there was division. And that a state cold never be in safety, where there was tolleration of two religions. For there is no enmytie so greate as that for religion. And they that differ in the service of God, can never agree in the service of theire contrie.

On the other hand, everyone would have admired the Lord Treasurer for those words (again attributed to him by his anonymous biographer) with which he declined Mary Tudor's offer of a place on her council. He was, he said,

> tought, & bound to serve God first, & next the queen. And if her service shold put him out of Gods service, he hoped her majesty wold give him leave to choose an everlastinge, rather then a momentarie service. And for the queene she had byn his so gracious ladie, as he wold ever serve, & praie for her in his heart; &, with his bodye & goods, be as ready to serve her defensce, as anie of her loyall subjects, so she wold please to graunt him leave to use his conscience to himself. . . . [29]

In sum, it was a matter of self-preservation for the state to enforce uniformity of religion, but the conscience of the subject was to be preserved inviolate. In Satyre III, Donne brings to consciousness this impasse, which lies embedded—unavowed, inarticulate—in Burghley's utterances. For the salvation of your soul, you must ("of force"), says the grave man into whom Donne has projected himself, choose one religion, "unmoved" in your conscience by "lawes still new like fashions" (56–57), and yet, he adds, you *are* "forc'd" by the state to accept as true ("allow") but one religion. The religion you choose, he concludes, must be the right one. Right one, we ask, by which standard—that of the unmoved individual's conscience or of the enforcing regime's prerogative? The austere voice of Satyre III only responds with the same dark enigma: the "unmoved" individual must, though "forc'd," choose the right religion.

A closely related text produced by an older contemporary, who was Donne's equal perhaps in acumen and also in dedication to statesmanship, assists in placing Satyre III within the Elizabethan discourse on faith by statute.[30] It was probably in 1589 that Francis Bacon (like Donne, filling a secretarial role for a member of the Privy Council) drafted a famous letter on Elizabeth's policy in "ecclesiastical causes" for the signature of Sir Francis Walsingham. This letter, addressed to a French public official, was designed to meet criticism that Elizabeth's policy exhibited "inconstancy and variation."

> I find . . . that her Majesty's proceedings have been grounded upon two principles:
>
> 1. The one, that consciences are not to be forced, but to be won and reduced by the force of truth, with the aid of time and the use of all good means of instruction and persuasion.
>
> 2. The other, that the causes of conscience, when they exceed their bounds and grow to be matter of faction, lose their nature; and that sovereign princes ought distinctly to punish the practice or contempt, though coloured with the pretence of conscience and religion.
>
> According to these principles, her Majesty at her coming to the Crown, utterly disliking the tyranny of Rome, which had used terror and rigour to seek commandment of men's faiths and consciences, though as a Prince of great wisdom and magnanimity she suffered but the exercise of one religion, yet her proceeding towards the Papists was with great lenity, expecting the good effects which time might work in them. And therefore her Majesty revived not the laws made in the twenty-eighth and thirty-fifth year of her Father's reign, whereby the oath of allegiance might have been offered at the King's pleasure to any subject, though he kept his conscience never so modestly to himself; and the refusal to take the same oath without further circumstance was made treason. But contrariwise her Majesty, not liking to

make windows into men's hearts and secret thoughts except the abundance of them did overflow into overt and express acts or affirmations, tempered her law so as it restraineth only manifest disobedience, in impugning and impeaching advisedly and maliciously her Majesty's supreme power, and maintaining and extolling a foreign jurisdiction. ... But when about the twentieth year of her reign she had discovered in the King of Spain an intention to invade her dominions, and that a principal point of the plot was to prepare a party within the realm that might adhere to the foreigner, and that the seminaries began to blossom and to send forth daily priests and professed men, who should by vow taken at shrift reconcile her subjects from their obedience, yea and bind many of them to attempt against her Majesty's sacred person; and that by the poison which they spread the humours of most Papists were altered, and that they were no more Papists in conscience and of softness, but Papists in faction; then were there new laws made for the punishment of such as should submit themselves to such reconcilements or renunciations of obedience. And because it was a treason carried in the clouds and in wonderful secrecy, and came seldom to light, and that there was no presumption thereof so great as the recusance to come to divine service; because it was set down by their decrees that to come to church before reconcilement was to live in schism, but to come to church after reconcilement was absolutely heretical and damnable; therefore there were added new laws containing a punishment pecuniary against such recusants, not to enforce conscience, but to enfeeble and impoverish the means of those to whom it rested indifferent and ambiguous whether they were reconciled or no. . . . [31]

Bacon's effort to keep clear the distinction between conscience and faction becomes tortured as he confronts the increasing severity of Elizabeth's legislation against Catholics. He wrestles with the central issue of Satyre III, the conflicting imperatives of the state and the individual conscience—the need to retain integrity by maintaining their separate jurisdictions, and yet their unavoidable trespass into each other's domain. Since Bacon's letter for Walsingham forms part of an actual diplomatic exchange with a skeptical outsider, Bacon is at a disadvantage by comparison with Donne. In his impersonation of Walsingham, Bacon is compelled to state the regime's policy with greater rhetorical coherence than the policy itself could achieve in practice. Donne, however, projecting himself in a poem—and not a dispatch—into the mind of a Privy Councillor can at least choose his own occasion, and he chooses to impersonate the powerful leader in his capacity as an example to insiders, to skeptical Englishmen, who need to be persuaded that they can live within the Elizabethan Settlement and, despite its incoherence, retain their integrity. Hence, Donne is free to speak openly of an impasse which Bacon (though as disabused as any statesman of his time) is forced to obfuscate. Donne enacts the part of the Privy Councillor speaking to troubled friends of the regime, while Bacon assumes the voice of a Walsingham or a Burghley taking on potential enemies.

Bacon's troubled awareness of the thin ice on which he is skating manifests itself in the balancing act performed by his sentence structure. It is impossible, for instance, to comprehend despite Bacon's rhetoric how the fine of twenty pounds per month (a year's salary at the time for a parish schoolmaster),[32] which was imposed by the 1581 parliament for refusal to attend establishment services, could have left the Catholic conscience unforced, and especially the conscience of those wavering Catholics for whom reconcilement might have been a matter "indifferent" or "ambiguous." And yet Bacon's narrow premises and lockstep antitheses march willfully on as if no such troubling details and unseemly realities existed. If—says Bacon—to have been reconciled *to* Rome by a Jesuit or a seminary priest is the same as to have been severed *from* one's obedience to the Queen,[33] and if refusal to attend establishment services is the surest sign of such reconcilement, then the twenty-pound fine is punishment for treason. It is not religious persecution. The Catholic conscience can be tolerated, but any ambiguity, on the subject's part, as to his obedience to the Queen cannot be. In theory—according to Bacon—Elizabeth meant only to discourage disloyalty, not to force lukewarm Catholics to accept the state religion, nor did she wish to persecute even the most obstinate for their religious beliefs. The trouble with the theory, of course, was that in reality Catholic consciences could not be separated from Catholic subjects and left free while the subjects were fined and threatened and disenfranchised in ways too numerous to go into here. There is not the slightest hint in Bacon's letter that the Queen's policy coerced not only Catholic consciences but troubled even loyal conformists. Instead, the exquisitely balanced clauses pile up layer on layer of mystification.

The principal danger of engaging in such discourse lies not in one's vulnerability to sensible rejoinders like Cardinal Allen's that the Queen's policy was "the very torment of all English consciences"[34] but in being taken in by one's own rhetoric, and Donne was to experience this danger himself in *Pseudo-Martyr*. Torment, in this case, with one's immortal soul at stake, is better than self-delusion. It is one thing, as Donne's friend Henry Wotton put it in his punning definition of an ambassador, to lie abroad for your sovereign; it is quite another to deceive oneself with one's own propaganda. This is the difference between Castiglione's advisor to princes and the "quaint Castilio" of Marston's satire. It distinguishes Kent from Oswald, Horatio from Guildenstern. It also distinguishes the choice of an illusion from the choice of a religion.

Satyre III represents the healing discourse necessitated by exercises of the sort that Bacon and other English secretaries engaged in. Satyre III heals because it acknowledges the disjunctive and the incoherent in public affairs and analyzes the inducements to self-deception created by a state religion. Donne begins with a protestation, on the part of the grave man for whom he speaks, that his detachment is sincere, not merely a pose of diplomatic reserve or philosophical aloofness. Powerful emotions cancel each other out and leave him pensive. Compassion for his fellow human beings neutralizes his impulse to deride them, and yet "brave scorn" dries up his compassion. He can neither weep with Heraclitus nor laugh with Democritus and be a wise philosopher. However, the ambiguity of line 3's close suggests that it may not be wisdom to be wise in the sense that they are. Philosophical aloofness may only be another example of the self-deception practiced by Mirreus and company. In any case, Democritus and Heraclitus are "blinde Philosophers," whose "merit of strict life" (12–13) got them into heaven, not their opinions. Finally, "brave scorn" falls by the way with that patently rhetorical question asked in line 4. Obviously, "railing" will do no good, because those "worne maladies" would not have had time to become "worne," to become stale and hackneyed, if such a simple solution were effective. Instead, the scorn of Juvenalian satirists reveals itself too clearly as rhetorical bravery—ornament, that is—designed to make the satirist look good, and not real courage aimed at reform of society. In four lines, Donne obliterates the conventional postures of satire, as if to say that postures and conventions are the problems here and cannot serve as solutions.

The problem acknowledged in Satyre III is that religion should amount to more than a posture, more than a theatrical illusion, more than attendance at the approved services in order to avoid a fine or other penalties, and yet the existence of penalties, the intrusion of political power into the spiritual realm, must leave even the loyal adherent of the Settlement in doubt as to whether attendance at services is a matter of conviction or convention, of conscience or convenience, of truth or illusion. How can even the loyal conformists of Donne's generation, baptized into the state religion—much less the Catholic convert—adhere to the establishment and be reasonably certain that they retain their integrity, that their decision is made in the forum of conscience, and not in the political and economic market place? For Egerton and Donne, both converts from Catholicism, this must have been a consuming question, and it was for the older man to set an example to his sons' and his secretary's generation. This explains the stress in Satyre III on fatherhood: first, in the images of the "fathers spirit" in heaven (11) and the son "whom hee taught so easie wayes and neare / To follow . . . " (14–15) and, then, in the more complex image of the father who, questioned by his son, must, in turn, question his father to get an answer in what amounts to a process of historical inquiry. Donne's use of the father figure in Satyre III dramatically implicates the grave man himself in the historical developments leading to the impasse his words reveal.[35]

The father speaker, rendered dispassionate by his conflicting emotions, begins his admonition with a useful message: the only thing to fear, he says, is failing to be afraid of what is truly frightening. "This fear great courage, and high valour is" (16), and reveals "brave scorn" for the moral cowardice it really is. It is courageous to fear damnation. Courageous to know your real foes and face them—the world, the flesh, and the devil (33–42). The speaker, one feels, gets so caught up in these pieties that he forgets when he refers to "thy fathers spirit" that his secretary's father and step-father were Catholics and that—if he *is* Egerton—his own father was a Catholic. But this so often happens when we generalize. We forget how implicated we are, how implicated our generalizations are, in the business of ideology, in the business of justifying norms which insure our security and material comfort. The grave man intends with his words only to register a commonplace criticism of the times: sons of Christian fathers are leading lives less Christian than pagan philosophers. However, his generalization about fathers taken within the specific context of his times betrays the issue he is evading. If men of his secretary's generation are more courageous about fighting Spain in the Low Countries and the New World, about sailing to discover the North-west Passage, and about fighting duels, than they are about practicing religion, it has much less to do with pride and greed or any aversion on their part to the general tenets of Christianity, than it has to do with a skepticism brought on by the religious controversy specific to their times. The speaker must bring himself—or be brought—to realize that the time has long gone by, in late Elizabethan England, when an appeal to the general principles of Christianity is enough to overcome profound spiritual malaise.

When he admonishes, "Seeke true religion" (43), one can almost hear his youthful listeners, perhaps at table in York House, bring him back into the historical moment with a simple question, which he repeats, "O where?" From this point, his discourse grows thick with specifics, and he acknowledges that the malaise of the younger generation (and its skepticism in the figures of Phrygius and Graius) is grounded in a history so recent that he himself has played a large role in it. Those "lawes still new like fashions," enacted in parliament after parliament during Elizabeth's reign and enforced by men like himself, can have, he admits, the same influence as the "ragges" (47)—the ceremonies, legends, and images, the whole rich panoply of externals—by which Catholics are seduced into idolatry, and which induce a sanctimonious iconoclasm, a reactive plainness, in equally deluded Calvinists. His equation of "the statecloth where the Prince sate yesterday" (48) with those rags of Rome confirms his admission that laws sanctioned by the Queen's prerogative can have a powerfully mesmerizing quality. His reference to those conformist "Godfathers," whose ministrations at the font are no less coercive than a guardian's financial leverage (59–62), not only contains none of the respect of his former reference to fathers, but constitutes as clear an acknowledgment as possible of the establishment's ability to force consciences. The speaker of Satyre III, once forced to focus on particulars, acknowledges everything that the Walsingham whom Bacon impersonates struggles to conceal. The voice of the grave man, the father and elder, heard in Satyre III sounds poignant, even bitter, inasmuch as it is the voice of a father acknowledging the death of paternal authority by its own hand, by its own involvement in the creation and enforcement of those statutes with which the establishment, in defending itself, assaulted the consciences of its own followers.

If Mirreus and company—the younger generation—find superficial reasons to choose a religion, as if religion were an earthly mistress, and if they find a thousand ways to evade serious spiritual questions, the blame can be laid at the door of a civil authority that committed adultery upon their consciences. In a fascinating drama of reversals, the grave man of Satyre III finds himself answering the very same charge that he had leveled against the youthful speaker of Satyre I. Now, it is he and his generation who must answer for having made a "fondling motley humorist" of religion itself, and it is the young man whom he had once rebuked for inconstancy who is answering in his behalf—who drafts a statement similar to Bacon's in every respect except that it is addressed to worried friends of the establishment and delivers a far more idealized picture of the governing authorities.

The next mention of fathers is more positive, but it swiftly moves beyond those actual fathers whose spirit will be met in heaven and seeks paternal authority in grandfathers and, by extension, in more distant ancestors. Moreover, it follows upon that pivotal acknowledgment of impasse, "but unmoved thou / Of force must one, and forc'd but one allow; / And the right . . . ," which sums up the description of spiritual malaise in the preceding twenty-five lines and opens the way, with the abruptness of a leap of faith, to an affirmation of the Settlement. The appeal to that truth which is "a little elder" (73) is identical to the appeal implicit in the first proposition that Elizabeth required her Catholic bishops to debate at Westminster in 1559: "It is against the worde of God, and the custome of the auncient churche, to use a tongue unknown to the people, in common prayer. . . . "[36] By referring to the custom of the ancient church, Elizabeth sought to revise once and for all and silence Catholic discourse on the subject of forefathers, just as the grave man of Satyre III revises his own understanding of paternal authority. His earlier invocation of fathers to be met in heaven, he realizes (at the prompting of his youthful listeners), is perilously close to such invocations, for example, as that of Bishop Scot of Chester, who spoke against the Settlement in the parliament of 1559:

> But nowe I do call to remembraunce that I did here yesterday a nobleman in this house say . . . that our fathers lyved in blyndness, and that we have juste occasion to lament their ignorance: whereunto me thinkethe it may be answered, that if our forefathers were here, and heard us lament their doings, it is very lyke that they woulde say unto us as our Savyour Christe said unto the women which followed hym when he went to his death, and weepted after him, *Nolite flere super nos, sed super vos.*[37]

The crucial realization of Satyre III's grave man is that he and his Christian forefathers did indeed live in blindness—albeit a papist blindness, and not the pagan blindness of those "blinde Philosophers"—and that one cannot so simply invoke paternal authority as he did earlier in his discourse and Bishop Scot did in opposing the Settlement. One must seek a truth which is "a little elder."

One must seek to be among "those blessed flowers that dwell / At the rough streames calme head" and not abandon one's "roots" (103–105), which are planted in the ancient church preceding Rome. Donne makes the same point with an architectural metaphor in the *Essays in Divinity* when he asserts that the Church of England has kept "still the foundation and corner-stone" of the Christian religion "Christe Jesus" and has abandoned "the spacious and specious super-edifications which the Church of Rome had built thereupon."[38] One must go back to the basic elements of the older structure. Satyre III's second reference to fathers differs from its first in that it invites, rather than evades, historical inquiry: "in strange way / To stand inquiring right," the grave man or Egerton declares, "is not to stray; / To sleepe, or runne wrong, is" (77–78).

It is obvious, though, that swimming upstream or dismantling old buildings encounters resistance. "On a huge hill, / Cragged, and steep, Truth stands, and hee that will / Reach her" must take pains. It is no accident that Satyre III's last line begins with the word "power," and, of course, that power is spelled out in the Acts of Supremacy and Uniformity and in those various statutes, "new like fashions," enacted in support of the Church of England. What so suddenly justifies the speaker of Satyre III in thinking that "mens unjust / Power from God claym'd" (109–110)—especially if it is English power—can be resisted, the mountaintop be attained, souls be saved from perishing? Donne's answer—or rather the answer he attributes to his older speaker—is that the acknowledgment of impasse is in itself enough to justify his confidence and validate the process of historical inquiry. It is the only justification. Admitting that one is "forc'd" and yet must be "unmoved"—and not pretending that one is not forced—is the only way to obtain "hard knowledge" (86) and "keepe the truth which thou'hast found" (89). Alertness to the inducements to self-deception in one's world insures that one's soul will not "be ty'd / To mans lawes, by which she shall not be try'd / At the last day" (93–95). The healing utterance which Donne finds for his speaker is generated by the same code governing the debates of Castiglione's courtiers: salvation lies in the disabused awareness of stalemate, impasse, the incoherent, the self-contradictory, in human affairs.

One can never be certain of one's own sincerity in choosing a state religion. One will always be subject to charges of hypocrisy, leveled (of course) by outsiders, but most of all by the self against itself. This is the plight of the establishment person with a conscience, of persons like Donne and—as he would wish us to believe—Egerton, and the only relief lies in open admission that the freest exercise of one's will, leading—one thinks—to salvation, may, under the pressure of a state religion's powerful material inducements, be an act of self-deception leading to spiritual death. "Lecherous humors" may bring on adultery and hypocrisy. This is the impasse, and not to face the uncertainty, not to look into the vortex, is to be swallowed by it, to be "given to the streames tyrannous rage" and, if not consum'd in going" (105–108), to be lost at last in a sea of illusions.

The Looking Glass

Satyre III represents an extraordinary act of self-abnegation. It is one thing to lose oneself in Christ in order to find oneself, as the Gospel according to Matthew urges, but to let an Egerton, despite his status in the world, become "the disposer of [one's] verie thoughts" must occasion severe doubts. Satyre IV records those doubts, the doubts of Angel Day's English secretary, and in so doing constitutes Donne's own reflections on the type of self-fashioning which Jonathan Goldberg observes in Donne's later works. That the authority figure through whom Donne speaks in Satyre III is idealized does not remove the doubts. It only intensifies them. How could secretaries with the intelligence of Bacon and Donne have gotten through the day without idealizing their superiors? Their inducement to see in Walsingham and Egerton finer qualities than were actually present must have been enormous. Their own self-respect depended on the existence of superior personal qualities in those social superiors to whom they sold their intelligence. Otherwise they were Coscus.

Satyre IV's anxious—at moments, frenzied—tone and its phantasmagoric parade of disturbing images records a malaise inseparable from the very social mimesis which Donne's world valued so much and which he practices in Satyre III. In his passage from Satyre II to Satyre III, Donne traded the mimetic tradition in poetry of poems imitating poems for a social mimesis in which selves constitute themselves by impersonating other selves in a manner equally as conscious as the poetic, and ironically he produced one of the richest formal satires in the history of a poetic genre. Also, by acting the role of a revered older contemporary, with whom he had much in common, he succeeded in thinking through certain spiritual problems more confidently perhaps than he could have *in propria persona*—problems of the convert which were to trouble him to the end of his days.[39] However, he also laid himself open to a charge starkly summed up in a poem by one of his fellow satirists, William Goddard:

> *Dartus*, if thou'dst a Courtier learne to be,
> Then take a glasse; that booke shall straight teach thee.
> Looke in thy glasse, and frowne, or skowle, or smile
> And shalt see one doo soe another while,
> Laugh thou, there's one will laugh: shedd thou a teare
> A teare ther's one will shedd; I dust thou heare?
> Thy bodie bow, gape, winke, or nodd thy pate,
> Do what thou wilt, ther's one will imitate.
>   *To great men (if thou wilt a Courtier bee)*
>   *Thou must doe, as thy shadowe dus to thee.*[40]

The speaker of this wicked little poem stands far more aloof from the foolish Dartus than Donne could have claimed to be, and hence his tone of mock seriousness is arch and derisive, with nothing of the anxiety that readers detect in Satyre IV.

It was a courtier that Donne sought to be. Imitating the Egerton figure in his third satire, he fashions himself as a great man's mirror—to be sure, no ordinary mirror hung where anyone in the house can be reflected in it, but a mirror for that closet or private chamber (according to Day's metaphor of the secretary) where only the great man's reflections touch it. Still, in Day's discourse, there is that opening, that fissure, down which the trusted intimate, the secretary as friend, may slide, only to wind up at the bottom of his fall a zealous imitator—an employee, at best, and, at worst, as Satyre IV puts it, "a priviledg'd spie" (119) or "a licenc'd foole" (228). The impasse dealt with in Satyre IV leaves the zealous secretary, who fashioned himself in Satyre III as a great man's alter ego, in doubt as to whether he has not ended up the great man's despicable shadow. The image of the wax museum in lines 169–174 lends his doubt the appropriate dash of horror.

A better explanation is available for the extreme loathing—at moments, nausea—that Donne feels in the presence of his interlocutor in Satyre IV and for his insulting tone toward him than that Donne confused Juvenalian diatribe with the urbane, conversational mode of Horace and produced an awkward hybrid.[41] Donne was too subtle a craftsman to commit such a blunder, and especially in a work like the *Satyres,* which he took pains revising and presented to at least one powerful patron, and possibly two (if Milgate's conjecture about the presentation to Egerton is correct). At the risk of introducing a jarring anachronism, I would suggest that the taunting tone of Satyre IV's speaker toward his interlocutor, and yet his fascination with him, his inability to walk away from him, resembles nothing so much as the bearing of Dostoevsky's Raskolnikov toward his double and evil angel, the corrupt Count Svidrigaylov. The nightmarish entrance of this interlocutor in lines 117–119 ("Towards me did runne / A thing more strange, then on Niles slime, the Sunne / E'er bred"), as if he were summoned from the supernatural to punish Donne for his visit to court, recalls the materialization of Svidrigaylov in Raskolnikov's room, apparitionlike, as if emerging from the sick man's guilty delirium.[42] Even the first words of this interlocutor, "Sir, / I love your judgement" (51–52), spoken as if in conscious rebuke and contradiction of Donne's insistence during the preceding thirty-three lines on his strangeness, recall Svidrigaylov's assumption that he has found an accomplice in Raskolnikov. Actually, the comparison with Svidrigaylov may not be so anachronistic as it seems at first glance. In *The New Age of Old Names,* printed in 1609, Joseph Wybarne quotes lines 17–23 of Satyre IV as a description of the Antichrist and suggests that the courtier-interlocutor's relationship to Donne is the same as that of Archimago, Duessa, Orgoglio, and the Soldan to Spenser's heroes.[43] Moreover, in the late 1630s, a poem by Clement Paman imitating Satyre IV refers to this courtier-interlocutor as a devil haunting Donne.[44]

In sum, the interlocutor of Satyre IV, unlike the buffoon of Satyre I, poses a real threat, and the John Donne narrating Satyre IV is aware of it. This John Donne, as opposed to the deluded self narrating Satyre I, is aware that his interlocutor represents dreadful potentialities in him-

self, and he reacts, therefore, with a frenzied volley of insults designed
to ward off a peculiarly insidious evil spirit. The frenzy of these insults
is betrayed by the way that some of them misfire. It is hard, for instance,
to work up resentment toward Donne's courtly double when Donne
compares him to victims of English xenophobia and religious intoler-
ance (23–29). Instead, one hears a note of hysteria in Donne himself,
who is usually sympathetic in the *Satyres* to victims of persecution. One
even wonders if the image of the disguised Jesuit refers to a guilty uncertainty on Donne's part as to his own religious leanings. Is he a recent
convert to the Settlement or is he a Catholic in disguise? Whatever the
case, the images of monstrosity and disease with which Donne describes
this courtier convey a sense of loathing so deep and so consuming as to
seem to derive, less from the conventional satirical impulse to revile the
sins of others than from an anxious dread of one's own hidden sins.
Donne depicts himself in Satyre IV as having shed the complacency of
the bookish satirist of Satyre I, of the self-styled contemplative spirit,
and as experiencing the anguish of self-scrutiny in the domain of political action, where no one's hands are clean and one has to genuinely
worry about being drained of subjective autonomy.

Whether, in Satyre III, Donne served Egerton as a flattering mirror or as an accurate—and therefore honestly complimentary—one, the
courtly interlocutor of Satyre IV, with his language of "complement,"
gives Donne a horrifying image of himself. There are more indications
that this courtier is a member of Donne's class and a shadow self than
merely Donne's sense of imprisonment (154), or his inability to walk
away from him, or even their shared preoccupation with clothes, as
when Donne first brags that he despises showing off new clothes at court
(7) and then sneers at the courtier for wearing a worn-out velvet jerkin
(29–34). Even in matters as subtle as the courtier's insistence on the appellation of dignity, "Sir," when he addresses Donne, a class solidarity
is hammered home and an identity is established. With this title, the
courtier, at first meeting, calls attention to their shared identity as gentlemen (51), and then, when Donne gives a moral lecture on the virtues
of solitude, the courtier squeaks, "O Sir" (73), as if to remind Donne
that it is in the definition of a gentleman to find it sweet to talk of
kings, to be interested in the noblest members of his class, to be in and
of society. Furthermore, when the courtier calls the guardian of the
tombs at Westminster Abbey "base, Mechanique, coarse" (81), he is reminding Donne that he should find it sweet, not only to talk of kings,
but to do so—in case Donne did not know—with other gentlemen, with
other members of his own class. He is returning Donne's insult in a
rather subtle way—that is, by ignoring the insult and by taking Donne

seriously in his claim that he can talk just as well of kings with the keeper of the tombs as with a fellow gentleman. Anyone who could make such a claim needs help.

That Donne is aware of the riposte, aware that he is being given an implied lesson in gentlemanly deportment, becomes apparent when he himself makes irritated use of the appellation in letting his interlocutor know that talk of French fashions is not—or, at least, should not be—obligatory conversation among gentlemen (87). One can almost hear the duelist cry touché, but, of course, the irony of this exchange is that Donne reveals himself, at this point, to be touched, or tainted, just as much as his interlocutor, by the amour propre of his class. A similar nuance can be felt in the exchange over foreign-language acquisition, when the courtier suggests that "a poore gentleman" by traveling may surpass the great linguists of his time, and Donne replies, "If you'had liv'd, Sir, / Time enough to have beene Interpreter / To Babells bricklayers, sure the Tower had stood" (60–65). The use of "Sir" here is sarcastic. The "Makeron" (117) has no title to the title, because he is an audacious fool and presumes upon it—he is an associate of bricklayers (again Donne sneers). However, Donne *is* entitled to the title and by censuring the "Makeron" demonstrates his superior qualifications. This squalid tit-for-tat, this class-conscious sparring culminates in lines 143–144, when the courtier begs a crown—"Sir, can you spare me?"—and parries Donne's insulting reply with "Nay, Sir," as if to remind Donne for the last time that he is, despite his hypocritical hauteur, talking to his semblance, to his brother, to a fellow beggar at court. He is looking into a mirror and this time it is hanging in a madhouse.

How different the use of "Sir" is in Satyre IV from its use at the opening of Satyre II to address the grave man. Donne uses it there to establish a solidarity with the grave man and to exalt himself thereby, but in Satyre IV the tables are turned and it is directed at him, as a sign of complicity, by a person who represents everything loathsome in public life, by an intelligencer, a malcontent, a flatterer, a beggar. That Donne has learned a humiliating lesson in the course of his anguishing conversation is proven by the adjustment of his vision that makes the "Makeron" seem not quite so strange to him as at first sight. Donne realizes that there are "more strange things then hee" (152) at court. In fact, there is evidence in Donne's early correspondence, written during the Egerton years, that Donne was quite as avid for gossip about the court as this garrulous courtier assumes him to be. In a letter written in 1600, probably to Henry Wotton, he mocks his own hunger for news:

> methinks now y^t y^{ey} err wittyly wch teach that saints see all mens action in god as in a mirror. for I am sure y^t if I were but glorified wth y^r sight

I should gather many particulars of carieres & altibaxos (as y^t fryer sayes) wherein fortunes tumblers are exercised at & from ye Court, for I hunger to know who & why & when doth what. . . . when I have drunk one potion more to my health & weaked my self I shalbee strong enough to find y^o at Essex or rather then not at all at Court where you shall find me (a miracle in y^t place) y^r honest frend.[45]

This letter is amusing for its betrayal of the allure that court gossip had for Donne—amusing, that is, as external evidence of Donne's similarity at one time to the courtier whom he derides in Satyre IV. It also provides a lighthearted, informal treatment of the issue of integrity, which Satyre IV enfolds in a nightmarish, hallucinatory discourse. Here, if courtiers are like mirrors, they are like God reflecting all things to the initiated vision.

Still, for all its lightheartedness, the comparison of court gossip with the privileged vision accorded saints explains only too well Donne's depiction of himself as paralyzed by those tales of "When the Queene frown'd, or smil'd, and . . . what / A subtle States-man may gather of that" (99–100). Saints do not breed so much idolatry among Catholics as courtiers do among each other when they lay claim to esoteric knowledge, to inside information, about secular centers of power. Neither in this letter nor in Satyre IV does Donne represent himself as immune to this idolatry. If he learns anything in Satyre IV, it is that he was wrong to think that he "went to Court; But as Glaze which did goe / To'a Masse in jest" (8–9). He went in earnest with the rest of the congregation as a fellow idolater. Donne may "belch, spue, spit, / Looke pale, and sickly like a Patient" (109–110) and "sigh, and sweat" like a woman in labor "at sight of loathed meat" (115–116) when his double plies him with courtly conversation, but Donne is a courtier too and perhaps a trifle sick of himself.

In another early letter, again probably written to Henry Wotton and clearly dating from the year 1600, Donne proves himself to be quite the "subtle States-man" satirized in line 100 of Satyre IV who has a sharp eye on the Queen's moods:

The Court is not great but full of iollyty & revells & playes and as merry as if it were not sick. Her m^{tie} is well disposd & very gratious in publique to my Lo: Mountioy my lo: of Essex & his trayne are no more mist here then the Aungells wch were cast downe from heaven nor (for anything I see) likelyer to retourne. He withers still in his sicknes & plods on to his end in the same pace where y^o left us. the worst accidents of his sicknes are y^t he conspires wth it & y^t it is not here beleevd. That wch was sayd of Cato y^t his age understood him not I feare may be averted of y^r lo: that he understands not his age: for it is a naturall weaknes of innocency. That such men want lockes for themselves & keyes for others.[46]

No "triviall houshold trash" here (98), the Queen's frowns and smiles. There is genuine compassion for Essex in this letter, the commander with whom Donne sailed on the Cadiz expedition, but the condescension of the shrewd political analyst mutes it. Donne may begin by calling the court sick, but Essex failed at court, and Donne condemns him for it. His "innocency" is the opposite of admirable. Although, in lines 181–185 of Satyre IV, Donne expresses revulsion at the theatricality of the court ("All are players"), he condemns Essex for not having been a competent player, for not having dissembled his feelings enough. He lacked a lock for himself. Nor did he ever learn to read the Queen's expressions. He lacked the key, and hence he failed to understand his age. Consignment to an outer darkness is the punishment for failing to be a proper player. The simile of the fallen angels, like that of the saints in the previous letter, stresses the peculiar allure of the court, its aura of being inhabited by creatures who appear to be slightly more (or less) than human. When, like Essex, one has been in favor there and fallen, there is no middle ground to land on. The court is the only place worth being. Nothing else compares. Banishment means relegation to the torments of an inconsequential life—and they were real torments for Donne once he came to know Essex's plight more feelingly.

What is implicit in Satyre IV, with its trip to court, its retreat to Donne's home only to continue the entrancement (157) in a bitter meditation, and finally its return to court a "second time . . . that day" (177–178), is made explicit in Donne's letters. There is no exit from a hell which is also the only paradise in sight. Either one is a courtier, or one is an asshead. "As divers others destroyed first there owne townes & burnt theire ships to quench all hope of revenging, so am I in this warfare enforced to fight it out bycause I know not whether to run," declares another of these early letters.[47] So much is at stake in the struggle to succeed at court that all else seems ashes and dust. The epistolary statement most closely resembling Satyre IV prefaces the report on Essex quoted above:

> I am no Courtier for w^(th)out having lived there desirously I cannot have
> sin'd enough to have deserv'd that reprobate name: I may sometymes
> come thither & bee no courtier as well as they may sometymes go to
> chapell & yet are no christians. I am there now where because I must
> do some evill I envy y^r being in ye country not that it is a vice will make
> any great shew here for they live at a far greter rate & expence of
> wickednes. but because I will not be utterly out of fashion & unso-
> ciable. I gleane such vices as the greater men (whose barnes are full)

scatter yet I learne that ye learnedst in vice suffer some misery for when
they have reapd flattery or any other fault long there comes some other
new vice in request wherein they are unpracticed.[48]

The first sentence so closely parallels the reference to Glaze and his visit
to Mass (8–16) that Donne appears to have had his satire in mind, or
else the letter in mind when he wrote the satire. Even without the report
on Essex, the movement of Donne's thought is the same as in Satyre IV.
He begins by insisting that he is not like everyone else at court and ends,
despite the jocular tone, by confessing his implication in court crimes.
He begins by avowing that he is in the court world but not of it and ends
by admitting that he is contaminated. His fellow courtiers are, in the satire's terms, "burnt venom'd Leachers" (134) passing their disease to him
and to others who must remain in fashion, not simply to be sociable, but
to survive in their careers. The truth is that there is "no token of worth,
but 'Queenes man'" (235)—despite the satirist's contempt for Elizabeth's
athletic halberdiers.

The general issue of integrity is the same in Satyre IV as it was in
Satyre III. How does one preserve a conscience in public life? However,
here it is expressed specifically as revulsion at the mental operation of
the secretary which Donne performed in Satyre III. Donne expresses
genuine torment in Satyre IV over the process of defining oneself as the
reflection of a great man at court, even an Egerton. At the center of
Satyre IV, Donne has fled from court and rebukes himself for his cowardice:

> Low feare
> Becomes the guiltie, not th'accuser; Then,
> Shall I, nones slave, of high borne, or rais'd men
> Fear frownes? And, my Mistresse Truth, betray thee
> To th'huffing braggart, puft Nobility? (160–164)

These lines are interesting because Donne is talking himself into a return visit to court, and not because there is any hint that Donne regards
Egerton, or his like, as huffing braggarts. It is not Egerton (if indeed
Egerton were the great man for whom he was speaking in Satyre III)
whom Donne fears. What he fears are his own motives. Has he, in fashioning himself as the great man's spokesman, done so from motives of
self-interest, not service, and therefore done no better than if he had
been serving "puft Nobility"? How anguishing if, in having offered
himself to be an Egerton's mirror, he now found himself mirrored in the
"privileg'd spie" who so annoys him! The spy has no doubt that he and
Donne are alike. What evidence does Donne have that they are not? Going back to court that same day and facing the same thing in a Macrine

or a Glorius does not prove one's courage. Bravado may be all that is involved, because one has to go back anyway if one wishes to be a public servant. In fact, Donne's second trip turns out to be more nightmarish than the first and produces the same result: Donne shakes "like a spyed Spie" (137). He spies himself, that is, as the despicable shadow in Goddard's satire, the "licenc'd foole," and not the authorized spokesman.

The impasse is intractable. One cannot think one's way out of it. It is, in fact, the same one that Thomas Greene stresses in his reading of Book II of *The Courtier*. If, according to Federico Fregoso, loving the Prince means that the courtier "in his wil, maners and facions" must be "altogether pliable to please him" (p. 123), or if, according to Angel Day, being the perfect secretary means allowing all one's thoughts and desires to be shaped by one's employer, what is there to distinguish the secretary or the courtier from a hired sycophant? What is to distinguish Francis Bacon writing that letter for Walsingham's signature from a groveling toady? The letter may be written in Baconian prose, but it follows the workings of Burghley's mind, as expressed in *The Execution of Justice in England* (1583), with looking glass accuracy. The only difference between Donne's treatment of this impasse and Castiglione's is that Donne achieves a much greater dramatic intensity—an urgency commensurate with the fierce competition for places at Elizabeth's court in the late 1590s. In such circumstances, Donne recognizes that there is no way to persuade oneself of one's own integrity. One cannot play Horatio to one's own Hamlet. One has no right to take on the tone of the preacher (237–241), as his earlier self did in Satyre I. Like the author of Maccabees, Donne cannot know if his assumption of the great man's voice in Satyre III has succeeded as he wished it to. He can know it to have merit in the abstract as a poetic fiction (which is what he means when he refers to the "knowne merit" of his work), but it will not have served its purpose unless an actual Egerton acknowledges that he has spoken well on his behalf and authorizes him to speak in the future. This is what he hopes for: that "some wise man shall / . . . esteeme my writs Canonicall" (243–244). Release from the impasse has to come from without. No state of mind, only history itself, can draw one out of the looking glass of morbid self-doubt and crippling self-consciousness. The person in whose image one is fashioning oneself must make one's poems histories and oneself a valid statesman by accepting the poems and oneself in full recognition of the ambiguity of the poems and of one's own honest confrontation of fearful contradictions within the regime. If one can be hired on those terms by those who make history, then one's poems are not belied by history—they are history.

This welcome entrance of history is what happens in Satyre V, which is much less a poem than a history. The satires leading up to it are poetry historicized, or poetry as history. Satyre V is history as poetry. The tormented introspection has ended momentarily. The historical Egerton has hired a secretary and authorized him to speak in full awareness of his secretary's critical, disabused insights into the regime. Satyre V sets the other satires in perspective, and is anything but "a hastily-put-together occasional piece."[49] It renders them comprehensible. It causes us to realize that Satyres I through IV, by reflecting shrewdly on the contradictions of public life, were at once presenting Donne's credentials and testing the regime. By announcing the secretaryship with Egerton, Satyre V brings this drama to a happy conclusion: Donne and the regime have passed the test represented by Castiglione's discourse. York House lives up to the standard set in Urbino, where critical discourse and self-reflection take place. This is why Donne introduces Castiglione and Egerton in the same breath. If Egerton enters this five-part drama as the deus ex machina, it is only because there is another god behind him and the god is a text. Long after his employment with Egerton, Donne presented his satires to the Countess of Bedford in the hope that they would produce a result similar to the one they dramatize—that is, gain him her acceptance on terms which would preserve his integrity and demonstrate hers. The ambitious young man depicted in the *Satyres* knew how to set a price on his services. His ambitions were anything but simplistic.

2

Aesthetic Play

In the opening pages of *The Courtier*, Emilia Pia has no sooner chosen the first evening's game and its first player than she makes up a rule which governs to the end. Federico Fregoso, who proposed the game of defining a courtier, would have liked to proceed along lines set down by "Philosophers schooles" for "him that keepeth disputations" (p. 29), but Emilia has a better kind of evening in mind. We learn, in fact, that she would probably have agreed with Donne about intellectual pastimes: "To know how to live by the booke is a pedantery, & to do it is a bondage," the young John Donne pronounces, "for both hearers & players are more delighted wth voluntary then wth sett musike."[1] However, Emilia goes beyond spontaneity to describe a method which Donne will employ with dazzling effect in his *Elegies* and *Songs and Sonnets* and hints of which we have already observed in his *Satyres*, with that dramatic presence of a grave man to whom Donne responds, for whom he speaks, against whose influence he struggles before being hired by him away from poetry and into history.

> Then the Lady Emilia saide laughing unto Lewis count of Canosse: Therfore for leesing anye more time, you (Counte) shall be he that shall take this enterprise upon him in forme and manner as sir Fridericke hath declared. Not for that wee know ye are so good a Courtier that you have at your fingers ends that belongs therto: but because in repeating everie thing arsiversie, as we hope ye wil, we shal have somuch the more pastime, and everie one shall be able to answere you.
>
> Where if an other more skilfull then you should take it in hand,

there should bee nothing said against him for telling the truth, and so should we have but a cold pastime. (p. 30)

With his clever reply (that the truth will never go unchallenged where Emilia is), Ludovico parries Emilia's barb, but he admits, when the laughter dies down, that the task before him is too difficult. He is glad to decline the offer of a day to prepare himself, for fear that he might do "as he did, that stripped himselfe into his doublet, and leaped lesse ground than he did before in his Coate" (p. 31). He is admitting that Emilia's method will spare him embarrassment whether his discourse fails or succeeds. The arsiversy method, he admits, will be not only entertaining as parody of the form that Federico would use but merciful in sparing him the dangers of high seriousness.

Best of all, it enables the players to bait each other, as Ludovico immediately sets out to do by insisting that the courtier be of noble birth. He knows that his argument (which is anything but new) is one-sided—arsiversy, as it were—but he provokes Gasparo Pallavicino to come in with the other side, so that then he himself may score the depressing point that in a fallen world of appearances and first impressions noblemen by birth will be received in society sooner than commoners with exceptional qualities. Far from attempting to gloss over the impasse, the two courtiers acknowledge it with their daring game and provoke each other to explore its depths. This grounding of his discourse in a world of appearances enables Ludovico to move on to that chilling delineation of grace involving *sprezzatura* which constitutes the true fascination of his contribution to the courtly entertainment. He demonstrates that Emilia knew her player when she chose him, not Federico, to begin the game.

This process, instigated by Ludovico and Emilia, by which the courtly players provoke and supplement each other's contributions, carries the assembly through several evenings and serves Castiglione as a major generative principle—like the movement toward impasse—of *The Courtier*'s narrative. One speaker after another lures his cohorts into rounding out the discourse that he has begun and into leaving him an opportunity to score a telling point. Much of Book III's interest lies in the Magnifico Giuliano's exchange with Gasparo, in which it is difficult to tell who has best provoked whom to draw unexpected conclusions. If the Magnifico manages to describe the court lady as anything more than an ornament and an inspiration to men, he is more indebted than he knows to Gasparo's provocations. Finally, on the fourth evening, Ottaviano Fregoso codifies the process as an aesthetic of provocation, which enables the courtier to capture the attention of his prince and tell him the truth:

In this wise may hee leade him through the rough way of vertue (as it were) decking it aboute with boughes to shadow it and strowing it over with sightlye flowers, to ease the griefe of the painefull journey in him that is but of a weake force. And sometime with musicke, sometime with armes, and horses, sometime with rymes and meeter, otherwhile with communication of love, and with all those waies that these Lords have spoken of, continually keepe that minde of his occupied in honest pleasure: imprinting notwithstanding therein alwaies beside (as I have saide) in company with these flickering provocations some vertuous condition, and beguiling him with a holsom craft, as warie Phisitions doe, who many times when they minister to yong and tender children in their sicknesse, a medicine of a bitter taste, annoint the cup about the brimme with some sweete licour.

The Courtier therefore applying to such a purpose this veile of pleasure, in every time, in every place, and in everie exercise, he shall attain to his end, and deserve much more praise and recompence, than for any other good worke that he can doe in the world.

Because there is no treasure that doth so universally profit, as doth a good prince. . . . (p. 165)

There is more to this passage than the familiar Lucretian sugared-pill theory of teaching, as the sixteenth-century translator recognizes. Flickering provocations—in the original the word is "illecebre"—imprint virtuous conditions. While Hoby's translation makes Ottaviano seem the inventor of a Renaissance version of subliminal advertising, it also clarifies the aesthetic play that Castiglione advocates and his book exemplifies and that Donne was to adopt in his secular poetry—provocative play, scarcely perceptible as provocation, inciting the mind to form conclusions which it will receive as its own, though they were imprinted by someone else. The courtier as consummate diplomat induces the other side to draw, not its own conclusions, but those which he implants in the course of recreation.

Possibly because of the distinction that Castiglione lent this provocative play, it assumed a place in two of the most important sixteenth-century English treatises on poetry. George Puttenham's *The Arte of English Poesie* describes synecdoche in the following terms: "it encombres the minde with certaine imagination what it may be that is meant, and not expressed."[2] Synecdochic poetry provokes the mind into a game of filling in the blanks and deceiving itself, once it has performed the task, that the ensuing device is of its own conception. Sidney's much greater authority lay behind the same idea of poetry, and especially in that passage of the *Apology* where he states that the reader "shall use the narration but as an imaginative ground-plot of a profitable invention"—

the invention to be the reader's supplementation of the poet's text.[3] Here Sidney seems to translate into Elizabethan English Roland Barthes's concept of writerly writing.[4] However, Sidney limits the reader's range of creativity to what is "profitable" under norms which, in Barthes's view, literature should challenge.

To the extent (which was not great) that Donne interested himself in literary theory, Sidney and Puttenham could be said to have offered him an influential example of a code of courtly conduct derived from Castiglione that serves also as a rule of poetic composition. And yet the extreme—as we shall see—to which Donne took the practice of pro-vocative play suggests, if not complete independence of their influence, at least his customary free-handed, aristocratic disdain of literary rules. With his rearticulation of Castiglione's aesthetic of the "flickering provo-cation," Donne actually plays the literary decorum game backwards. In-stead of supplying his readers with circumstances for which *he* then dis-covers a suitable utterance (instead of indoctrinating them, that is), he supplies only the utterance and forces *them* to match it with suitable con-siderations of time, place, purpose, and person addressed. This is a freer, less moral game than Sidney had in mind, a wicked game perhaps, and one of which Barthes might have approved. It is the risky game that am-bitious courtiers had to play in order to survive—the game, as we have seen, at which Donne found Essex incompetent. Essex had neither the key nor the lock, neither the ability to perceive in utterances the circum-stances giving rise to them nor the ability to restrain himself and pro-ceed by suggestion, letting his objectives form in the minds of others as if they were not his, but theirs.

More than fifty years ago, Pierre Légouis based an important study of Donne's lyrics on a conception that parallels the aesthetic of provoca-tion depicted in *The Courtier* and that still challenges our understanding of many poems in the Donne canon, as well as the capacity of modern criticism to describe the experience of reading the *Elegies* and the *Songs and Sonnets:*

> ... in many of the Songs and Sonnets there are two characters; the second is indeed a mute; or rather his words are not written down; but we are enabled to guess how he acts and what he would say if he were granted utterance. The way in which Donne gives us those hints is both very clever and very modern. More important still ... is the ef-fect produced on the speaking character by the presence of a listening one, whom he tries to persuade and win over. What seemed at first dis-interested dialectics, indulged in for truth's sake, or at least as 'evapo-rations' of wit, sound quite differently when the reader realises this dumb presence.[5]

The hints referred to by Légouis may have their modern counterparts, but they are, in historical context, Donne's version of those "flickering provocations" described by Ottaviano. All that follows in this chapter stems from a conviction that Légouis defined a major feature of Donne's poetry—one that derives from Castiglione, and yet is so difficult to explain in the usual literary critical ways that an excursus into the theory and practice of another Elizabethan art form will prove illuminating. The peculiar expressivity of Castiglione's courtiers and Donne's poetry (as Légouis describes it) has parallels in Donne's England in the practice of court painters like Nicholas Hilliard and Isaac Oliver (both of whom painted Donne's portrait) and in art theory as it was transmitted from Italy to England in the later years of Elizabeth's reign. A discussion of Donne's relationship to the court painting of his time will help to illustrate his peculiar rearticulation of Castiglione's aesthetic play.

Courtly Art

The evidence of Donne's interest in the visual arts is plentiful. He had his portrait painted more often throughout his life than any other major English poet of his time, his choice of artists was always impeccable, and he was a sufficient connoisseur of painting to own by the time of his death, among at least twenty other paintings, in all probability an original Titian.[6] As a connoisseur, Donne was everything that Castiglione required of a perfect courtier and was also in perfect conformity with aristocratic taste of his time in the visual arts. Moreover, his early verse letters explicitly compare his poetic practice with the painting of portrait miniatures and suggest that he considered the exchange of verse letters similar to the exchange of portrait miniatures among the ruling class.[7] Letters and miniatures heralded an inner circle of alliances, an aristocratic coterie. Based on observation of the latest stylistic developments in court painting and on an awareness of the avant-garde in art theory, Donne's practice of the ancient *ut pictura poesis* tradition was yet another means of fashioning an aristocratic self, and hence it helps to define the peculiar courtliness of Donne's secular poems.

Although I have no wish to pin an art historical label on Donne's poetry, a Mannerist art treatise provides a bridge between his poetry and its sister art. However, as we shall see, the conception pertinent to Donne's courtly aesthetic, though contained in the treatise in question, is not quintessentially Mannerist; instead it represents a transmission of High Renaissance values—particularly those of Leonardo da Vinci— into the early seventeenth century and probably helps to define the naturalism and dramatic expressivity of the Baroque much better than it does the distinctive features of any artworks which are widely recognized as Mannerist. In 1598, Richard Haydocke—another ambitious place seeker—published his translation of Giovanni Paolo Lomazzo's *Trattato dell'arte della pittura, scoltura, et architettura* and in a modest way made history thereby, since this is the first translation into English of an Italian art treatise. It is likely that Donne was familiar with Haydocke's achievement. By 1598, Donne had almost certainly sat for the famous Lothian portrait, and if current opinion of the Marshall engraving is reliable, Donne had already sat for a portrait by the dean of the Elizabethan limners, Nicholas Hilliard.[8] Anyone with Donne's inquisitive mind and his demonstrated interest in the visual arts would have been keenly interested in the most important publication of his time in the field of art theory in England. Even if he was not familiar with Lomazzo, it does not make much difference, since Nicholas Hilliard's admiration for Haydocke' translation of Lomazzo is indisputable,[9] and Donne's early admiration for Hilliard is on record in the opening lines of "The Storme" addressed to Christopher Brooke:

Thou which art I, ('tis nothing to be soe)
Thou which art still thyself, by these shalt know
Part of our passage; And, a hand, or eye
By *Hilliard* drawne, is worth an history,
By a worse painter made; and (without pride)
When by thy judgment they are dignifi'd,
My lines are such: 'Tis the preheminence
Of friendship onely to 'impute excellence.

These lines are interesting, apart from the reference to Hilliard, because they reveal that early in his life Donne was aware of Italian art theory to the extent that he knew the hierarchy of genres postulated for painting by Alberti, with history painting taking precedence over portrait painting. A similar example of Donne's knowledge of art theory—again an early example—occurs in "Satire IV" (204–206), where Dürer's rules for achieving perspective are ridiculed along with courtly assheads overly fastidious in their choice of fashions. This treatment of Dürer's rules accords well with Lomazzo's and also Hilliard's rejection of them. In the work of Hilliard and of his student Isaac Oliver, the great court painters of the age, Donne, the poet of courtliness, had vivid examples before his eyes of everything that could have been of interest to him in Lomazzo's newly translated treatise on painting, sculpture, and architecture.

Conveniently, Hilliard himself, in his own treatise on the art of limning, directs our attention to the passage in Lomazzo that is of special interest in connection with Castiglione's art of provocation and with Légouis's description of Donne's peculiar evocative powers.[10] When

Hilliard comes to his discussion of the portrayal of the emotions, he refers the reader to the Second Book of Lomazzo on actions and gestures, and there in the first chapter one finds a famous anecdote about Leonardo da Vinci:

> But to returne thither where I left: I am of opinion, that insomuch as these motions are so potent in affecting our mindes, when they bee most artificially counterfaited, we ought for our bettering in the knowledge thereof, to propose unto us the example of Leonard Vincent, above all others: Of whome it is reported, that he would never expresse any action in a picture, before he had first carefully beheld the life, to the end that he might come as neere the same, as was possible: whereunto afterwards ioyning art, his pictures surpassed the life.
>
> This Leonarde (as some of his friendes who lived in his time have given out) being desirous on a time to make a table, wherein hee would expresse certaine Clownes laughing: (although hee never perfected it more, then in the first drawght) he made choise of some clownes for his purpose, into whose acquaintance after he had insinuated himselfe, he invited them to a feast, amongst other of his friendes, and in the dinner while, he entered into a pleasant vaine, uttering such variety of odde merry conceites, that they fell into an exceeding laughter (though they knew not the reason hereof;) Leon. diligently observed all their gestures, togither with those ridiculous speaches, which wrought this impression in their mindes; and after they were departed, withdrew himselfe into his chamber, and there set them down so lively, that they mooved no lesse mirth in the beholders, then his jokes did in them at the banquet.[11]

According to Lomazzo (and in this passage Haydocke translates him literally), a painting can seem livelier than life itself if it succeeds in evoking in the beholder a response identical to that of its figures to whatever experience, seen or unseen by the beholder, moves them in the precise ways in which the painter has chosen to depict them. Leonardo's clowns evoke in us a response identical to that which we would have if we were able to hear one of his jokes. For a Hilliard or an Oliver, for a painter of portrait miniatures, Lomazzo's anecdote about Leonardo had a special relevance, because the portraits had to exhibit extraordinary empathic power. First, they had to awaken, in the particular persons to whom they were given, feelings corresponding to those depicted in the features of the givers, and second, they had to awaken in the casual beholder an admiration for the unseen men or women who could inspire the feelings depicted in the givers' features. Instead of the laughter called for in Lomazzo's example of Leonardo's drawing, the portrait miniatures had to inspire the appropriate response in their particular addressees and an admiration for the addressees in their casual beholder, and hence they would serve as persuasions and compliments.

Donne's poetry, according to Légouis, achieves its extraordinary liveliness by a similar process. However, in the poetry, speaker, reader, and addressee correspond to sitter, casual beholder, and addressee in the paintings, and so the poetry succeeds, not merely in expressing the emotions of various speakers with exceptional dramatic clarity, but also in evoking in the reader an image of a silent second character—the addressee—whose words or actions influence the speaker's behavior. This goes beyond Lomazzo's requirements for painting, to be sure, and even seems to suggest, in terms of Lomazzo's anecdote, that the poetic equivalent of the expressive painting should actually enable the reader to reconstruct the jokes that made the clowns laugh. The poem should go beyond the speaker's responses and stimulate the reader's imagination to reconstruct, using only the barest of hints, the very experience that gave rise to those responses. In this respect, Donne's poetic, as Légouis defines it, may be a shade more complex and supple than Lomazzo's aesthetic or Castiglione's "flickering provocations," but in all three cases the work of art—this being the courtier himself in Castiglione's text—succeeds or fails according to how effectively it seizes control of the reader's, the beholder's, or the prince's response. The courtly poem or painting must shape its affective reality with extreme precision, and in doing so, bring us into intense participation in the life of its sitters or speakers—into participation in the movements of their minds—and thereby cause us to participate in the process of its own creation. In certain modern aesthetic terms, it could be said that Donne drew from contemporaneous painting and art theory the rudimentary principles of the "open work," which presents itself as a challenge to our creative capacity to engage in the process of completing it according to rules it itself lays down.[12] In modern art historical terms, it could be said that Donne found in contemporaneous art theory suggestions for a style that attempts to achieve an integration of the beholder's reality with the space defined by the work of art.[13] I am suggesting that, under the influence of a courtly aesthetic, Donne adapted this style to his poetry and, in the process, created a version of the literary Baroque.

As for a precise example of the kind of art that inspired Donne and that parallels his poetic accomplishment, Nicholas Hilliard's portrait of an unknown youth against a background of flames, in the Victoria and Albert Museum's collection of miniatures, springs to mind (fig. 1). For the purposes of this discussion, it has the double advantage of illustrating Lomazzo's doctrine of expression and of being a close visual equivalent of the Petrarchan love lyric. In *The Portrait in the Renaissance*, John Pope-Hennessy uses the youth with flames as one of his two examples

Fig. 1 Nicholas Hilliard's "Youth in Flames." Courtesy V&A picture library.

(the other being Hilliard's famous portrait of a youth leaning against a tree, also in the Victoria and Albert Museum) of portrait miniatures that are like sonnets in that they are minuscule and capable of becoming "the incandescent record of an emotional relationship."[14] Actually, this portrait of a youth against a background of flames exhibits certain qualities that invite an even closer comparison with Donne's love poetry than with very much love poetry written prior to the 1590s.

One is struck, first, by the intense privacy and intimacy of the image. The youth's gaze is not directed toward us—the museum-browsing public—but toward the young woman whose portrait he wears over his heart and at this moment he is clasping, as if to signal to her with this gesture his devotion. We have the impression that we have come upon a scene that was not meant for our eyes, just as we have the impression that we are overhearing the words of the speakers in Donne's love poems, words never directed toward us as a general readership, but toward a specific, though fictional, young woman who has evoked them and who now totally absorbs the speaker's attention.

Another related similarity of Hilliard's miniature to Donne's poetry lies in its instantaneity. The image is of the stolen glance, familiar to readers of Renaissance love poetry, but rendered with greater vividness and immediacy in this portrait than in the poetry. The body turned to the left and the head also turned to the left—but much less so than the body, as it seems to follow the eyes, which have become riveted on the beloved, who must be imagined as standing to the right of the youth—suggest a spontaneous emotion and change of expression coming over him when the beloved enters his presence. Along with the positioning of the figure, the peculiar vertical and horizontal asymmetries of the face also suggest motion and change, just as the abrupt, colloquial opening lines of most of Donne's love poems represent an unpremeditated reaction on the part of the speaker to something that someone— usually the beloved—has just said or done. In this respect, Donne resembles Hilliard's "curious drawer," who must "wach, and as it [were] catch thesse lovely graces, wittye smilings, and thesse stolne glances which sudainely like light[n]ing passe and another countenance taketh place. . . . "15

A third quality of Hilliard's miniature, which arises from those already described and is inseparable from them, provides the most significant connection between this painting, Donne's poetry, and Castiglione's art of provocation: the portrait is not self-contained. Instead, the woman to whom the image responds determines its design and purpose. To borrow Donne's phrase, this portrait aims to perform witchcraft by a picture. In Lomazzo's terms, it aims to evoke in the woman at whom it gazes a corresponding emotion; as a work of art, it consciously declares its success to depend on its ability to seize control of, and complete itself within, the affective reality of its addressee's response. The effect of this on us—as we peek intrusively at this private drama—is to make us wonder what the woman is like who can evoke the emotions we see portrayed on the youth's face. Does his longing look produce the desired result, and who must she be to have inspired such passion? So we strain our eyes—a little foolishly—to make out the image in the miniature that he wears on the chain around his neck. Of course, this is precisely the effect that Légouis distinguished in Donne's love poems, which purposely lack self-containment insofar as they cause us to attempt to reconstruct the words and actions used by an otherwise silent woman to evoke the words of a poem's speaker, to evoke those words that actually delimit the poem on the page before our eyes.

Such imaginative reconstruction on the part of the reader is essential to the detailed interpretation of many of Donne's love poems. Thinking about these poems as one thinks about the miniature paintings makes reading them a courtly recreation. In the balance of this chapter, I shall, therefore, turn to the close study of a few poems, and I shall also turn to a pair of typical twentieth-century responses to Donne's poetry that reveal how the poetry provokes its readers to engage in the sort of game approved by Emilia Pia and her circle at Urbino. Moreover, I hope to show that an awareness of Elizabethan art theory and miniature painting helps us to comprehend the wholeness of each poem as it performs its function as a courtly entertainment. The temptation to break Donne's poems into pieces, to take passages out of context, and to regard these fragments as having sufficient life to reveal the experience of the whole poem is great, because no other poet of the time, except Shakespeare, presents so heterogeneous and large a collection of intricate metaphors, as Donne does, within the space of a short poem. If readers are the least bit sluggish, they may find themselves mesmerized by the brilliance of a single conceit into substituting a part for the whole, a conceit for the poem, and this is almost always to subvert the purpose of the conceit, which is to stimulate concentration, contemplation, imaginative involvement in the whole experience of the poem—an experience, as we shall observe, that extends in a precise manner beyond the written words into the fictive circumstances that give rise to them.

"On his Mistris"

This elegy, one of the most enjoyable, and also the richest, of Donne's poems, exhibits all the qualities of privacy, intimacy, instantaneity, and imaginative expansion that Donne's poetry shares with contemporaneous miniature painting, and so it serves as a good preliminary example of the demands made on the reader by Donne's courtly style. Although it is not my purpose to take particular issue with any critic's reading of this or that poem, it is useful to cite Frank Kermode's remarks about "On his Mistris," because they represent a counterpoint to the approach offered here. Kermode characterizes the poem as serious in tone, and in a way he may be correct, but he bases his judgment on the opening twelve lines, and says, "we're not required to imagine that Donne himself was about to go on a dangerous journey and that the girl was proposing to dress up as a man and follow him, but again, it's a set piece in a way."[16] The *whole* poem, however, is the best evidence of its seriousness, or lack thereof, not any of its parts. Possibly, we are not required by this poem to imagine anything about "Donne himself," but we are under pressure. If we adopt Kermode's view that the opening twelve lines are earnest in tone, we must somehow make them accord with the young woman's preposterous proposal to dress up as a page, and also with the bawdy comedy of lines 31 through 41, in which the speaker admon-

ishes her that the seductive French may penetrate her disguise only too
literally and that the lascivious Italians will pursue her without making
any distinction of gender. The beauty and earnestness of such phrases as
" . . . if thou dye before, / From other lands my soule towards thee shall
soare" and "bee not strange / To thy selfe only" must be assimilated to
the comic situation, for it is more than likely that they owe their power
to the surrounding comedy. Of course, the assimilation can be achieved
only if we see the poem as a complete entity, and we cannot see it as such
unless we respond to those hints that suggest its unstated dramatic context. In other words, we must get beyond the strangeness of the monologue before us in order to enter imaginatively into the experience of the
speaker and the young woman.

Here the hints are fairly obvious. Even if the speaker did not use the
stage metaphor in lines 35–36 (referring to the French as "the rightest
companie / Of Players which uppon the world's stage bee"), the young
woman's proposal to dress up as a page should remind us of certain
Shakespearean comedies. It is hard to imagine how readers of Donne's
time could have failed to make this connection. Viola of *Twelfth Night*
and Rosalind of *As You Like It* come to mind, but Julia of *The Two Gentlemen of Verona* actually has more in common with the young woman of
this elegy, because she dresses up as a page and pursues her Proteus all
the way to Milan. The earlier date of *The Two Gentlemen of Verona* is
likely to make it more contemporaneous with Donne's poem, but dates,
historical connections, and possible intimations of Shakespeare are not
my point. Surely, Donne's contemporaries, aware of this commonplace
of romance literature, would have responded with laughter to the word
"page" in its punch-line position riming with "rage," for it represents a
comic anticlimax to all that earnest exhortation in the preceding lines.
Actually there was something fustian about those lines to begin with,
with their begging and conjuring by this and by that and their unswear-
ing and their overswearing, and as for the "impetuous rage" which the
speaker attributes to the young woman's love, one cannot help but think
it to be more the product of his swaggering than of her feelings.[17]

Perhaps this is the dramatic situation: a separation is imminent, and
the speaker and the young woman are unhappy about it, but they are
easing their sorrow, as people often do, by making fun of themselves,
and their way of doing so is to playact. One imagines the young woman
as having cast herself in the role of Julia—or of any other similar heroine
of Renaissance romance—and as having recited some such lines as these:

A true devoted pilgrim is not weary
To measure kingdoms with his feeble steps;

> Much less shall she that hath Love's wings to fly,
> And when the flight is made to one so dear,
> Of such divine perfection. . . . (*TGV,* II.vii.9–13)

So then the speaker is called upon to reply in a suitably histrionic style, and of course (having been invented by Donne) he does, extemporizing in such a way as to sustain the comedy and express his affection as well. Throughout this poem, hyperbole and melodrama create humor designed to ease the pain of parting, and they also represent a concession that the love between the speaker and the young woman is so great as to render a direct statement of their unhappiness inadequate. When the speaker admits that it is only "flatterye" to suppose "that absent lovers one in th'other bee," he is acknowledging an awareness and sensitivity in his beloved too refined to tolerate the ordinary consolations as anything but hollow, and he is crediting her with a sense of humor about her sensuality. This young woman is, as Virginia Woolf recognized, "as various and complex as Donne himself."[18] The closing line of the poem is especially powerful, because in its plain straightforwardness it lapses from the romantic posturing of the preceding lines, as if to admit that even the most ingenious playacting can furnish only a temporary cessation of sorrow.

As an elegy, "On his Mistris" provides the illusion of immediacy, spontaneity, agon, and irony, and hence lends itself to the approach taken here. The influence of Latin elegiac poetry on Donne's style and treatment of subject matter makes itself felt everywhere in the secular lyrics. However, there is no clear antecedent in Latin elegy for the imaginative expansion that readers of "On his Mistris" are required to exert on the text if they wish to comprehend its unity. This phenomenon is much more easily explained by Lomazzo's treatise, by observation of similar phenomena in the court painting of Donne's time, and most of all by comparison with the aesthetic play governing Castiglione's rendering of the dialogue at Urbino. The passage from *The Two Gentlemen of Verona* that the young woman of "On his Mistris" might have recited to provoke her lover's response corresponds with those jokes in Lomazzo's anecdote that made the clowns laugh. Reading Donne, we go beyond empathy with his speakers to creation of the unstated circumstances that make them say what they do. Of course, Donne could have been more explicit about those circumstances, he could have engaged in description and narration, but he restrained himself, purposely denied himself the privileges of his medium and, under the influence of a courtly aesthetic, restricted himself to the limitations of visual art, to the seizure of a critical moment of time, in order to achieve that "forcibleness, or Energia" to which Sidney refers.

Poems like "On his Mistris" cause the imagination to bring to the surface invisible, inaudible contexts which enable us to return to the words on the page and see them as more coherent than they had appeared at first glance. We "see" them in the sense that we come to understand certain relations among them which would have remained hidden if the imagination had not discovered their dramatic context. The poems integrate themselves with our mental space, seize control of our responses, and use us to complete themselves in a more precise way than can be observed of literature in general. It is as if most of Donne's poems come to us speaking the opening words of "The Storme": "Thou which art I . . . , / Thou which art still thy selfe. . . . " This phenomenon of confusion between metaphysical planes, between that of the work of art and that of the beholder, is customarily thought of as an effect of the Baroque and usually labeled "open form" or "imaginative expansion" (the term preferred in this study), but Lomazzo, generally regarded as a Mannerist painter, describes it in his anecdote about Leonardo's clowns, and we can see it in operation in the portrait miniatures of Hilliard and Oliver. Castiglione's aesthetic of provocation informs Donne's poetry, but Donne's peculiar rearticulation of Castiglione adapts to literary uses a proto-Baroque style in the visual arts.

Although the portrait miniatures were primarily icons of power and wealth (and one thinks of Elizabeth's many portraits, along with Isaac Oliver's unfinished one—unfinished apparently because it was not iconic enough for her requirements), many of them exhibit a strange poignancy. Their subjects gaze out at and respond to the special circumstances and specific people of a vanished world. We can no longer reconstruct their context with sufficient vividness. They appear to have forgotten that they are portraits to be looked at, and instead, with their absorption in concerns exclusively their own, cause us to surrender, not to suspend disbelief in their reality, but to surrender belief in our own, as the space around us seems to form itself momentarily into a room or outdoor setting of a magnificent country house where intimate glances and revealing expressions pass like lightening over the faces of ladies and nobles gathered for some festive occasion. They seem the speechless participants at a soiree like the one attended by their Italian cousins at the Palace of Urbino. Examples are almost too numerous to choose among, but Hilliard's portraits of his wife Alice and himself (fig. 2) are striking because the limner appears to be using his paintings (as Donne used his poems) to represent himself as a member of the aristrocracy that employed him. Donne's *Satyres* have the same effect as these portrait miniatures, inasmuch as the absorption of the young secretary in his employer's world and that grave man's concern with a disillusioned younger generation exclude us if we do not take our place at

Fig. 2. *Left:* Hilliard's self-portrait; *right:* portrait of Alice Hilliard. Courtesy V&A picture library.

table in York House and share their concerns. In courtly poetry as in courtly art, imaginative expansion causes the reader to formulate unseen images and unspoken words. In reading poetry that exhibits this feature, we go beyond the word on the page and beyond suspension of disbelief in the reality of our imagination's incarnation of that word in image, sound, and sense, and we find ourselves in the act of formulating unspoken, unwritten words to which we lend fictive incarnations of their own. We surrender. We undergo *ecstasis*, move outside ourselves, and the artistic illusion becomes our reality, pressures us to make it our reality, if we wish to comprehend the relations among its parts. It becomes the ground we receive in exchange for that which we surrendered, for that which we were standing on a moment before we came within the influence of the poem or painting.

In a haunting passage of his treatise on the art of limning, Hilliard wonders how the painter can catch the "lovely graces" and "stolne glances" of his sitters "without an affectionate good judgment and without blasting his younge and simpel hart."[19] Here the painter of portrait miniatures adapts to his own circumstances Horace's influential dictum, "Si vis me flere, dolendum est primum ipsi tibi."[20] Hilliard is saying that the artist must share his subject's emotions if he desires the portrait he is painting to evoke corresponding emotions in its addressee, and he is also saying that this can be dangerous for the artist, because he must also share his subject's sufferings. To be sure, this is an exaggeration of Horace's advice, but the same exaggeration is to be found in Lomazzo's treatise, where it reaches proportions great enough for Rensselaer Lee to suggest that it sounds like "a kind of *reductio ad absurdum* . . . of the modern theory of empathy."[21] However, it was probably Hilliard's and Lomazzo's exaggeration of the empathic powers of the artist that caught Donne's eye. Certainly, this would help to explain Donne's peculiar variation on the courtly aesthetic of provocation—his new kind of poetry—which denies readers access unless they experience the life of each speaker so thoroughly that they can judge his circumstances without having to have them described.

Modern Instances

If John Donne's secular lyrics are the provocative, courtly performances that I have claimed them to be, there should be evidence in their critical history of that imaginative expansion so central to the courtly aesthetic. The poems should have induced even their twentieth-century readers to engage in the game of completing them according to the rules, hints, or provocations that they themselves furnish. We should be able to find repeated instances of poem and criticism engaging each other in ways similar to those in which Ludovico da Canossa, as we have seen, engages Gasparo Pallavicino in Book I of *The Courtier*, or Gasparo himself later engages the Magnifico Giuliano during discussion of the court lady. As Carew puts it in his percipient elegy, we should be able to observe the poems committing holy rapes upon the critical will, and indeed, it could be said that the courtly exchange, as Castiglione understood it, characterizes twentieth-century Donne criticism. Whether the critic strains to demonstrate that the speaker of "The Canonization" is really the *adversarius* of Satyre I, "talking back to his friend the satirist and triumphantly announcing at the end that the situation has completely changed and that their former positions in relation to each other have altered in a way that . . . could hardly have [been] anticipated,"[22] or the critic argues movingly that a speaker-casuist in the poems is attempting to allay the doubting conscience of the addressee with an argument that their particular case requires adjustment of universal moral law,[23] Donne criticism, from the ridiculous to the sublime, gives countless examples of critics provoked to create, by way of imaginative expansion, specific dramatic contexts for Donne's poems. The problem is to choose among all the examples.

The following case of imaginative expansion in action involves a poem—"Communitie"—that closely resembles one of those flickering provocations described by Ottaviano. Conveniently, the critic whose imagination this poem expands is concerned throughout her study with the morality of Donne's poems and therefore likely to detect whatever virtuous conditions they can be said to imprint. N. J. C. Andreasen, admiring the poem's "witty audacity and insolent ingenuity" and noting the challenge it delivers those whose conduct is guided by the type of moral truism it makes serve its immoral purpose, imagines

> another young lawyer at the Inns of Court reading the poem, recognizing the challenge to discover the trick in the argument, and saying something like this: "Ah yes, but 'prove' and 'use' do not mean the same thing, as you try to pretend; you cannot say that we are obliged to consume 'things indifferent' just because we are obliged to test them. And further, 'things indifferent' are not amoral, as you try to imply; you begin by using the phrase in its commonplace sense, which assumes that there are things whose goodness or badness may change according to their context and situation; but this sense does not assume that notions of goodness and badness are totally irrelevant, only that they are relative and that things may be blamed or praised as circumstances warrant; but you, changing the meaning later in the poem (and cleverly refusing to use the phrase again lest your reader recognize your equivocation), try to show that because women are neither absolutely good nor absolutely bad, one is justified in treating them as if they were worthless; all you are permitted to conclude, if you do not shift the meaning of 'things indifferent,' is that all men must test the worth of each woman (not consume, but test) in order to determine whether the particular circumstances of her condition and nature make her good or bad or perhaps a mixture of both. It is very ingenious, the way you try to hide all this inconsistency by your complex series of syllogisms, which make the poem seem logically impeccable. But it won't work in the long run, for moral truth is one thing and sin is another, and no amount of ingenuity can make them seem identical for very long. That is undoubtedly the point of the first two lines, which are your own private joke, your way of hinting that the advocacy of sin is all a game. For, as you say, 'Good wee must love, and must hate ill, / For ill is ill, and good good still. . . .'"[24]

The poet-courtier imprints this edifying discourse in the critic-prince. Of course, Andreasen is aware of the provocation, which she explains by citing Donne's tenth paradox on the relationship between fools and laughter. The speaker of "Communitie" is a solemn fool, according to Andreasen, who provokes laughter in the wise, proving thereby the truth of the old adage, *Per risum multum possis cognoscere stultum.* Where the fool is there will be much laughter—of the wise, that is.

Andreasen's invention of a sparring contest between two young law students at the Inns of Court illustrates perfectly the point I have been making about courtly aesthetics. However, her explanation of comedy in a poem like "Communitie" does not accord well with its ingenuity, which she herself admires. Poems like "The Indifferent," "Communitie," "Woman's Constancy," and "Confined Love" possess the ingenuity of the author of *The Paradoxes and Problemes*, not the foolishness of the objects of his wit. The exchanges of Gasparo Pallavicino with the Magnifico Giuliano in Book III of *The Courtier* resemble much more closely Donne's exchange with Andreasen in "Communitie" than do the antics of a fool diverting wise men. There is evidence that Gasparo is intentionally provocative in Book III and succeeds brilliantly in making his point. A word or two about his technique sheds light on the effect of Donne's poem on his modern critic.

First of all, it must be remembered that Gasparo's reason for wishing to dispense with discussion of the court lady is that to him it seems self-evident that she should be endowed with the same accomplishments as the courtier (p. 188). Giuliano disagrees, declaring that her purpose "above all other thinges" is to "gently entertain all kinde of men with talke worthie the hearing . . . " (p. 190). Ironically, throughout Book III, the professed defenders of women—the Magnifico Giuliano and Cesare Gonzaga—emerge as much less their friends than their apparent enemy, Gasparo, whose demeanor in the discussion of the court lady is framed by the ladies' mock assault on him at the end of Book II and their dancing with him at the beginning of Book IV. This is not how we treat people who regard us as inferiors. In Book III, Gasparo is only retaliating against the ladies with a mock assault of his own, just as the speaker of "Communitie" delivers a mock assault on the faithfulness of lovers. In neither case is it the provocateur who exhibits solemn foolishness.

By forcing him to defend his lavish praises of women, Gasparo provokes Giuliano to abandon his belief in essential differences between courtiers and court ladies. Suspecting that Giuliano's praise vouches more for the refinement of his own sensibility than for any real qualities of women, Gasparo taunts him. Gasparo recognizes the contradiction between those praises and the actual role that Giuliano assigns to women. He does not, however, engage Giuliano in a serious debate. He plays with him. Whichever arguments he deploys, whether that women are defects of nature or that men correspond to form and women to matter, Gasparo slyly assigns responsibility for them to certain wise men who left them in writing—the very sort of pedants for whom Emilia Pia and court society have little tolerance. He prods Giuliano into solemn refutations of authorities for whom no one has much respect anyway. One imagines the youthful Gasparo (who died at the age of twenty-five) winking when he suggests that Giuliano should abstain from his abstruse, philosophizing rebuttals—the very pedantry into which he has provoked him—because the ladies will be unable to understand (p. 199).

They understand only too well what is going on. Gasparo makes this suggestion after he has provoked Giuliano to deliver that fascinating speech on the perfection of human nature as a union of the male and female, which are defective apart from each other. Giuliano's solemnity is comical here, not because of his speech's substance, but because it is so at odds with his position at the outset of the dialogue and he is so unaware of his volte-face. Gasparo has reduced Giuliano to an unwitting acceptance of parity between the sexes and brought him almost one hundred and eighty degrees around from his starting position. Similarly, Donne's critic finds herself provoked by the speaker of "Communitie" into a solemn rebuttal whose tone accords ill, not only with the poem, which satirizes solemnity of tone in moral discourse, but also with her own admiration of the speaker's ingenuity.

Gasparo is at his best when he provokes Cesare Gonzaga into a ponderous defense of the self-evident—which is that women profit the world in more than the bearing of children and are no less continent than men. In the context of the Urbino gathering, these propositions are self-evident for the simple reason that the Duchess Elisabetta, legendary in her time for chastity, presides and is both childless and inured to living like a widow with her sickly husband. Nevertheless, Cesare takes up the banner in defense of women's continence. One imagines Gasparo winking again, and especially when Cesare finally gets around to citing the Duchess as one of his examples. It is no wonder at this point that she is unable to resist showing offense (p. 231). However, my point is that Gasparo provokes Cesare and Giuliano in the same way that "Communitie" provokes its modern critic into an excessive discourse on morality.

Donne himself, in a letter probably written to Henry Wotton in 1600, provides the best guide to reading poems like "Communitie." He is speaking of his *Paradoxes*, but his words apply equally well to most of the poems that Andreasen categorizes as Ovidian:

> . . . indeed they were made rather to deceave tyme then her daughth[r] truth: although they have beene written in an age when any thing is strong enough to overthrow her: if they make y° to find better reasons against them they do there office: for they are but swaggerers: quiet enough if y° resist them. if perchaunce they be pretyly guilt, y[t] is there best for they are not hatcht: they are rather alarums to truth to arme her then enemies: & they have only this advantadg to scape fro being caled ill things y[t] they are nothings: therfore take heed of allowing any of them least y° make another.[25]

They are not hatched, they do not have the brilliance of solid gold inlay, rather theirs is the specious glitter of gilding. They are "swaggerers," like the speaker of "Communitie" or like Gasparo, and their purpose, "there office," is to serve as those "flickering provocations" of which Castiglione speaks in Hoby's translation. It is remarkable to find such a clear statement of authorial intent coming from Donne—in his time perhaps the poet least given to literary disquisition. However, it is not remarkable that the statement accords so well with an aesthetic laid down in the principal courtesy text of Donne's age. If Wotton really were the recipient of Donne's letter, Donne was writing to one of the more successful courtiers and diplomats of the time, a poet of considerable talent and a slightly older contemporary, in whose career Donne might have seen his own wildest dreams materializing. For Donne, there did not exist a more appropriate person in whom to confide his poetic intentions.

If poems like "Communitie" play with their readers in much the same lambent, elusive, insinuating ways in which Castiglione's courtiers play with each other, the poems for which Donne is best known provoke their modern critics to more strenuous exercises of the imagination. It takes ingenuity to evoke a young inner barrister at the Inns of Court debating a case, but the imagination finds itself under greater pressure when confronted with a poem like "A Valediction: forbidding Mourning." In his rejoinder to John Freccero's learned reading of this poem as a statement (in figurative terms of death and resurrection) that the lovers will eventually enjoy reunion, David Novarr stresses the poem's dramatic and bawdy contexts, as opposed to its metaphysical, astronomical, and alchemical ones. Novarr notes the fragility of gold leaf and argues that the compass image enters as a concession on the speaker's part that his lady's grief over the separation is justified. Just as the legs of a compass do not have to rejoin each other for the circle to be drawn perfectly, the poem's collocation at its close of such words as "stiffe," "foot," "center," "erect," "firmnes," and "circle" stresses love's physical and ephemeral manifestations in a bawdy counterpoint to that interassuredness of the mind on which the speaker has insisted. According to Novarr, the speaker concludes his high-minded argument with a concession that no love precludes mourning. Novarr then asks what the effect must be on the young woman of the speaker's attempt to prove the impossible.

> What effect does the compass image have on the lady? She will see that Donne has made a concession, will appreciate that he is being responsive to her in making one. Still, the concession, it turns out, is not truly one; Donne continues to try to prove the same point he has made before. But, since he has got hold of such a striking image, since he is arguing logically rather than associatively, he has caught her attention

and she starts to follow his step-by-step demonstration. The compass image is probably absurd and ingenious enough to distract her. She weeps still, we may imagine, but more quietly, for she is listening intently. Donne's words confuse her; she blushes, perhaps, for though his words say one thing, they remind her of another tune. When he ends, she is aware of a flaw in his argument, and she is aware that he must be very much aware of another point as he writes his counterpoint. She understands that he is not without feeling, that he is so sensitive to her feelings that he has used all his resources to make a case he can't make successfully, that his solicitude and love for her are reflected in his attempt to calm her. In some measure, he has succeeded. She appreciates his high-minded expression of what their love means to him; she sees how much he cares for her in the pains he has taken for her; she sees that for all his effort to prove otherwise, he, too, feels that sadness and weeping at parting are natural and human. She may even smile a little through her tears as she realizes that, for all his artful manipulation, her lover, too, knows that compasses are not made of flesh and blood.[26]

Novarr experiences the life of the poem's speaker so intensely that the speaker's circumstances and his interlocutor emerge in Novarr's imagination to complete the poem. A silent woman emerges whose refined sensibility makes the poem possible, whose sensibility is—in the profoundest sense—the poem's subject, but a subject inaccessible to a passive reader. Novarr furnishes a perfect model of the reader as creative participant responding in the most sophisticated ways to the courtly art of provocation. The exchange between the speaker and the young woman resembles that of the couple in "On his Mistris" who do their best to divert each other in order to allay the grief of separation.

In reconstructing the dramatic context of "A Valediction: forbidding Mourning," Novarr responds to those hints of which Légouis speaks—in this case, the word "if" opening the seventh stanza with a concession and that series of words with bawdy connotations associated with the compass image. The poem to which I shall turn to conclude this chapter contains similar hints for the reader, but it also exercises the courtly reader's literary connoisseurship in an amusing way. One of the major hints with which it provokes imaginative expansion consists of an apparently recherché allusion to Latin elegiac poetry. Not Ovid, Propertius, or Catullus, but the much less obvious Tibullus serves Donne's turn in provoking his readers to experience the mental workings of a young woman whose sensibility could also be said to be refined, but not in quite the same ways as that of the young women suggested in "On his Mistris" or "A Valediction: forbidding Mourning."

Courtly Comedy

Most readers of Donne's Elegy VII ("Tutelage," in Gardner's nomenclature) would be inclined to agree that Tibullus' epigrammatic "Ipse miser
docui, quo posset ludere pacto / custodes: heu heu nunc premor arte
mea!" sums up rather well the dilemma of the poem's speaker.[27] Robert
Burton's free translation of Tibullus' lines captures their humor: "Wretch
as I was, I taught her bad to be, / And now mine own sly tricks are put
upon me."[28] This is the sort of irony that Donne's readers—those youthful Inns of Court connoisseurs of the erotic in poetry and elsewhere—
must have looked for in the elegiac mode, with a speaker lashed by his
own invective when he attacks, for having been unfaithful to him, the
very woman whom he has schooled in the art of infidelity. A conventional reading of Elegy VII, drawing on Tibullus' sixth elegy of his first
book as a model for Donne's poem and expecting to find a speaker en-
meshed in ironies typical of the Latin elegiac tradition, must insist on
an adulterous relationship between the speaker and the young woman
whom he castigates for having betrayed him, and yet the burden of critical opinion banishes adultery from the poem and also, thereby, much of
its dramatic power. The case for adultery in Elegy VII helps not only to
demonstrate the truth of one critic's judgment that, in the elegy form,
"Donne's accomplishment, from the outset, lies in a full understanding
and use of the dramatic speaker,"[29] but also reveals the poem to be a brilliant example of Castiglione's aesthetic of provocation, with a speaker
provoked by a silent woman and provoking us in turn to reconstruct her
point of view. Every detail of the poem contributes to the peculiar pressure that we are under in its presence to recreate the comic drama of
which it is the turning point.

   Helen Gardner notes that this poem "may owe something to Tibullus, 1.6.5–14," but she claims that it is "more innocent" and that "only
'Jealousy' among Donne's *Elegies* is concerned with adultery."[30] The
lines of Tibullus cited by Gardner contain the distich quoted above and
they also set up a dramatic situation enabling the speaker of Tibullus'
elegy to urge, in a whimsical apostrophe, the very husband whom he has
been deceiving to trust him with the guardianship of his wife. She
has become interested in other men besides the two of them and only in
this way will they succeed in keeping Delia faithful to them alone. The
husband will be unable because Delia is using those very tricks that
worked on him when she was the speaker's "faithful" mistress. Obviously, it is the speaker who, having taught her all those tricks, is the right
man for the job, if only there were a way to persuade the husband. As it
is, he must stand by and suffer Delia's infidelity along with that lumpish

husband whose inept guardianship had once worked in his favor. Reduced by his "own sly tricks" to an irksome camaraderie with his former victim, he proposes a ridiculous partnership. It is easy to imagine the virtuosity of this poem's comic eroticism as having won for it an avid following among those "frolique Patricians" at the Inns of Court.

Ovid, whose admiration for this elegy of Tibullus is recorded in the *Tristia* (2.447–464), describes the dilemma of the *praeceptor amoris* in words which became proverbial for Donne and for every Renaissance love poet in England and on the Continent: " . . . neque enim lex aequior ulla est, / quam necis artifices arte perire sua" (. . . nor is there truly any fairer law / than that the artificer of destruction should perish by his own art).[31] In Elegy VII, what could Donne owe to Tibullus if not an awareness of the dramatic possibilities of having a speaker whose expertise in adultery renders him just as deceived as all those husbands whom he had always scorned? Could there be a more nearly perfect case of poetic justice? Could there be—to use Sidney's terms—a better ground plot for the imagination to act upon, creating, if not necessarily a profitable invention in the moral sense, at least a brilliant psychological portrait of illicit sexual behavior?

It is curious that Gardner should cite Tibullus' poem as a possible model for Elegy VII and then should exclude adultery from Donne's concerns, for there is nothing in Tibullus' elegy, except for the predicament of the adulterous *praeceptor amoris* worsted by his own precepts, that Donne could not have found in Ovid and Propertius—the more popular models for elegy in his time. Certainly, in Propertius, Donne had observed the stance of the poet vis-à-vis his readers as the teacher of love's lore, and had also observed the sometimes ironic, at other times desperate and defensive, coupling of this stance with a representation of the beloved as utterly faithless. As for the theme of instruction in the various ruses to be employed in furtive love affairs, Donne had Ovid's *Amores* and *Ars amatoria* before him, and the *Ars amatoria* could also have furnished a model of the *praeceptor amoris*' fear of turning over dangerous weapons to the female—and therefore, enemy—camp. "Arma dedi Danais in Amazonas; arma supersunt / Quae tibi dem et turmae, Penthesilae, tuae" (Arms have I given to the Danaans against the Amazons; arms are left over / which I should give to your troops, Penthesilea, too) (3.1–2), or "Ponite iam gladios hebetes; pugnetur acutis. / Nec dubito telis quin petar ipse meis" (Now lay down the dull swords; let the battle be fought with sharp ones. / Nor doubt I but that I myself may be struck by my own darts) (3.519–520). The notion that lessons in love bestowed on the female sex might turn to the instructor's painful disadvantage was available to Donne through Ovid; however, the love quadrangle, consisting of the *praeceptor amoris*, his mistress, her husband, and the shadowy fourth party with whom she uses her lessons to deceive both husband and poet-lover, is peculiarly Tibullan, and it represents a dramatic situation that Donne, among English elegiac poets, would have been the first to appreciate and the best qualified to develop to its greatest effect. Due to Donne's use of certain flickering provocations, Tibullus' Delia returns, in Elegy VII, to sample life in an English boudoir.

Contending with the school of thought that would banish adultery from the poem best reveals its provocativeness. Read without regard for the courtly aesthetic which Donne absorbed from Castiglione, Elegy VII yields a scenario which Frank Kermode describes, with a speaker indignant over having managed to seduce a very naive, stupid young girl and over having done the hard work of preparing her for sexual pleasure, only then to see her marry someone else who must become the beneficiary of his good offices.[32] Read, on the other hand, with some curiosity concerning the point of view of the silent woman who is the object of the speaker's tirade (and who is present during it to be called an idiot and a fool and to be reminded of her many debts), the poem yields a rather different picture. One becomes sensitive to those hints or clues for reconstructing the poem's dramatic context. The plurals in lines 27 and 29, "strangers" and "others," suggest that there might be more than one interloper in the speaker's "blis-full Paradise," while the simple past tense of "Inlaid" (22), set in grammatical parallel with the past perfect tense of "have with amorous delicacies / Refin'd" (23–24), suggests that the young woman was married *before* the speaker met her. Furthermore, the "houshold charmes" in lines 15 and 16 can with no difficulty be understood to refer to the young woman's domesticity, by which she was spellbound into absolute fidelity to her husband until she met the speaker of the poem.[33] Then lines 13 and 14 would mean that her ignorance, since she is a "lay Ideot," was such that she was unable even to recognize a seducer until the speaker taught her how, and so she treated her would-be seducers as if they were friends, saying that she would go wherever they asked as long as her friends agreed to go along. Then the various lessons detailed in lines 3 through 12 would make sense, for the speaker is reminding her that he had, not only to seduce her, but to teach her how to recognize and respond to a seducer in the first place, and to respond with secrecy. His job was arduous.

So the scenario takes a drastic departure from Kermode's description. This is the altered dramatic situation: A man is having a tantrum over the fact that his mistress—a young married woman who was married when he met her, though she was abysmally naive—has learned her lessons on illicit love from him so well that she has proceeded to jilt him and to take on new lovers. She has grown altogether too "subtile" in the lore to which he introduced her, and he is incensed at her ingratitude, at her apparent ignorance of the great debt she owes him. After all, he says, your husband reduced you to a private pasture for domestic cattle to graze in, while I refined you into a Garden of Eden, so it is clear that you owe me much more than you owed him when I first met you, but you are unjust—you are treating me just exactly as you treated him (20–27). It is implied, of course, that her husband, dull and sexually inept, held her in ignorance until the speaker-seducer with Promethean dexterity—at least in his opinion—descended on her and imparted the heavenly secrets of sexual fulfillment. The inciting action of this little drama is the assault that the young woman has launched on the *amour propre* of the speaker by taking on new lovers, and the flood of words—the poem itself—is the speaker's feeble retaliation.

In essence, apart from the charge of ingratitude, the speaker bases his counterattack on an analysis of the young woman's character. In the opening line, he says, with apparent redundancy, that she is "Natures lay Ideot." Gardner glosses this as "ignorant simpleton by nature," and A. J. Smith offers "ignorant uninitiate in the workings of nature,"[34] but neither paraphrase accounts well for the speaker's regarding her, paradoxically, as "too subtile" in the practice of love's "sophistrie." The speaker appears to have a particular variety of simpleton in mind, or at least, a peculiar characteristic of idiocy not inconsistent with subtlety and sophistry, even if his usage renders the terms ironic. In "The True Character of a Dunce," which first appeared in the 1622 edition of the *Overburian Characters*, Donne himself provides the best gloss on the speaker's analysis of the young woman's character. The origin of the word *dunce* in the sixteenth century as a term of derision to describe followers of Duns Scotus, the "Doctor Subtilis," is familiar to students of the Renaissance. According to the *OED*, it had become in Donne's time synonymous with "caviling sophist" and "hair-splitter," and it was used of any asshead incapable of taking in the new learning of the humanists. So, on the surface, it would seem that the speaker of Elegy VII, as *praeceptor amoris*, must have in mind a type of "Ideot" similar to a dunce. However, Donne's own words establish the similarity and supply the context demanded by his courtly aesthetic:

> He is meere nothing of himselfe, neither eates, nor drinkes, nor goes, nor spits, but by Imitation, for all which he hath set-formes and fashiones, which he never varies, but stickes to with the like plodding constancie, that a mill-horse followes his trace. . . . Hee speakes just what his bookes or last company said unto him, without varying one whit, and very seldome understands himselfe. You may know by his discourse where he was last, for what he heard or read yesterday, he now dischargeth his memory or Notebooke of, not his understanding, for it

never came there. What he hath he flings abroad at all adventures, without accommodating it to time, place, persons, or occasions. He commonly loseth himselfe in his tale, and flutters up and down windless without recovery, and whatsoever next presents it selfe, his heavy conceit seizeth upon, and goeth along with, how ever *Heterogeneall* to his matter in hand. His Jests are either old flead Proverbs, or lean-esterved-hackney *Apothegmes*, or poore verball quips. . . . [35]

Of course, this calls to mind immediately the "broken proverbs" and "torne sentences" with which the young woman, according to the speaker of Elegy VII, used to make "ill arraid" conversation before she met him and he instructed her in this and other matters. However, it also suggests that one reason for her remaining an "Ideot," or dunce, in his estimation, is precisely the "plodding constancie" with which she received his instruction and has gone on to apply it. "Too subtile" in that "sophistrie" she has indeed become in the sense that she has fastidiously, rigidly, undiscriminatingly adopted her seducer's behavior as her own. She remains "Natures lay Ideot" in his opinion, just as she was before, because she is still by nature the incompetent simpleton prone to hold relentlessly to any idea, whether she understands it or not, just as long as it has done the hard work of penetrating her thick skull. Just as she was once pertinaciously and obtusely faithful to her husband, she has now become likewise promiscuous, flinging her seducer's instruction "abroad at all adventures, without accommodating it to time, place, persons, or occasions"—and especially to persons!

In a sense, the speaker of Elegy VII is throwing up his hands and asking what can be done with a person who will remain true to her plodding nature no matter how much you try to do for her. It is easy then to see how his gradual descent into the barnyard imagery with which the poem closes constitutes an admission of defeat, though it is not so easy to tell how aware he is of the full extent of his defeat. After all, he has had to admit from the outset that she has been a very exact pupil, so he cannot in justice accuse her of having done anything contrary to his instruction—at least according to the letter of it, if not (in his benighted opinion) the spirit. If by imitating him she is now as much a libertine as he, and if he now finds himself treated as he once persuaded her to treat her husband, he must not complain too loudly, because he will only identify himself all the more directly with that husband who would have fenced her into his barnyard and made her all his own. However, the thundering crescendo of indignation into which his wounded ego has driven him appears to have blinded him to this irony. His angry self-portrait compels us to imagine the play of expressions on the young woman's face as she listens to his tirade. Elegy VII ends, the reader suspects, with the inaudible laughter of a young woman whose intelligence is perfectly adequate to her needs. The poem provokes the reader to entertain the young woman's point of view and to reconstruct it from the various clues that Donne makes available.

This interpretation of Elegy VII suggests that Donne read Tibullus' poem carefully, imitating it with the independence in literary matters which one would expect of the speaker of Satyre II or of the young man who idolized Sir Christopher Hatton. On the one hand, he retains the ironies implicit in the position of the *praeceptor amoris* vanquished by his own skill in adulterous love. On the other hand, the courtly aesthetic prompts him to achieve a dramatic immediacy missing in Tibullus' elegy when he shifts the speaker's attention to the young woman herself instead of leaving his words as a soliloquy, or as an apostrophe to the husband. Hence Elegy VII gives the impression of being part of a spontaneous dialogue taking place in the heat of conflict, and the reader has the pleasure of witnessing the speaker become step by step more and more ensnared in the trammels of his faulty argument and his false position. Add to this the fact that Donne's adaptation of Tibullus enables the reader to probe facetiously the psychology of the faithless young woman, and the conclusion becomes compelling that Donne, with the opening words of his poem, invites comparison with Tibullus for the purpose of provoking his courtly readers to immerse themselves in the speaker's and the young woman's experience. If this conclusion is true, Donne might easily have felt himself at liberty to develop his poem along dramatic lines unique to his conception of the speaker's dilemma, all the while confident that his readers' recognition of the classical model would render any laboriously explicit statement about adultery unnecessary. Donne compliments his courtly audience in the process of inviting them to join in the aesthetic play.

If a virtuous condition must be said to be imprinted by this flickering provocation, one could point to the chastity and humility to be learned from observing the speaker become more and more foolish. At least, Donne could have excused his courtly entertainment with such an appeal to the *utile et dulce*. In actuality, the foolish figure of the discomposed lover suggests the opposite of that graceful detachment—*disinvoltura*—advocated throughout *The Courtier*. The wounded lover, by insisting on the extraordinary efforts he made to educate his mistress, flaunts his art and exhibits *affettazione*—or "curiosity," as Hoby translates the term—which is the opposite of that *sprezzatura*, or "recklessness," so vital to the perfect courtier and the subject of the next chapter. As a courtly recreation, Elegy VII presents its untowardly speaker as having started out a courtier and graduated, under his mistress's tutelage, an asshead.

3

Sprezzatura *or Transcendence:*
From Travesty to Palinode

Travesty

For students of English Renaissance literature, *sprezzatura* comes to mind in connection with Sir Philip Sidney, whose letter to his sister, printed with the first edition of the revised *Arcadia* in 1590, is a famous example:

> Here now have you (most dear, and most worthy to be most dear lady) this idle work of mine, which, I fear, like the spider's web, will be thought fitter to be swept away than worn to any other purpose. For my part, in very truth (as the cruel fathers among the Greeks were wont to do to the babes they would not foster) I could well find in my heart to cast out in some desert of forgetfulness this child which I am loth to father. But you desired me to do it, and your desire to my heart is an absolute commandment. Now it is done only for you, only to you: if you keep it to yourself or to such friends who will weigh errors in the balance of goodwill, I hope, for the father's sake, it will be pardoned, perchance made much of, though in itself it have deformities. For indeed, for severer eyes it is not, being but a trifle, and that triflingly handled.

At a distance of four centuries from the Sidney charisma and with our knowledge of the intensive revision to which the *Arcadia* was subjected, we can be excused for feeling momentarily miffed at what appears to be an insult to our intelligence delivered by a haughty aristocrat. We know that Sidney worked on the *Arcadia* in both versions for almost nine years. We know that he studied Minturno in order to achieve the epic effects of the revised version. In sum, we know that Sidney labored and studied over what he calls a "trifle," and hence we are inclined to charge him with insincerity, just as we are to charge Castiglione himself with deceitfulness when he advocates this *sprezzatura* of which Sidney seems too fond.

However, Sidney, born to public service, heir of the Earls of Leicester and Warwick, son of the Lord Deputy Governor of Ireland, understood, when he wrote the letter to his sister, that he possessed by ascription a status in life recognized by all as far more important than the poetic role he assumed in writing the *Arcadia*. In fact, it would have been apparent to everyone that his achieved status as poet merely masked or loosely disguised—"travestied," in the root sense of the word—his status by ascription in the Elizabethan state. Hence, nothing could be more sincere and self-aware on his part than to admit the trifling nature of his poetic achievement. A much commented upon passage early in Book II of *The Courtier*, in which Castiglione attempts a refinement of his earlier definition of *sprezzatura* as nonchalance, illustrates Sidney's position perfectly and draws a connection between *sprezzatura* and the concept of travesty.[1] Federico is explaining the conditions under which the courtier may undertake certain exuberant dances:

> I will not say but hee may . . . also dance the Morisco and braulles, yet not openly unlesse hee were in a maske [*fuor che travestito*].
>
> And though it were so that all men knew him, it skilleth not, for there is no way to that, if a man will shew him selfe in open sights about such matters, whether it be in armes, or out of armes. Because to be in a maske [*lo esser travestito*] bringeth with it a certaine libertie and licence, that a man may among other things take upon him the forme of that he hath better skill in, and use bent studie and preciseness about the principall drift of the matter wherein he will shew himselfe, and a certain recklesnesse [*una certa sprezzatura*] about that is not of importance, which augmenteth the grace of the thing, as it were to disguise [*come saria vestirsi*] a yong man in an old mans attier, but so that his garments be not a hindrance to him to shew his nimblenesse of person. And a man at armes in forme of a wilde shepeheard, or some other such kinde of disguising, but with an excellent horse and well trimmed for the purpose, because the minde of the lookers on runneth forthwith to imagin the thing that is offered unto the eyes at the first shew, and when they behold afterwarde a far greater matter to come of it than they looked for under that attire, it delyteth them, and they take pleasure at it. (p. 99; original in brackets)

Sidney's family status is disguised (*travestito*) by the role he assumes as poet in writing the *Arcadia*, just as the young courtier is disguised as an old man or the soldier as a rustic shepherd. The letter to his sister might be termed a looseness in the garment enabling the spectator to discern the greater reality beneath—the reality of his social status. By masquerading as a poet, Sidney takes on "the forme of that he hath better skill in," and no matter how much study and care he uses, he is still *only* masquerading as far as the spectator is concerned. In fact, his excellence as a poet inclines the spectator to believe, on the one hand, that he would be an even better poet if poetry were his chief occupation, and, on the other hand, that he must be truly superlative at being what he actually is, a soldier-statesman, if he can do so well at something which is *only* a masquerade. Anything he did as a poet, no matter how brilliantly, could only parody, or travesty (in the modern sense of the word), the immeasurably greater reality of his ascriptive being. In Sir Philip Sidney's position, the important thing was to know what one had skill in and to practice it as if masquerading, and transcendence would come of itself, since what one really was—by birth—would always be taken to be greater than anything one could achieve.

John Donne, the son of an ironmonger and stepson of a physician, did not have it quite so easy, even though the ironmonger was prosperous and the physician prominent. Nothing quite so simple as Sidney's letter to his sister would serve Donne's purpose, because Donne himself was nothing if not what he had achieved. He was his deeds' creature. As an excellent poet he ran the risk of having poetry be regarded as his chief occupation, unless with that poetry itself he were able to suggest something greater beneath or behind it. No status by ascription to which he could casually refer and by comparison with which the poetry would seem a brilliant trifle lay ready to be discerned beneath a poetic masquerade. *Sprezzatura*, or the appearance of having transcended ordinary human limitations, Donne had to exhibit in the most paradoxical of ways by making the very thing which he had skill in—poetry—seem easy and unstudied, a trifle, with respect to his talents and motives, but not such a trifle per se that lookers-on would fail to be awed by his accomplishment. The apparent ease with which he brought off a number of extremely difficult poetic performances had to make his talents and motives seem transcendent. Then the payoff would be admission to that "club of the happy few," as one critic puts it,[2] whose members were the leaders of society and shapers of public opinion—a club to which Sidney belonged by birth.

Hence, Donne's poetry provides better examples than Sidney's of *sprezzatura*, according to Castiglione's primary definition of the term in

Book I of *The Courtier*. The following passage is often quoted, yet so significant in this context that it requires quotation again:

> But I, imagining with my selfe often times how this grace commeth, leaving apart such as have it from above, finde one rule that is most generall, which in this part (me thinke) taketh place in all things belonging to a man in word or deede, above all other. And that is to exchue as much as a man may, and as a sharpe and daungerous rocke, too much curiousnesse, and (to speake a new word) to use in everye thing a certaine disgracing to cover arte withall, and seeme whatsoever he doth and saith, to doe it without paine, and (as it were) not minding it.
>
> And of this doe I believe grace is much derived, for in rare matters and well brought to passe, every man knoweth the hardnesse of them, so that a readinesse therein maketh great wonder.
>
> And contrariwise to use force, and (as they say) to hale by the haire, giveth a great disgrace, and maketh everie thing how greate so ever it bee, to be little esteemed.
>
> Therefore that may bee saide to be a verie arte, that appeareth not to be arte, neither ought a man to put more diligence in any thing than in covering it: for in case it be open, it looseth credite cleane and maketh a man litle set by. (pp. 45–46)

This definition of *sprezzatura* applies to Donne, and not to Sidney, who did not have to go to such lengths. As we have seen, Sidney had licence to use "curiosity," because his social status could never fail to make poetic achievements seem trifling. Sidney had only to make sure that his poetry was acceptable, which he more than accomplished. Donne, however, did not have license to use "bent studie and precisenesse" without at the same time finding means to conceal his efforts, for there was nothing beneath the garment of achievement to catch men's eyes, no ascriptive being of outstanding importance. He was not free to write an *Apology for Poetry* or to engage in controversies over the merits of quantitative verse in English. To bring off that transcendence which was Sidney's practically for the asking, Donne had to write outstanding poetry and conceal, not only its difficulty, but the seriousness of his commitment to creating it in the first place. For Donne, poetry had to exhibit *sprezzatura* in the most rigorous sense, creating awesome illusions of freedom and power, while, for Sidney, poetry was a trip to a costume ball.

I would hesitate to claim that John Donne's secular poetry represents the strictest case of literary *sprezzatura* in the English Renaissance, but I will argue in this chapter that Donne went to greater extremes than any of his contemporaries to achieve that apparent transcendence which defines *sprezzatura*. "To his Mistris Going to Bed," not at first glance a poem suggesting the transcendence of human limitations, is, in fact, a perfect example of *sprezzatura* attained through travesty—but travesty as Donne, not Sidney, had to practice it. The hyperbolic contrast throughout this poem between *them* and *us*, between the laity and love's initiates graced with their mistresses' favor, suggests a burlesque treatment of Castiglione's contrast between his courtly adept, basking in the "imputed grace" of his aristocratic employer, and those untowardly assheads—those "busy fooles"—who labor for favor to no avail because their punctilious industry is too apparent. However, the burlesque in this poetic striptease cuts deeper than satire of courtliness.[3] The object of Donne's travesty in "To his Mistris Going to Bed" is his own poetic style—precisely that aesthetic of the flickering provocation discussed in the preceding chapter. While undressing his mistress, Donne dresses his own poetic style in a burlesque costume and sends it to the courtly masquerade.

Comparison of "To his Mistris Going to Bed" with an extreme example of imaginative expansion in the visual arts will illustrate the travesty Donne accomplishes of that art of provocation central to the courtly poetic. The sculpture of Gian Lorenzo Bernini represents the highest development of that peculiar expressivity defined in Lomazzo's anecdote about Leonardo da Vinci and his clowns and adopted by court painters in Donne's England. Bernini's David (fig. 3) causes us to move around his pedestal until we get into the right position to see him and then, perversely, rivets our attention on an imaginary giant in the distance. This David appears to have forgotten that he is a statue to be looked at, and instead, with his total absorption in the act that he is about to perform, causes us to surrender—not to suspend disbelief in his reality, but to surrender—belief in our own, as the space around us forms itself into the valley between the armies of Israel and the Philistines. No other sculptural representation of David causes us to feel so strongly the presence of Goliath. Nor is it easy to think of a poem that causes us to feel quite so strongly the presence of a naked female body as "To his Mistris Going to Bed."

Not a single word, however, in this poem of forty-eight lines offers the slightest clue as to the actual appearance of the female body over which the speaker grows more and more excited. In this sense, the speaker is an erotic David and the young woman his Goliath, for he no sooner gives us a glimpse of himself at the opening of the poem than he glues our eyes on a young woman whose body we must visualize solely through the medium of his anticipation, and like David with his sling drawn taut ready to fire, the speaker has his erection, to which he calls our attention at regular intervals throughout the poem in lines 1–4, 12, 24, 32, and finally in line 44, this time in a manner most pertinent of all to the question of imaginative expansion. However, with line 25,

Fig. 3. Gian Lorenzo Bernini's "David." Courtesy
Galleria Borghese.

there begins the famous passage of the roving hands in which, as Frank
Kermode observes, "an authentic sense of sexual excitement enters the
poem."[4] Now, it may be true that sexual excitement reaches a high pitch
in these lines, and especially in line 26, but with the speaker's having
established the image of his erection throughout the preceding 24 lines,
it is difficult to agree with Kermode's implication that the poem's eroticism has been somehow inauthentic up to this point. On the contrary,
we have been led up to it through a striptease, the salient details of which
we ourselves have been provoked to create, using each article of dis-
carded clothing as an indication of which part and how much of the
young woman's anatomy we should visualize. Hence, we come to line 25
in the course of an imaginary voyage of erotic discovery. We have sup-
plied the poem with a young woman of our dreams, so to speak, and now
we are requested, not merely to look at her, but to touch her—"behind,
before, above, between, below." In his literary, more illusionistic medium, Donne is more audacious than Bernini. He invites us to stroke
Goliath's beard.

The impact of "To his Mistris Going to Bed" derives from precisely that imaginative expansion on the reader's part which characterizes the courtly aesthetic. However, it is far from a "vertuous condition" that is imprinted by this "flickering provocation." The symmetrical use of the parturition metaphor at the beginning and the end of the poem in lines 2 and 44 imprints quite another image. It is tempting indeed to regard this metaphor as willful—to put it mildly—since the poem is interested in every aspect of the procreative act except procreation itself, but, of course, this is the point of the metaphor: it disorients readers, compelling them, by way of imaginative expansion, to perform a sex-change operation in order to regain their bearings. The latter part of line 2 ("I in labour lye") evokes the image of a woman with a swollen pelvis writhing in labor, but we know that the image is being used of a man lying in bed as a woman undresses. So readers must in their imagination switch the sexes, but in doing so, they cannot avoid transferring to the male image the piquant details of the female image, and hence they are left staring at the swelling and surging of a gargantuan tumescence. That Donne may have had in mind the medical belief of his day that sperm contained homunculi only fixes this image with greater precision. To continue the comparison with Bernini, we are left with a David whose sling is loaded with a boulder.

For authenticity, the eroticism of line 2 is equaled only by that of line 44, where Donne's peculiar articulation of the courtly aesthetic asserts its influence again, only this time with the added force lent it by the reader's memory of the full effect of the parturition metaphor in line 2. Of course, the midwife image functions very directly as a request of the young woman to bare her bottom and assume a certain posture, but there is also something rather strange about it, since it suggests an image of the young woman as pregnant and about to give birth. Now this, we say to ourselves, is impossible, it presents an impossible obstruction, and no sooner have we said this than we commence to unscramble the metaphor, removing the obstruction and reversing the directionality of the birth image in order to make a submergence where previously an emergence was in question. In fact, if our memory serves us, we will perform this imaginary insertion on the imaginary young woman with that very same imaginary organ which we discovered in the birth image of line 2, and having done this, we will have brought Goliath down.

"To his Mistris Going to Bed" is self-satire on Donne's part. It is an exuberant travesty of the courtly aesthetic which he himself practiced with so much brilliance, and it is also a send-up of the Horatian *utile et dulce*. The speaker's erection, which this poem as "flickering provocation" imprints in the reader's imagination, may be of utility to the imaginary young woman and pleasurable, one hopes, but a reader look-

ing for the infusion of a "vertuous condition" would have to look elsewhere. The poem resolutely refuses to let its content be taken seriously,
even if we are dazzled and entertained by the talent of its author. If anything about the poem is to be taken seriously, it is the talent of its author,
who so casually and adroitly parodies his own art—who, though a consummate poet, treats his own poetry as if it were a toy or pastime. What
other extraordinary talents, we ask, must such a person have if he can be
so nonchalant about what he does so well, and, of course, the moment
that we ask this question we must acknowledge that we have come under
the spell of Donne's *sprezzatura*, ascribing to him transcendent gifts
which he has not had to demonstrate. We judge that there must be something else beneath the poetic masquerade—something, perhaps, like
Sidney's inherent social distinction—which transcends endeavor.

A Lesson in Deportment

The *adversarius* of "The Canonization" is just such a busy fool or mala-
pert asshead as the ones whom the speaker of "To his Mistris Going to
Bed" scorns. The contrast between *them* and *us* in the latter poem is the
central issue in "The Canonization." Some people are canonized and
some are not, some have it and some do not, the poem argues. To draw
the difference as sharply as possible, "The Canonization" exploits a
mélange of Christian and Neoplatonic ideas in the same way that "To his
Mistris Going to Bed" uses the ideas that the soul must be separated from the body to experience "whole joyes" and uses also the Protestant doctrine of Christ's imputed grace—the transferral, that is, of
Christ's righteousness to humans—necessary for human salvation. In
the elegy, the religious metaphors, which may be "derisive"—as John
Carey claims—but are not "defensive,"[5] stress the difference between
the chosen or elect among lovers, graced with their mistresses' favors,
and those busy fools fascinated with jewels and fashions who must sweat
to purchase what the elect find bestowed on themselves with no struggle. A social elite, capable of sophisticated self-mockery, is contrasted
with the assheads who plod along until time, "which . . . must make a
calfe an oxe," turns them into clergymen, lawyers, and nervous husbands. "The Canonization" differs from "To his Mistris Going to Bed"
in that, after a breezy opening, it settles into a deeply serious consideration of distinctions among people and a deployment of its spiritualiz-
ing metaphors that has real majesty. The speaker makes his untowardly
adversarius party to a meditation and a lesson on conduct out of Castiglione.

Efforts to read "The Canonization" as an account of Donne's feelings about the disastrous consequences for his career of his marriage to Ann More have led to such gross anomalies of interpretation that Donne criticism should make a pact to cease and desist.[6] There is no evidence internal or external enabling us to date this poem even to within a decade. Moreover, if we take the mention of ruined fortune in the first stanza as an autobiographical reference to his marriage, we must also conclude that Donne was an aged sybarite, palsied, bald, and gout ridden, when he wrote the poem and that he is blaming all these symptoms of a dissolute life on poor Ann. If, on the other hand, we ignore irrelevant biographical material and focus on the language of social life which Donne articulated in most of his secular lyrics, if we focus on social codes instead of biographical data, a more straightforward understanding of the speaker emerges. We see that he is making a distinction at the outset between his love and that lust of which the *adversarius* accuses him. *If* he were palsied or bald, *if* he had the gout or his fortune were ruined, *if* he had given himself over to damnable lust and all the evident signs were upon him, *then* (he is saying) anyone would have a right to admonish him, but since that is clearly *not* the case, his accuser should mind his own business. The tone is ironic, in keeping with the condescension required of a courtly adept addressing a busy, social-climbing fool. Opening and closing each stanza of his lecture with the rhyme word "love," the speaker is, in effect, drumming the distinction into his accuser's thick skull. In any case, no appeal to biographical circumstance is needed to make sense of the poem's opening.

The opening line, however, has figured in a controversy more troubling than the biographical one. In the course of a sweeping study of the balance between worldliness and spirituality in Donne's poetry, Murray Roston compares the opening of "The Canonization" to the stunned figure of Paul lying in the foreground of Caravaggio's *Conversion of St. Paul*. Roston argues that poem and painting are examples of the Mannerist effort "to subvert the firmly established this-worldliness of the Renaissance and to replace the current faith in vigorous self-assertion by an introspective yearning for revelatory truth."[7] Donne's poetry, according to Roston, even the secular poetry, exhibits a tendency to dematerialize the physical universe and a "tormented striving towards a more satisfying spiritual reality beyond the empirically verifiable world."[8] Almost simultaneously with Roston, Robert Ellrodt was comparing Donne with Tintoretto and discerning the same trait of religious mannerism. On Tintoretto's *Last Supper*, Ellrodt is especially persuasive:

Dans le tableau du Tintoret deux sources de lumière se conjugent et semblent rivaliser: la lumière artificielle de la lampe et la lumière surnaturelle du divin. De même le peintre maniériste n'a-t-il accentué les aspects naturalistes—serviteurs, animaux domestiques et nourritures terrestres—que pour rendre plus saisissante l'angélique invasion des serviteurs celestes. Et si l'espace est rigoureusement clos, c'est que, dans le mystère eucharistique, le spirituel s'incarne dans le sensible, l'infini s'enclôt dans un étroit espace, l'éternité palpite en l'instant vécu. C'est le paradoxe fondamental, que Donne transpose en certitudes triomphantes de l'amour profane avant de le reprendre en poésie sacrée. C'est aussi l'image de l'alliance qu'il réalise entre le sens aigu des choses terrestres et charnelles et le désir lancinant d'une irruption de la transcendance dans ce monde opaque et tangible.[9]

[Two sources of light come together in Tintoretto's painting and seem to compete with each other: the lamp's artificial light, and the supernatural light of the divine. Accordingly, the mannerist painter has stressed the naturalistic—the servants, the domestic animals, the terrestrial nourishment—only to render all the more striking the angelic invasion of the celestial servants. And if the space is rigorously closed, that is because, in the mystery of the eucharist, the spiritual is incarnate in the palpable, the infinite is enclosed in a narrow space, eternity throbs within the living moment. This is the fundamental paradox that Donne transforms into triumphant certainties of profane love before taking it up again in religious verse. It is also the image of the bond which he achieves between a sharp sense of carnal, terrestrial things and a piercing desire for transcendence to burst into this dark and tangible world.]

For Ellrodt, "A Nocturnall upon S. Lucies Day" (to which I shall turn after discussing "The Canonization") is the superlative example of Donne's mannerism.

Both Ellrodt and Roston, but particularly Roston, find in the Mannerist John Donne an answer to the "dissociation of sensibility" school of Donne criticism, as it is codified in Basil Willey's *The Seventeenth Century Background:*

I think that something of the peculiar quality of the "metaphysical" mind is due to this fact of not being finally committed to any one world. Instead it could hold them all in loose synthesis together, yielding itself, as only a mind in free poise can, to the passion of detecting analogies and correspondences between them.[10]

Against this notion of the detached—unified and unifying—sensibility, Roston and Ellrodt oppose the picture of John Donne as passionately committed to a spiritual reality presentiments of which he strives to contain in his poetry. According to Roston, the shock device of the opening line of "The Canonization" prepares the reader for a subversion and a sanctification of the everyday. For Roston and Ellrodt, irruptions of transcendence into this dark, tangible world are the true subjects of Donne's poetry.

"The Canonization" will always offer tantalizing opportunities for debate over the balance of this-worldliness and otherworldliness in Donne's poetry. My own position in this controversy is close to Roston and Ellrodt's, because their description of religious mannerism can be transposed (with one major exception) to the courtly context. It is precisely the effect of *sprezzatura* to make eternity seem to palpitate in the lived instant. The fundamental paradox of *sprezzatura* is also that of religious mannerism as Ellrodt describes it. Possessors of *sprezzatura* have the sharpest possible sense of things mortal and mundane, and yet we appreciate this acuity in them only because of their apparent transcendence of all mundane endeavor. In fact, *The Courtier* ends with just such an irruption of transcendence into a narrow space—the Urbino drawing room—as Ellrodt perceives in Tintoretto's *Last Supper*. The supernatural light of Bembo's discourse has blinded his auditors to the natural light of sunrise, leaving them astonished at the rapidity with which natural time has passed while they had a glimpse of eternity. Possibly Castiglione should be regarded as a mannerist author to the extent that *sprezzatura* dominates his depiction of the perfect courtier. However, Ellrodt's and Roston's stress on religious mannerism would be almost as unsuitable to a description of *The Courtier* as it is to Donne's secular poetry, even to "A Nocturnall upon S. Lucies Day" and "The Canonization." In the final analysis, *sprezzatura*, or transcendence, in *The Courtier* as in Donne's secular poems, aims at a triumph, not only over this world, but *in* this world. In "The Canonization's" terms, one dies to this world, not the better to see God in the next, but to be seen and worshiped by humans in the here and now, to be evoked as a pattern of the sublime in mortal affairs.

More in accord with the secular character of "The Canonization" would be a comparison of its opening with Bernini's portrait of Cardinal Scipione Borghese (fig. 4), who, though a churchman, is the image of the senior diplomat, administrator, statesman. Although it is almost as difficult to contemplate the Cardinal saying, "For Godsake hold your tongue, and let me love," as it is to imagine a talking horse in Caravaggio's *Conversion of St. Paul*, the subject has at least a secular aura and the setting can be construed as courtly. It is impossible to guess what has suddenly seized the Cardinal's attention, but it must be important if it can jolt his composure. By means of a visual conceit, the concentricity of the folds in his cloak as they ripple away from the slightly tilted face with its parted lips and arched eyebrows implies a previous state of profound stillness, of dignified poise. Paradoxically, the disruption of this

Fig. 4. Gian Lorenzo Bernini's "Cardinal Scipione Borghese." Courtesy Galleria Borghese.

state portrays it best, because the observer is forced to imagine it as it was before the disruption occurred. The shimmering rhyme scheme of "The Canonization," with its couplets and triplets and its five stanzas all beginning and ending with the same word, gives the same impression as the folds of the Cardinal's cloak. It attests to the presence of a poise and profound harmoniousness which the *adversarius* has momentarily disrupted.[11] From the point of the disruption, the poem returns to that state, and as the speaker makes his return he spells out the nature of that calm which the *adversarius* mistook for raging lust.

The movement of "The Canonization" can be charted from its use of the word "approve" at the close of the first stanza to the reappearance of that word at the close of the fourth. In the course of telling his accuser in the first stanza to mind his own business, the speaker notes that the accuser is the sort of person who goes about approving and disapproving of virtually everything. In the sixth line, he is an "observer" in the sense of being a follower of secular and religious dignitaries, and in the eighth line, he "contemplates," with an overtone of religious worship, power and the money power coins in its image. The speaker's point is that the accuser observes and contemplates, but is not himself observed or contemplated, lends his approbation, but is not himself approved, worships, but is not worshiped. On the contrary, the speaker, by the time we come to the end of the fourth stanza, finds himself and his lover "approved" by all as saints of love. In the several stanzas leading up to the pronouncement of canonization, the speaker converts the Petrarchan love-saint formula from panegyric to something more even than "a declaration," as Donald Guss puts it, "of the principles by which lovers live in a hostile world."[12] The speaker brings that world to its knees.

Paradoxically, the second stanza insists that Petrarchan conceits are nothing but conceits. The speaker turns the tables on his worldly accuser by suggesting that the accuser, not he, is the one who has trouble distinguishing between fantasy and reality, the one who has perhaps been reading too much poetry. The exhibition of *sprezzatura* in "The Canonization" could be said to begin at this point, and in a profound sense for which the ironic, nonchalant treatment of poetry is only a preparation. Clay Hunt is surely correct in emphasizing that the speaker here begins to dwell on the vanity of worldly affairs, the uncertainty and instability of this life, filled with floods, plagues, wars, and wrangling lawsuits.[13] Which of us is the more realistic and reasonable, myself or you, the speaker asks his accuser—which of us truly appreciates this world of power and wealth for what it is? Certain persons may devote themselves to amassing goods, to procuring a comfortable life, but in light of the precariousness of everything, is it not also reason, and reason of a higher order, to be able to turn one's back on the world and, at a cost to oneself, seek a transcendent calm? In any case, who is respected in this unstable world—those who accumulate things subject to loss at any moment, whose own avarice increases the instability they shun, or those who recognize a need for the stable and permanent and who value transitory things accordingly? The Troilus who looks back from the eighth sphere with a mixture of pity and contempt for the things he sought so passionately in this life wins our respect more than the abject creature bewitched by Cressida's eyes, but we are inclined to attribute majesty to the Troilus who can be in this life and far above it at the same time, who can die to this world and yet be in it, enjoying its benefits with a detachment that increases the pleasure. This secularized *contemptus mundi* (a flagrant oxymoron) characterizes *sprezzatura* and forms the core of the speaker's lecture to his maladroit critic.

Possibly, it is from the *Dialoghi d'amore* of Leone Ebreo that Donne and his speaker draw their distinction between the lower, self-preserving reason counseled by the *adversarius* and that higher reason of the speaker which impels a lover to neglect his present state in pursuit of something higher.[14] The *Dialoghi d'amore*, in any case, does provide an explanation of the paradox which has fascinated twentieth-century readers of "The Canonization"—that is, the speaker's assertion of a love both spiritually transcendent and, at the same time, exceptional for its heightened eroticism. In the usual Neoplatonic scheme—that of, say, Ficino in his *Commentary on the Symposium*, Bembo in *Gli asolani*, or Castiglione himself in *The Courtier*—transcendent spiritual love occurs after the attraction to bodies has been left behind. Ficino may introduce the concept of the *Geminae Veneres* and Castiglione limit himself to consideration of aged courtiers, but the contemplative takes precedence over the propagative Venus. However, a curious, and peculiarly modern sounding, passage of the *Dialoghi d'amore* argues that spiritual lovers may actually experience greater physical desire than their carnal counterparts, and this precisely because of their spiritual love. In quoting this passage, which is imposingly difficult in the original, to support a different view of "The Canonization" from my own, Donald Guss arrives at a clear translation:

> such love [spiritual love] is a desire for perfect union between lover and beloved, which union is impossible without total inter-penetration. This is possible in souls which are incorporeal: for pure spirits can inter-penetrate, unite, and become one through mental means, which are most effective. But in separate bodies, which return to separate places, such union and penetration of the beloved increases the desire for union, for it cannot be perfectly achieved. And the mind, which does achieve an entire union with the beloved, leaving itself and becoming her, is left more desirous and anguished than before because it cannot have perfect bodily union.[15]

Unlike carnal lovers who can be sated after coition because they sought nothing more, spiritual lovers are left after physical lovemaking with an increased desire for union. The imperfection of physical union, of which spiritual lovers are aware due to their experience of mental union, anguishes the mind and body and makes them more desirous than before. So Donne's lovers "dye and rise the same," burn like tapers and fornicate like flies, because they are "made such" by love—by their spiritual love—not by the lust which their critic attributes to them. Turning their backs on the world, devoting themselves to transcendent spiritual union, they have paradoxically acquired to a heightened degree one of life's keener pleasures.

This lesson—which is the lesson of *sprezzatura*—of turning away from the world in order to receive its greatest blessings is one which is probably wasted on the *adversarius* of "The Canonization." In the third stanza, the speaker confronts his critic with an array of their culture's symbols of transcendence—eagle, dove, phoenix, and hermaphrodite—as if to admit that subtlety is wasted on such a fool and that only an overwhelming catalog of particulars will make any impression at all. Despite some impressive attempts,[16] scholars have not been able to exhaust the meanings of Donne's quasi-emblems. They are infinitely suggestive of divine love and harmony—whether Trinitarian, Neoplatonic, prelapsarian, or Petrarchan—and resolutely ambiguous, permitting this-worldly, sexual interpretation. They drive home the paradoxical argument of "The Canonization" that this world's benefits go to those who appear to have transcended their material limitations. It is *their* pattern of harmony that is begged from above when materialists like the *adversarius* have increased the discord below. The occupants of "halfe-acre tombes" and the personages of chronicles may have amassed wealth, but they will not be revered so much as those who lent rich materials an unexpected shape, who left in the form of a "well wrought urne" or a sonnet—or, as Castiglione would have it, in the memory of evenings in Urbino—a presentiment of the infinite contained in a narrow space where eternity palpitates as often as we direct our attention there.

Palinode

"A Nocturnall upon S. Lucies Day, being the shortest day" is an example of *sprezzatura* carried to such an extreme that it would lose its character if it went one degree further and would become something else entirely. Language itself undergoes an interrogation so rigorous in this poem that oxymoronic formulas like "secularized *contemptus mundi*" seem inadmissible or facile as descriptive terms. Here, a detached posture threatens to become genuine detachment, and *sprezzatura* to become genuine *contemptus mundi*. "A Nocturnall upon S. Lucies Day," according to one reader, is a "black mass said in honor of a patron saint of nothingness,"[17] while another finds "good reason to suppose that despair will inevitably turn into new life, just as spring must return after winter, just as the longest night must give place to day."[18] Is the poem a dramatic monologue spoken by an idolatrous lover drowning in self-pity, or must we regard the speaker's despair as transcended by a new understanding of love and by a detachment more profound than that which is described in "The Canonization"?

If we lean toward the latter view, which is, I believe, the correct one, we must substantiate it somehow, and neither the biographical nor the purely aesthetic approaches lead anywhere but to a darkness almost as absolute as the darkness described in the poem. Many of Donne's poems invite explication, but this one does not. Apart from a title (curiously like a sermon's title) alluding to the liturgy and to the festival day of a saint, the poem concentrates on the paradoxical task of creating ever more explicit images of nothingness. Our understanding of "A Nocturnall" has been improved by study of its liturgical quality, but the relevance of Lucy, the Syracusan saint and martyr, to the poem's central paradox has generally been denied, or else treated in the vaguest terms. However, the love-saint thesis of "The Canonization"—the very title of the "The Canonization"—argues that the presence of a real a saint in one of Donne's love poems should be heeded. By focusing on the St. Lucy legend, it should be possible to corroborate that reading which sees the poem as depicting a "transition from the dead darkness of despair to the deep darkness of resigned expectation."[19]

Gardner's surmise that "A Nocturnall" was written as a compliment to Lucy Bedford on a theme possibly suggested by her is implausible, because the poem's theme—the death of a beloved woman—is among the least likely to have been proposed in sixteenth- or early-seventeenth-century England.[20] It is remarkable that English poets of the Renaissance avoided this theme, which was so popular among their Italian predecessors and contemporaries.[21] In any case, the evidence for linking the poem to Lucy Bedford or Ann More is so slender that our persistence in evoking those women's names only testifies to the poem's grip on our imagination, not to the efficacy of biographical criticism. Since we cannot date "A Nocturnall" with anymore confidence than we can date "The Canonization," we must, in order to retrieve its historical context, read it too in light of contemporaneous social codes, not biographical circumstance.

Only one woman is named in "A Nocturnall"—the legendary Lucy of Syracuse, martyred in the early fourth century, whose story was available to Donne in the *Legenda aurea* of Jacobus de Voragine. Of course, the poem supposes the death of a woman of Donne's own time, but by the closing stanza she has become associated with Lucy, and for the purposes of present-day readers, she must be regarded as another—perhaps the final—manifestation of that woman to whom such poems are addressed as "The Dreame," "The Good-morrow," "Aire and Angels," "Sweetest love, I do not goe," and, of course, "The Canonization." She is the good woman of *The Songs and Sonnets,* the one with whom the restless speaker of those poems imagines a union transcending change, and now, in "A Nocturnall," he grapples with the imagination of her death, testing the veracity of his claims for their love—the veracity of those claims that he made in "The Canonization"—and he seeks a festival vision.

Since the feminine pronouns of the poem's closing lines expropriate Lucy's eve for this beloved woman, one naturally wonders what might have been the association that Donne wished to conjure. Despite the claims of "The Canonization" that its lovers having died to this world, are martyrs ripe for sainthood, neither they nor the woman of "A Nocturnall" qualifies for the distinction in quite the same way as St. Lucy. In fact, the introduction into "A Nocturnall" (through allusion to the Lucy legend) of actual Christian martyrdom, fraught with the intensest physical suffering, and the speaker's hesitancy to make grandiose claims set the poem against "The Canonization" as its *contrapposto*. Still, certain general ideas about martyrdom are as relevant to "A Nocturnall" as the process of canonization in the Roman Catholic Church is to understanding the development of "The Canonization."[22]

In all ages, for instance, a psychological, anthropocentric view of martyrdom has interpreted the martyr's victorious struggle against his oppressors' efforts to make him recant his faith as the soul's triumph over the body—the spirit's victory over carnal impulses. The climax of the Lucy legend involves such a victorious struggle. The young woman stands so firm in her faith against the threats of Diocletian's governor that God rewards her with a corresponding physical firmness, so great that not even a team of oxen can drag her to the brothel to be defiled. In the closing stanza of "A Nocturnall," the speaker envisions himself as having won a similar victory over his carnal impulses when he bids farewell to those "lovers, for whose sake, the lesser Sunne / At this time to the Goat is runne / To fetch new lust . . . " (38–40). Here, of course, a further expropriation has taken place. The speaker may claim the saint's vigil for his beloved, but he claims the martyrdom for himself. Her death has been his martyrdom, and together they are, he is implying, canonized by love.

One must hasten to note, however, that the characteristic Donnean hyperbole and equivocation carry with them none of the confidence exhibited by the speaker of "The Canonization." "Death" has no double meaning in "A Nocturnall." It is the signifier of irrecoverable loss. The final stanza of "A Nocturnall" expresses hope, not affirmation. The uncertainty of the speaker's position is made emphatic by another idea, to which Donne alludes, also central in all times to the subject of martyrdom. The anthropocentric view of martyrdom may briefly enable the speaker of "A Nocturnall" to claim victory, but the claim holds good only if we are convinced by his words that his grief over the beloved's death is so crushing that it disables now and forever his carnal impulses. The association of his grief with a martyr's suffering depends on hyperbole and the blurring of categories. However, the poem is uncompromising. It introduces into the midst of the speaker's rhetorical efforts to attain affirmation the most rigorous standard by which a martyrdom can be judged—the Passion itself.

The play on the word "Sunne" in the opening lines of the poem's final stanza evokes an idea of martyrdom centered, not on man, but on

Christ, according to which the martyr participates in the suffering and death of Christ and in turn Christ repeats the Passion in the martyr's body and conquers the devil there. All of the emphasis here is on suffering and death, on the expiation of sin and the redemption of humankind as a whole. St. Lucy in flames and prophesying the fall of Diocletian, despite the sword plunged in her throat, bravely imitates Christ, and she merits her self-proclaimed status as intercessor with Him for her fellow Syracusans in the future. On the other hand, the speaker of "A Nocturnall" and his beloved have neither suffered much by comparison with Lucy nor imitated Christ in any significant way—unless, that is, the falling and rising in bed of "The Canonization" can be taken seriously in this context. The speaker of "A Nocturnall" may claim that his "Sunne" is brighter than the sun, but he has to admit that it has no power of renewal. His familiar play on words calls attention, not to a similarity between himself or his beloved and Christ, but to the black abyss separating him and her from the Son. In the end, it calls attention to itself— to the fact that signifiers may sound the same and signify no analogy thereby. Rhetoric cannot bridge human death and the death of God. The Christocentric view of martyrdom denies the lovers their canonization and ironically subverts the very wordplay responsible for its presence in the poem.

These traditional views of martyrdom—the Christocentric and the anthropocentric—lay bare the tension in "A Nocturnall" between the human intensity of the speaker's suffering and his wish to regard his suffering as significant in a more than human sense. One wonders which causes him more suffering, the loss of his beloved or his inability by the usual poetic means to endow the loss with satisfactory significance. In the story of St. Lucy, the tension between human suffering and the suffering of God is resolved; however, in the speaker's story, human loss resists religious interpretation. In "The Canonization," intense human emotion suggests an array of spiritual concomitants; in "A Nocturnall," the stark reality of death calls them all into question. The speaker's intense desire to universalize his personal loss clashes with religious truth to the point where his metaphors subvert themselves. In this sense, the poem can be said to embrace the controversy that has arisen over it in Donne criticism. Desolation and expectation, like resisting poles of a pair of magnets, are wrenched together at the conclusion of "A Nocturnall," and perfectly respectable close readings of the poem may emphasize the one or the other emotion depending on the reader's temperament. However, the purely aesthetic reading that emphasizes expectation must do so at the cost of neglecting the poem's anti-rhetorical, anti-aesthetic religious content. So far, then, the consideration of martyrdom's relevance to Donne's concerns in "A Nocturnall" brings us to the impasse that we find in modern criticism, but at least it gives us some authority for concluding that the impasse is in the poem, as well as in the criticism, and it whets our curiosity as to the specific relevance to "A Nocturnall" of St. Lucy's martyrdom. It may also provide us with a way of breaking the impasse.

A third conception of martyrdom, which G. W. H. Lampe in his essay "Martyrdom and Inspiration" terms a "pneumatology" of martyrdom, connects the Lucy legend with Donne's poem in a quite specific and compelling way. According to this conception, the martyr's words at the time of suffering are directly inspired by the Holy Spirit, and all the emphasis, as Lampe puts it, is on

> the confessor of Christ as a Spirit-possessed and prophet-like person. According to this tradition, it is the faithful Christian's testimony that is of central significance. To deliver it may well mean to incur death, but whether the result is death, a lesser penalty such as imprisonment or exile, or, exceptionally, release is comparatively unimportant. Death is almost incidental; it is the witness before hostile authorities that is the essence of 'martyrdom,' and the role of the Spirit is not primarily to bring consolation and strength in physical suffering, but to inspire confessors to proclaim the Lordship of Christ with uninhibited freedom (parrhesia).[23]

Although St. Lucy's story in the *Legenda aurea* illustrates other conceptions of martyrdom, it is clearly this one that Jacobus emphasizes. Almost half the story is given over to the triumphant debate in which Lucy reduces the Roman governor, Paschasius, to inarticulate fury with her inspired answers to his interrogation. Although Lucy's physical suffering is extreme and protracted in the story, no reader can doubt that Jacobus concerns himself most with Lucy's role as inspired witness of the Word. The story is about the authority that makes words meaningful.

The Lucy legend, viewed in this way, acquires a certain prima facie relevance to the work of all religious poets within the Christian tradition. However, one exchange between Lucy and her tormentor deserves quotation in full, because it points directly to the tension in Donne's poem between rhetoric and revelation. The exchange begins after Lucy has finished lecturing Paschasius on the true meaning of the word *corruption*.

> Paschasius dixit: cessabunt verba, cum perventum fuerit ad verbera. Cui Lucia dixit: verba Dei cessare non possunt. Cui Paschasius: tu ergo Deus es? Respondit Lucia: ancilla Dei sum, qui dixit: cum steteri-

tis ante reges et praesides etc. Non enim vos estis etc. Paschasius dixit: in te ergo spiritus sanctus est? Cui Lucia: qui caste vivunt, templum spiritus sancti sunt.[24]

To Paschasius' facile, but sinister, rhetorical play on "verba" (words) and "verbera" (lashes) and to the question as to whether she believes that she is God—which, according to the light of natural reason, is less a question than a conclusion—Jacobus has Lucy respond with the words of revelation out of Matthew 10:17–20 in the Vulgate of St. Jerome:

Tradent enim vos in conciliis, et in synagogis suis flagellabunt vos: et ad praesides et reges ducemini propter me, in testimonium illis et gentibus. Cum autem tradent vos, nolite cogitare quomodo aut quid loquamini. Dabitur enim vobis in illa hora quid loquamini. Non enim vos estis qui loquamini, sed spiritus patris vestri qui loquitur in vobis.

With her reply, Lucy disregards the authority of rhetoric and natural reason, just as surely as in "A Nocturnall" the allusion in the final stanza to the Son subverts the wordplay with which it is introduced and demolishes the sophistical argument with which the speaker has sought to convince himself that he and his beloved are martyrs. The instruments of a Paschasius are not enough, the speaker must admit, to make words meaningful.

"A Nocturnall upon S. Lucies Day" is a homily preached to a congregation of those "who shall lovers bee / At the next world, that is, at the next Spring" (10–11)—to a congregation of the lustful and the idolatrous—by a person who has learned from experience that natural reason and its instruments, rhetoric and dialectics, are inadequate to make a real connection between erotic desire in this world and the fruition of desire in that "next world" to which his beloved has departed. In "A Nocturnall," he bears witness to this truth and, in doing so, *prepares* himself for the role of martyr as witness of the transcendent Word. He has been a Paschasius; he will, he hopes, become a witness like Lucy.

In viewing "A Nocturnall" as a homily with the legend of St. Lucy as its subtext, we can (if we wish to succumb to the seduction) find a way to the biographical Donne along a route less speculative than the one positing a Lucy Bedford or an Ann More as the poem's subject. We are reminded, instead, of Donne at Mitcham (1606–1611) interesting himself more and more in theological questions with the composition of *Pseudo-Martyr* and *Biathanatos* and referring to his poems, in a letter to Henry Goodyer, as "evaporations" of his wit for which he will not condemn himself provided that "they be free from prophaneness, or obscene provocations."[25] Possibly he was suffering a moment of amnesia about

"To his Mistris Going to Bed" and several other poems like it when he wrote this letter, and "A Nocturnall" can be said to have been influenced by a concern with religious questions that was beginning to go beyond the academic and the polemical and to hit home with greater force than before. However, it must also be said that "A Nocturnall" only represents the most heightened instance of a detachment from poetry characteristic of Donne even in poems held by most critics to be among his earliest—like Satyre II—a detachment voiced as clearly in his early correspondence with Wotton as in the letter to Goodyer, and most easily explained as Donne's peculiar rearticulation of that *disinvoltura* so central to Castiglione's description of graceful conduct. Despite the powerful seduction in Donne's case of biographical criticism, we must retain our ability to contemplate two such dissimilar poems as "To his Mistris Going to Bed" and "A Nocturnall upon S. Lucies Day" as having been written within a short time of each other. We can do no otherwise until solid evidence of their dates of composition emerges, if it ever does. Seeing the poems as generated by the same social code makes that contemplation possible. The imagery of Roman ritual in both "The Canonization" and "A Nocturnall" may itself be a form of distancing. In any case, the point of this study is that most of Donne's poems—including "To his Mistris Going to Bed"—were *preparations*.

Donne depicts the speaker of "A Nocturnall" as reflecting on his past with remorse. When he tells his congregation, "Study me," he is presenting himself as a negative example. The alchemy metaphor, with which he directs his most caustic irony against himself, forms the center of the poem and drives home the lesson of St. Lucy's martyrdom that words as the products of natural reason have no authority. The crux of this metaphor lies in how one is to understand what the speaker means when he says that love's alchemical art ruined him and he is "rebegot / Of absence, darknesse, death; things which are not" (17–18). How did love's alchemy "expresse / A quintessence even from nothingnesse" (14–15) in the speaker's case? The answer lies partly in the question itself with its punning use of the word "expresse," and partly in the speaker's self-referential catalog in lines 22–27, listing floods, chaoses, and carcasses. In a literal sense, love the alchemist pressed or squeezed ("did expresse") a quintessence, which is the speaker himself, out of nothingness, which is the erotic relationship that his beloved's death has since taught the speaker was not what he thought it was; more figuratively, love brought the speaker to the *expression* of such preposterous claims for his erotic relationship that now, with his partner's death, he would indeed be the quintessence of nothingness if any of them were true. In "A Nocturnall," however, these claims are set forth in a spirit of bitter self-mockery, because with the beloved woman's death the speaker realizes that the religious and cosmological meanings he lent their love are false. He was using language to tissue over the void.[26]

Love's alchemical art is the rhetorical and dialectical procedure by which the speaker lent a false significance to his relationship with the beloved during her lifetime. If she had had infinite knowledge like God's, which he attributed to her in "The Dreame," or if she had been the angel he declared her to be in "Aire and Angels," strict logic would have required that her death, like the death of God, should have reduced him to a nothingness more complete even than the nothingness preceding the Creation. In "A Nocturnall," he entertains the possibility that he is that primal nothingness, but he does so sardonically, because, of course, he is still alive. Love has made a fool of him. He has been cozened by a quack, or more specifically, love prompted him to play the quack—the alchemist—with his strongest emotions, and now he is left shamefaced in his mourning clothes. The peculiar force of "A Nocturnall" lies not in any suicidal urges that critics have attributed to its speaker, but in the macabre spectacle he makes of himself as the man whose continued existence makes a lie of all his former utterances. In religious terms, "A Nocturnall" represents a confession and a bitter act of contrition; in poetic terms, it is a palinode. As courtly art, it is Donne's supreme example of *sprezzatura*.

The spiritual process undergone by the speaker of "A Nocturnall" is best explained by Donne himself in his sermon preached at St. Paul's on Christmas Day, 1621, on the text of John 1:8—"He was not that Light, but was sent to bear witness of that Light." Donne begins the sermon by warning against an overdependence on the light of natural reason by which some men have invented printing and artillery (which Donne regards as having saved lives by ending wars quickly), but others

> have found wherein the weakenesse of another man consisteth, and made their profit of that, by circumventing him in a bargain: They have found his riotous, and wastefull inclination, and they have fed and fomented that disorder, and kept open that leake, to their advantage, and the others ruine. They have found where was the easiest, the most accessible way, to sollicite the Chastitie of a woman, whether *Discourse*, *Musicke*, or *Presents*, and according to that discovery, they have pursued hers, and their own eternall destruction. By the benefit of this light, men see through the darkest, and most impervious places, that are, that is, *Courts of Princes*, and the greatest *Officers* in Courts: and can submit themselves to second, and to advance the humours of men in great place, and so make their profit of the weakenesses which they have discovered in these great men. All the wayes, both of *Wisdome*,

and of *Craft* lie open to this light, this light of naturall reason: But when they have gone all these wayes by the benefit of this light, they have got no further, then to have walked by a tempestuous Sea, and to have gathered pebles, and speckled cockle shells. Their light seems to be great out of the same reason, that a Torch in a misty night, seemeth greater then in a clear, because it hath kindled and inflamed much thicke and grosse Ayre round about it. So the light and wisdome of worldly men, seemeth great, because he hath kindled an admiration, or an applause in Aiery flatterers, not because it is so in deed.[27]

The speaker of "A Nocturnall" followed the light of his natural reason along the way of Craft only to find himself, by occasion of his flesh, plunged into "darke *clouds*, yea *nights*, yea long and frozen winter nights of *sinne*, and of the *works of darknesse*."[28] This is the lesson that his beloved's death has taught him, and he hopes that the long winter night of St. Lucy's Day will yield to a light different from that which led him into darkness. He hopes for an infusion of that spiritual light which Lucy symbolizes with her name, but he knows that there is a process of confession and expiation through which he must pass. In this Christmas Day sermon, Donne describes the process as a "denudation":

if we doe, by infirmity, fall into sinne, yet, by this *denudation* of our soules, this manifestation of our sinnes to God by *confession*, and to that purpose, a gladnesse when we heare our sinnes spoken of by the preacher, we have *lumen gloriae*, an inchoation of our glorified estate. . . . [29]

The speaker of "A Nocturnall" knows that if he wishes to experience a foretaste of that heavenly light in this world, he must confess and denude himself of his past sins as honestly in this world as he will in the next before the tribunal of Christ on the Day of Judgment. To this end, he abjures all his former utterances inspired by the light of natural reason, all those preposterous claims he had made for an erotic love, as so many "pebles, and speckled cockle shells." He denudes himself of those products of his imagination.

This process is not in itself a martyrdom, nor does the speaker of "A Nocturnall" go so far as to claim that it is. He is not the same man that he was in "The Canonization." Instead, he dedicates St. Lucy's eve to the beloved woman whose death has started him on the way *toward* a martyrdom which he conceives of as an inspired witnessing of the Word, like St. Lucy's martyrdom. The process is only a *preparation*, as he says, but the hoped-for reward will be a new kind of eloquence prompted by a shining in his heart of the light that Lucy symbolizes. The sermon that Donne preached on Easter Monday, 1622, on the text of II Corinthians 4:6—"For, God who commanded light to shine out of darkness, hath shined in our hearts, to give the light of the knowledge of the glory of God, in the face of Jesus Christ"—describes both the light and the eloquence as essential to the preaching of God's Word and Sacraments:

> And then there is *Vocatio Virtualis*, when having assented to that purpose of my Parents, I receive that publick Seal, the Imposition of hands, in the Church of God: but it is *Vocatio radicalis*, the calling that is the root and foundation of all, that we have this light shining in our hearts, the testimony of God's Spirit to our spirit, that we have this calling from above. First then, it must be a light; not a calling taken out of the darkness of melancholy, or darkness of discontent, or darkness of want and poverty, or darkness of a retir'd life, to avoid the mutual duties and offices of society: it must be a light, and a light that shines; it is not enough to have knowledge and learning; it must shine out, and appear in preaching; and it must shine in our hearts, in the private testimony of the Spirit there: but when it hath so shin'd there, it must not go out there, but shine still as a Candle in a Candlestick, or the Sun in his sphere; shine so, as it give light to others: so that this light doth not shine in our hearts, except that it appear in the tongue. . . . [30]

In "A Nocturnall," Donne repudiates the fusion of religious and carnal ecstasy which he extols in "The Canonization." He admits that there are no carnal martyrdoms or erotic saints. The dedication of this poem to St. Lucy and the dedication of St. Lucy's eve to his dead lover represent a calling out for an eloquence in which words have meaning because they are granted the authority of the Holy Spirit. This eloquence goes beyond the creation of well-wrought urns made of words, "hymns" by which lovers can be canonized for erotic love. It frees words from the paradox of imaging nothingness and is (as Chrysostom puts it in his homily on the words of Matthew 10:17–20 spoken by St. Lucy) as impossible to bind as the sunbeam. [31]

By quoting Donne's sermons, I do not wish to date "A Nocturnall," either as the product of the troubled Mitcham years, when Donne was lured and repelled by a vocation in the ministry, or as the product of his early years in the ministry, when his wife's death may have shaken his commitment only then to fortify it. Any of his wife's deliveries—not only the last one in the course of which Ann died—would in Donne's time have been enough to start him imagining the death of a beloved partner. "A Nocturnall" is as much an act of the imagination as any of Donne's other poems and equally undatable. In my reading, "A Nocturnall" carries to its logical (not biographical) conclusion a social code present in poems *thought to be* as early as "To his Mistris Going to Bed." Travesty and palinode, as subgenres, mark out a poetic terrain conducive to the representation of *sprezzatura*. What was lighthearted travesty of his own poetic style in one part of the terrain takes a serious turn in another part and becomes a principled renunciation of all poetic effects, but most specifically those for which Donne is best known.

Sir Philip Sidney's "Leave Me, O Love" or "Thou Blind Man's Mark," though moving poems and eye-catching for their uniqueness among his lyrics, lack the intensity of Donne's palinode, possibly because they succeed so well as conventional poetic renunciations of love. "A Nocturnall," on the other hand, is an unconventional renunciation of poetry in the face of searing loss. Sidney's poems exalt poetry as a medium by which to transcend emotion, while Donne's poem, paradoxically one of the greatest of the English Renaissance, spurns poetry as a trifling thing by comparison with deeply felt grief. Nor does Donne's poem content itself with mere statement, on the order of Sidney's letter to his sister. Instead, it proceeds, stanza by stanza, with a ruthless demonstration of its case, and it has the disorienting effect of casting many of the most compelling poems of *The Songs and Sonnets*—and especially "The Canonization"—in a pallid light. By comparison with "A Nocturnall," these other poems suffer from a certain theatrical artificiality. They dress life up as if for a masquerade in costumes whose hyperbolic colors call attention to a world transcending poetry—a world which Donne sought to master more than poetry and for which he was prepared at any moment to renounce his poetic gift.

4

Discerning Insincerity

In a passage of Book III of *The Courtier* recalling Beatrice and Benedick's exchanges in *Much Ado about Nothing,* Emilia Pia exposes the Unico Aretino's seduction technique. She suspects that his endless complaints about unrequited love are insincere—only a subterfuge, "a certaine kinde of discretion, to cloke the favours, contentations and pleasures which you have received in love, and an assurance for the women that love you and that have given themselves for a pray to you, that you will not disclose them" (pp. 244–245). She tells him that if he has real cause to complain of unkindness in women, it is due only to his technique's having worn thin with use. This confrontation dramatizes, more than elsewhere in Book III, the difficult position of the court lady. Again and again, it is said by Castiglione's males that women are more vulnerable than men, that women's lives are destroyed more easily by men than men's lives by women, that men should not slander women because of the irreparable harm women suffer from loss of reputation. However, the same men agree that the court lady must possess the beauty and affability that target her for seduction by that master of elegant subterfuge the very courtier whom they have been describing. In exposing the Unico Aretino, Emilia gives an object lesson in the discernment of insincerity—a lesson in the special vigilance required at court.

In Castiglione's world, Emilia's task is the most vexing. When clever dissimulation is a prerequisite of the right to speak truthfully, how can anyone be expected to distinguish the sincere from the insincere? To the extent that the court lady's task is shared by her male counterparts, they are unable to find a solution. (And the task is so perfectly shared that Book III's concerns add up to an allegory of the male power struggle at court, the unveiled truth being too bitter to coexist with a eulogy of Urbino.) Even the Magnifico breaks down when pressed by Federico Fregoso to give a rule by which the court lady may know a true lover from a false one:

> Howbeit in this I believe there can bee given no certaine rule, by reason of the diversitie of mens manners. And I wot not what I should say, but that the woman be good and heedfull, and alwaies beare in minde, that men may with a great deale lesse daunger declare them selves to love than women. (p. 238)

He does suggest that a paucity of words is a sign of sincerity (since true lovers are usually tongue-tied), but he then goes on to prescribe exactly which wordless gestures the courtier should use in order to be believed. No human behavior is exempt from impersonation. In order to judge a suitor correctly, the court lady would need to employ Hamlet's impossible criterion. She would need to know if her suitor's disposition had been shaken by thoughts beyond the reaches of his too calculating, too histrionic soul.

In her influential interpretation of *The Courtier*, Joan Kelly argues that "the Renaissance lady is not desired, not loved for herself. Rendered passive and chaste, she merely mediates the courtier's safe transcendence of an otherwise demeaning necessity."[1] Kelly does not mention Virginia Woolf, but her analysis of relations between the courtier and court lady resembles the analysis of male dominance in *A Room of One's Own*: the courtier's subordination of the court lady affords him a feeble compensation for the loss of freedom and power that his class has suffered with the breakdown of feudalism and the rise of central government under absolute rulers. In her subjection to the courtier, the court lady gives him an illusion of power, but she also reflects his impotence as the servant of princes. Kelly arrives at this bleak position by stressing the Neoplatonism of *The Courtier*'s conclusion, where Bembo describes the manner of loving to be adopted by an elderly courtier. The lady's Beauty, like the prince's Power, symbolizes God, and the courtier—says Bembo— serves her Beauty, as he does the prince's Power, hoping to be graced with the favor of the aesthetically pleasing and the politically influential. However, says Kelly, the actual prince and the actual lady mean little to him. The actual court lady, when not inspiring the courtier's introspective flights, provides him only a pathetic illusion of power while the actual prince constitutes a daily reminder of his vulnerability. So he serves not them, but what they symbolize, always preserving his "inner detachment from the actual." Even if Kelly appears to be confusing elderly with youthful courtiers and to be, thereby, palpably distorting Castiglione's text (which is, after all, a dialogue of youthful courtiers), her critique of *disinvoltura* sheds considerable light on the dilemma of the court lady dramatized in Emilia's debate with the Unico Aretino.

There must be a good form of detachment and a bad one, or Castiglione's court world would be a jungle. That it is not a jungle, even Castiglione's most casual reader will have noticed. One comes away from *The Courtier* with a sense of the sincere devotion to each other of the various participants in the dialogue and their commitment to the Duchy of Urbino and its ruling family. We know that the Medici turned against their old friends, but they were the exception. Kelly's stress on Castiglione's Neoplatonism leads us (though not in her essay) out of the gloom and into possession of a model of the good courtier as resembling Plato's philosopher-king. The good courtier returns from his contemplation of forms to the cave of the actual in order to share his vision with the actual lady and actual prince, shackled to their everyday lives and pressing concerns. He attempts to raise them to an understanding of that which they symbolize. This is Bembo's point in Book IV of *The Courtier*—a point which Kelly ignores (willfully, it seems). The bad courtier, on the contrary, obfuscates and deceives. His detachment—really a cold, devouring egotism—reduces the lady to an ornament for setting off his own attractions and the prince to a means of material self-aggrandizement. The good courtier helps the lady and the prince to profit from the inspiration which they provide, while the bad courtier uses them in a self-interested, self-promoting way. The power of the good courtier derives, not from dominance of the court lady or deception of the prince, but from his intellect's capacity to shape and mitigate the raw forces of the historical moment. The wise prince is able to distinguish between *disinvoltura* of the bad kind and the good—between inspired counselors and their impersonators. However, the court lady, so much more vulnerable than the prince, has to cultivate discernment as a matter of survival. This is the fascination of Castiglione's court lady and the feature that comes down through the sixteenth century to inform so many of Shakespeare's comic heroines, and especially the ones who disguise themselves as men.

If a Rosalind, a Portia, or a Viola—played on Shakespeare's stage by a boy pretending to be a woman pretending to be a boy—can be said to have disarmed the males in the audience at the Globe and enabled them to contemplate their own vulnerabilities, the same can be said of Castiglione's court lady. Her vulnerability to slander, her defenselessness, and her danger before the diversity of human types mirror the weakness of a male petty nobility in an age of despotism and mediate to these males issues too painful for them to address directly. Castiglione himself was for years barred from Mantuan territory, and his mother had to manage his estates, because enemies had slandered him to Francesco

Gonzaga. A reputation was a priceless commodity for the courtier as well as the court lady. On November 6, 1511, in the midst of Julius II's campaign against the French and well after being reconciled with Gonzaga, Castiglione sent a long letter to his family in which he reveals a new reason not to enter Mantuan territory, despite his mother's illness and her need to confirm negotiations for his marriage. He argues that he would be throwing away all his years of service to the Dukes of Urbino if he were discovered by the Pope to have set foot in territory sympathetic to the French. The Pope has declared his doubts of the present Duke's loyalty and named Castiglione as the conduit through which communication was held with the enemy. Malicious tongues have been at work, he tells his family, slandering him to Julius, so, in the name of a dearly purchased, fragile reputation, he must disappoint them.[2] Here Castiglione himself serves as an example of the dilemma which his discourse in Book III of *The Courtier* displaces as a problem specific to women.

Reputation was the courtier's currency in transactions with popes and princes, and loss of it could destroy him as swiftly as it could destroy a woman. He had to be as alert as the court lady to deceit, and he had to disarm others of their wariness toward him—whether the vulnerable like himself, with everything to lose, or the powerful, with so much wealth that the truth was the last thing they expected to hear. If the courtier failed to convince others of his sincerity, he was ruined, and yet it was common knowledge that the cultivation of false appearances was essential to his role at court. Everyone in Castiglione's dialogue knows that *disinvoltura*—nonchalance, detachment, premeditation, artifice— is essential to the courtier's performance, and yet it is a matter of self-preservation (self-promotion and entertainment too) for everyone to be as skilled as possible in exposing artifice. The courtier's business was casuistry.[3] Along with Renaissance defenders of poetry, he had to persuade prince and peers that his artifice was the exception to the rule that feigning is evil. Despite a plethora of baser motives attributable to his actions and obvious to everyone, he had to convince the world that he was the good courtier—the altruistic counselor—returning, like a philosopher-king, with a vision of the true and the real. This is the point at which Castiglione's courtier and Donne's lover converge, not only by reason of their extreme concern with the problem, but because Donne's erotic poetry and Castiglione's dialogue conduct the persuasion in the same way—by acknowledging, not evading, the problem, and by realistically admitting that altruism and self-interest are often difficult to distinguish. This may be the main reason that readers have always noted the intelligence that Donne's speakers attribute to the women whom they address. The exceptional speaker who insults a woman's intelligence usually winds up demonstrating his own mental deficiency—as in Elegy VII ("Tutelage").

Despite his nostalgia for the court of Guidobaldo and his need to depict it as a utopia whose cultural authority compensated for the political and military debacle of the opening decades of the Italian sixteenth century, Castiglione allows himself moments of uncompromising—even acerbic—reflection on human relations. In Book II, for instance, his discussion of the dangers of friendship explains the urgency of Book III's concern with the detection of insincerity:

> Therefore because it hath happened to mee more than once to be deceived of him whom I loved best, and of whom I hoped I was beloved above any other person, I have thought with my selfe alone otherwhile to bee well done, never to put a mans trust in any person in the worlde, nor to give him selfe so for a pray to friende how deare and loving soever he were, that without stoppe a man should make him partaker of all his thoughts, as he would his owne selfe: because there are in our minds so many dennes and corners, that it is unpossible for the wit of man to know the dissimulations that lye lurking in them (p. 119).

Nowhere more than in Book III do these "dennes and corners" of the mind enter the foreground of discussion, and nowhere is there a clearer acknowledgment that the dissimulation so necessary to the courtier's success, whether in cultivating provocative repartee or a nonchalant demeanor, is a double-edged instrument. In Book III, Urbino resembles Elsinore, and the court lady is left to determine who is painting an inch thick and who can truthfully say that he knows not seems. In Book III, to act is also to act in the stage sense, and to be, therefore, is too often not to be. In Urbino as in Elsinore, the court lady must be a skeptical Emilia Pia (and so must the courtier) or else drown in the "glassy stream" of treacherous impersonation. Of course, the result of Castiglione's veiled acknowledgment of Urbino's terrible flaw (he has, after all, camouflaged it in an updated version of the *querelle des femmes*) is that we believe him when he praises the place.

In John Donne's *Songs and Sonnets*, the peculiar forcefulness and the reality, often noted, of the female addressee is that of a wary, skeptical, highly intelligent Emilia Pia, and her world is the court, full of skillful seducers whose success in life depends on their feigning. Hence, the force of conviction that Donne's speaker achieves, the reality that he assumes for us and the sincerity with which his discourse strikes us, depends on his frank acknowledgment of the woman's risk. If—despite those "dennes and corners" of the mind of which she is all too aware—he is to convince her of his sincerity, if he is to persuade her that she is a genuine participant and coadjutor in whatever transcendence of their restricted lives he may enjoy, he must acknowledge her vulnerability. He must acknowledge that she may lose, not gain, from trusting him. She is too intelligent to tolerate evasions. If a poetic motto were needed for Book III of *The Courtier*, "A Lecture upon the Shadow" would serve well, with its admission that the feigning required of lovers to preserve their relationship in a hostile setting may imperceptibly—as imperceptibly as a shadow moving from west to east—turn inward against them and become mutual deception. This poem registers the fear felt throughout Book III that the feigning necessary to civilization may make a nightmare of human relations, unless a miracle occurs and the sun stands still—unless the courtier, by feigning, can bring to light redemptive truths.

The Good Courtier

In "The Exstasie," the speaker's acknowledgment of the real world of sex, conflict, and subterfuge cuts across the Neoplatonic vision of permanence shared by the lovers' disembodied souls.[4] And this motion against the grain wins for the speaker credibility, for the poem verisimilitude. Those "defects of loneliness" nullified by the "abler soule" (the single soul flowing from the lovers' individual souls) make themselves felt as strongly at the opening of "The Exstasie" as the deathbed imagery at the opening of "A Valediction: forbidding Mourning." The military imagery of the fourth and fifth stanzas registers as more than Petrarchan ornament. The lovers are armies seeking an "uncertaine victorie," and their souls go out toward each other as negotiators seeking to "advance their state." The ecstasy of the lovers begins in self-interest, conflict, and mistrust. The lovers are situated in the court world of isolation and mistrust, winning and losing, competition and dissimulation. They may gain a moment of transcendence, during which they know what they are composed of, during which their souls lie open to each other like the leaves of that book Donne mentions in his famous seventeenth meditation, but they must return to bodies and to a world of vicissitude in which no one can be certain who anyone else is or can know anyone else's intentions. It is the speaker's *acknowledgment* of this dilemma that lends his argument force and makes it persuasive—not merely to the obtrusive reader—but to the woman who he claims is his partner in transcendence. A physical love compatible with the spiritual love which they have briefly experienced is not, he admits, to be achieved in their courtly habitat without danger.

Poems like "The Good-morrow" and "The Sunne Rising" resemble "The Exstasie" in that their persistent reference to the world outside the lovers' bedroom increases the speaker's credibility. His readiness to consider dissonant elements encroaching on their private world distinguishes him from the seducer who seeks to conceal the dangers and get on with the enjoyment. In conceding that there are true fears, as well as false, the speaker of "The Anniversarie" resembles those of "The Goodmorrow" and "The Sunne Rising," and he shares with them the impulse to fashion a subjective universe apart from the squalor of the everyday. However, the speaker of "The Exstasie" does much more than his counterparts in these poems. Having had his world apart in ecstatic union with his beloved, and having seen at the same time the dangers of their social milieu, he proposes nonetheless to return to the everyday and to bring their vision into the realm of the physical and the social. Like Bembo's elderly courtier and Plato's philosopher-king, the lovers will return to the cave and help "weake men" break their chains and shed their illusions.

Still, even this is not all that he proposes. He couches his description of the lovers' return in Christian terms. By giving their spiritual love a physical expression, they will, like Christ when he assumed a human body, be enabling feeble mankind to look on "love reveal'd." In returning to their bodies, they will be like angels (figures of Christ) imprinting themselves on air in order to work heaven's influence. In sum, the speaker of "The Exstasie" describes himself and his beloved as having undergone together several stages of transcendence: first, they have made of their separate souls one soul and come to replace diffident conjecture with true knowledge of each other; second, in deciding to return to the world of illusions and reveal to weak men the nature of true knowledge, they have exhibited the generosity of Plato's philosopher-kings; third, in uniting the spiritual with the physical, they have, like Christ, lifted the taint from their small corner of the fallen world and may therefore serve, like the lovers of "The Canonization," as a pattern to other lovers. The hyperbole has grandeur, and yet the close of "The Exstasie" cuts across the transcendent vision with an ambiguous reassurance to the lady that no one will be the wiser once they have united their bodies as well as their souls, not even a lover who has had the same experience. Has the bubble of transcendence been burst, and do we detect a glint in the eye of the seducer, or does this concession to the need for secrecy in a world of slander, deception, and one-upmanship constitute an acknowledgment of the beloved's danger and of the fact that a personage of even Christ's importance was crucified for his troubles? The indeterminacy of the poem directly reflects the uncertainty of the court world as to the sincerity of its own motives, and the speaker's utterance—despite its resort to refined doctrine—carries the conviction of all speculation grounded in reality and in the humility of self-doubt.[5]

For all its exquisite tension, "The Exstasie" lacks the dramatic urgency and sense of conflict that readers are accustomed to in Donne's poetry. It is even difficult to judge whether its speaker is addressing the object of his desire, or both he and the woman—since it is a dialogue of one—are holding forth to each other with the same lecture simultaneously. However, there is a closely related poem, and one of the most controversial in the Donne canon, that raises all the questions introduced by "The Exstasie," but does so with the same drama we witnessed in Emilia Pia's exchange with the Unico. "Aire and Angels" is linked to "The Exstasie" in the same way that "The Funerall" is linked to "The Relique." Just as "The Funerall" analyzes the image of the lock of hair introduced in "The Relique," "Aire and Angels" glosses lines 57–60 of "The Exstasie":

> On man heavens influence workes not so,
>   But that it first imprints the ayre,
> Soe soule into soule may flow,
>   Though it to body first repaire.

Here heaven's influence in the form of an angel, a spiritual being, imprints itself on air, a physical substance, in order to manifest itself to humans, just as the lovers must assume physical bodies into order complete their union and manifest their love for each other as human beings. "Aire and Angels" modifies the analogy slightly, but intensifies the theologizing movement of "The Exstasie" and also develops the conceit of intelligences and spheres introduced in lines 49–52 of that poem. Most important of all, "Aire and Angels" has the dramatic immediacy of a response that a lover might make to a skeptical woman who has questioned his sincerity. If the Unico Aretino had been a poet of Donne's talent, he might have answered Emilia's charges with a poem like "Aire and Angels."

C. S. Lewis, Joan Bennett, Helen Gardner, A. J. Smith, Wesley Milgate, practically everyone who has risked a reading of "Aire and Angels" has treated the poem as if it were a touchstone for criticism of Donne's secular lyrics.[6] At present there could probably be no better validation of a critical approach to Donne than a convincing reading of this poem. The obvious danger here is of reading the poem in order to justify one's approach instead of concentrating on the poem itself. However, the criticism of "Aire and Angels" might lead one to wonder if such an entity as "the poem itself" exists at all. While there is general agreement about individual lines and about where the crux of the poem lies, interpretations manage nonetheless to look as if they could not have arisen from scrutiny of the same object. In reading interpretations of "Aire and Angels" from C. S. Lewis to the present, one loses the poem amid a fracas of conjecture about the nature of Donne's poetry. Therefore, I shall read the poem closely, beginning with a formalist approach to the actual text—which we must assume exists—and I shall, as much as possible, allow consideration of the poem as a courtly exchange governed by cultural codes to emerge from close reading. The poem itself is rich in ideas and in their rhetorical treatment, but this does not mean that it is the sort of text in which a reader should have overpowering difficulty getting his bearings. With the help of some information about angels that was common property in Donne's time and with close attention to the form of the poem, it should be possible, on the one hand, to arrive at a cogent reading and, on the other, to demonstrate that "Aire and Angels" is a good example of courtly discourse as defined by Castiglione.

First of all, it helps to observe that "Aire and Angels" may be a sonnet, not in any loose interpretation of the term, but in an exact and rather startling sense. The two fourteen-line stanzas make a double sonnet. Furthermore the rhyme scheme of each stanza (*abbabacdcddeee*) contains a six-and-eight division—the division of a Petrarchan sonnet turned upside down. Sestet serves as octave, octave as sestet. Accordingly, the sestets pose certain problems which the octaves undertake to resolve. The first sestet poses a difficulty love must contend with as a passion in search of an object, and the first octave solves this difficulty by having love discover its object in the woman to whom the whole poem is addressed. Then the second sestet poses a new problem involving love that has become aware of its object, and the second octave resolves the problem with a request of the woman that she manifest her love for the speaker of the poem, just as angels manifest themselves by assuming bodies of air. This is the poem in very broad outline viewed as a double sonnet. The outlines need to be filled in and reasons must be given for the radical exaggeration and distortion of the sonnet form here, but from the outset "Aire and Angels" can be viewed as orderly in form and in the development of its subject matter. It consists of two sonnets so closely linked as to comprise one poem.

The subject matter of the poem is inextricably linked to a conceit that compares the woman addressed in the poem to an angel, but this conceit, which is unusually detailed, cannot be understood unless the occasion prompting the speaker to use it is firmly grasped. Readers must adjust to the courtly code described in chapter 3 of this study and respond to the poem as a "flickering provocation," as a case of the decorum game played backward. Here Bennett first, and then Theodore Redpath and Smith, are very helpful in noting the similarity between the opening lines of "Aire and Angels" and those lines in "The Goodmorrow,"

If ever any beauty I did see,
Which I desir'd, and got, 'twas but a dreame of thee.

The lover whose voice we hear in "Aire and Angels" has had other lovers before he met the woman who, he now claims, is the only true object his love has ever had. He is in a familiar predicament. The impurity of his past behavior calls into question the sincerity of his love, and the whole poem, right down to the word "puritie" in the next-to-last line, will be concerned with this problem. The angel metaphor enters the poem from the start and is sustained with great rigor to the end as a defense against the charge of impurity and as a means of persuading the beloved to put her love to good use by redeeming a fallen man. While in "The Exstasie" the speaker compares himself to an angel along with his angelic beloved, here he admits that, though she is indeed an angel, he is less pure and in need of her benevolence. The speaker's dramatic situation (which the poem as courtly provocation forces us to reconstruct) gives rise to the metaphor and is suspenseful, quite specific, and certainly not without comic nuances.

In effect, the speaker of "Aire and Angels" is faced with a problem as difficult as numbering angels on the head of a pin, so it is not surprising that he should summon to his aid various angelologies, including those of St. Thomas Aquinas and Dionysius the Areopagite. However, his first desperate step toward a solution is the obvious one: to eliminate the indeterminate "any" of "The Good-morrow" and to substitute "twice or thrice," which is tantamount to saying that before he met the woman whom he addresses in the poem, there were not twenty or thirty women but only two or three of any consequence to him. This helps a little, but it is still not very convincing. He needs to diminish the importance of his past loves, but to do so without making himself appear a callous philanderer. A solution would seem impossible, if it were really necessary to arrive at a solution, but since all that is required is to convince the beloved, persuasion is the key—not proof. So the field is open to a display of sophistry just as long as it has an appearance of reason, and the speaker of "Aire and Angels," if he proves anything, proves himself to be a brilliant sophist. He blames the beloved herself for his past loves. She is so rare and exquisite that inevitably he made some mistakes in his quest for her, having "twice or thrice" mistaken his love's true object, limited as he is by his mortal senses. After all (he tells her), you are an angel.

From a strictly forensic standpoint, the purpose of the angel metaphor in the first stanza is to provide the lover with an excuse for the impurity of his past behavior when his love was still in search of its true object. There is a certain facetiousness and playfulness about the lover's stance as a defendant pleading his case. Assuming that the beloved is his accuser, he manages in the opening words of his defense first to diminish the extent of his crime, second to make his involvement in it appear the consequence of weakness, not intent, third to shift the responsibility for it to his accuser, and fourth to flatter his judge, for the beloved is also his judge. The pattern is extremely sophistical and would have been a source of delight by itself to those "frolique Patricians" whose favor Donne sought during much of his life. But the angel metaphor serves a purpose beyond sophistry and has another aspect altogether. It analyzes the experience of the lovers in a very important way, and from the start it prepares the beloved for the request that is to be made of her at the conclusion of the poem. The greater the analytic power of the metaphor the greater will be the speaker's success in making a genuine case for his sincerity.

Now a difficulty arises. In order to understand the more serious implications of the angel metaphor, it is necessary to reject the opinion of Bennett and Smith that the lover in "Aire and Angels" requests a return of his love. He is indeed asking the beloved to manifest her love for him, but that is not the same as asking her to return his love. He has no need to ask her to return his love, because he knows from the outset of his speech that their love is mutual. Her hesitation, based on a suspicion that she might be no different from his previous loves, strongly suggests that she is interested in him, that she returns his love, but that she is wary of expressing her love for fear of becoming another conquest. She fears those "dennes and corners" of her lover's mind in which dissimulations may be lurking of which even he himself is not aware. He understands her fear, and he also understands that it could not exist unless she desired him. There would be no reason for it otherwise. So he is able to begin his defense and his persuasion (the poem itself after we have responded to its provocation) with the assumption of a mutual love and then move on, with the help of the angel metaphor, to suggest that this mutual love existed before their first meeting and actually brought them together, although not before he had mistaken its object "twice or thrice." Within the framework of a conceit filled with implications, each one of which finds its development, the speaker is making the familiar (if always preposterous) observation that it seems as if they have always loved each other.

The opening lines of "Aire and Angels" are inexplicable unless the love described in them is mutual and unless the speaker is understood as saying that this love must have existed before any actual meeting between himself and his beloved. When he uses the angel metaphor to declare that his previous loves were merely imperfect manifestations of the woman upon whom his love has finally come to rest, when he describes them as voices or shapeless flames in whom he worshiped her, he is saying that her influence was at work in them guiding him to her before he had seen her or the two of them had actually met. She "affected" him through those other women, and in them he worshiped her, not them. Or else, allowing for the seventeenth-century double meaning of the word *affect*, he is saying that like an angel, before he knew her, she "had affection for him" and through it "influenced him" by manifesting herself imperfectly in other women. She was active in them, making them seem "lovely and glorious," even though now that he and she stand face to face they seem to him to have been nothing at all, so splendid is she, once fully manifested as herself. This is why he is able to say that he was going to *her* when he was going to them. The "thou" of line 5 refers to *her* imperfectly manifested in them. In general, he is saying that her love, like a divine influence, prompted him to love her in lesser manifestations of herself until he actually saw her, just as God's love communicated to humans by angels influences humans to love God in return, even though humans may err in selecting lesser objects for their love until they meet God face to face. In "Aire and Angels," the gallantry, the hyperbole, the sophistry of seduction coexist in fusion with the *fides quaerens intellectum* of a devout belief in truths exceeding reason. This is the same tension multiplied that we have already observed in "The Exstasie." The lover in this poem is using reason in order to understand his belief that he had always loved the woman whom he now sees, and that she had always loved him, and yet this noble effort stirs the suspicion that a simulacrum of logic may simultaneously be in deployment to effect a clever seduction. Where does perfervid analysis of a cherished belief end and extravagant sophistry begin?

A passage in Richard Hooker's *Of the Laws of Ecclesiastical Polity* is helpful to an understanding of the full significance of the angel metaphor in the opening lines of "Aire and Angels."

> God which moveth mere natural agents as an efficient only, doth otherwise move intellectual creatures, and especially his holy angels: for beholding the face of God, in admiration of so great excellency they all adore him; and being rapt with the love of his beauty, they cleave inseparably for ever unto him. Desire to resemble him in goodness maketh them unweariable and even unsatiable in their longing to do by all means all manner good unto the children of men: in the countenance of whose nature, looking downward, they behold themselves beneath themselves; even as upward, in God, beneath whom themselves are, they see that character which is nowhere but in themselves and us resembled.[7]

This contemporary, thumbnail angelology illustrates a feature of Hooker's thought that must have been appealing to Donne—an insistence on the immanence of the divine in human life. If Hooker is a trustworthy guide, the opening lines of "Aire and Angels" are a declaration on the lover's part that the woman's love for him is like an angel's love of mankind in that she has always longed to do him good, and by doing so, to resemble God. Her love is the kind practiced by superior beings out of consideration for their inferiors. Just as angels are purer than men, their love is purer in that it seeks to raise men up to a contemplation of things higher than themselves. On the other hand, the kind of love practiced by men, including the lover, is of necessity less pure, because in order to raise themselves up, inferior beings must call on the object of their love to lower itself. Otherwise they would be unable to perceive it with their senses and love it. Hence the first stanza of "Aire and Angels" insists that love assume a body. Human love—in order not to capsize, as the opening lines of the second stanza suggest—must perceive its object clearly. This is not to say that the human love practiced by the lover is impure; it is merely less pure than the angelic love that the woman has used to raise him up and draw him toward her. If the compliment to the woman contained in all this seems too earnest and too noble to square with sophistry of any sort, it should be remembered that the kind of thought that goes into the development of an angelology in the formal sense stems from a priori reasoning, and so does sophistry. For sophist and theologian, certain conclusions are foreordained, so it is not so difficult for the lover's discourse in "Aire and Angels" to pass back and forth imperceptibly between the blandishments of the seducer and the deductions of theology.

If one is to be as sophistical and as reverent as the paradoxical lover in "Aire and Angels," one must at least be passionately consistent about one's central argument, and the extraordinary symmetry in the double-sonnet structure suggests that consistency is important. If the lover declares his beloved to be an angel at the opening of the poem, she must remain an angel to the closing line. However, this is where the crux enters, and it is best to deal with it now in connection with the angel metaphor instead of delaying over details that can be treated along the way. Virtually every reading we have of "Aire and Angels," from Lewis to the present, gets caught in an exasperating contradiction that forces the lover to defeat the purpose of his persuasion. In Redpath's account of the closing octave, we have a clear example of how this contradiction enters interpretations.

> For love cannot inhere either in nothing or in things which are too concentrated and destructively brilliant. So the solution must be that

just as an angel (to appear to human beings) takes on a face and wings of air (not as pure as the angel, of course, but pure all the same), so my love must assume your *love* as its body, or, to vary the metaphor, my love must take your love as its sphere, just as an angel moves in and exerts control over a sphere (or, if we take "sphere" to mean *element*, "so my love must assume your love as the body or element in which it can act"). As a matter of fact, the perennial difference between male and female love *is* that women's love, though pure like air, is not quite so pure as men's love, which is as pure as an angel.

None of the critics is more detailed and learned on these lines than Redpath, no one has bothered to learn as much about angels as he has, but his reading has the disadvantage of forcing the speaker's love to become the angel and the woman's love to become air, with the word "love" both times carrying its primary meaning of passion in search of an object. So, according to Redpath, with Bennett and Lewis concurring, as well as Gardner and Smith, the speaker ends his delivery by attributing an angelic quality to himself, even though he had begun by calling the woman an angel and had remained consistent in this compliment up to line 25 ("So thy love may be my loves spheare"). One cannot help but agree with F. R. Leavis that there is something "blandly insolent" about this;[8] not that insolence should be denied a place in poetry any more than drunkenness or any other kind of disorderly conduct, but only that it would seem to be very much out of place in *this* poem.

It is true that the words of "Aire and Angels" are spoken by a lover whose mind is steeped in scholastic philosophy and rhetorical technique, but he is also a dramatic character—an elegant seducer whose success can only be measured in terms of the delicacy and intelligence with which he compliments the woman to whom his words are addressed. He will succeed with her only insofar as he is able to convince her that his sophistry is truer than reason and insofar as she accepts his compliment that she is an angel. In fact, her unquestioning acceptance of this compliment would, by itself, constitute an admission that she returns his love. If the lover calls his beloved an angel in his opening words, he must remain passionately committed to those words and at the same time make them express with great precision that which he desires: a manifestation, a physical expression, of the love that the woman has felt for him all along.

The last six lines of the poem accomplish this by comparing the embrace of a man and a woman to the coming together of an angel with air in order to manifest itself. In the eleventh line of the second stanza, the word "love" ceases to signify a passion in search of an object and comes to mean the object of a passion, just as in the eleventh line of the first stanza the word "thou" ceased to signify an imperfect manifestation of the beloved in other women and came to refer directly to the beloved. The symmetry is startling, but it is all part of the plan that a poem about harmonious love should see that harmony reflected in its form. In this, "Aire and Angels" strongly resembles "The Canonization." In the supposedly problematic eleventh line of the second stanza, the speaker's love *is* the woman and the woman's love *is* the speaker, so that a plain paraphrase of the line should read, "So may *I* be *your* sphere." Then the last six lines of the poem become a consistent development of everything that has been said in the whole poem. The lover is asking the woman, like an angel, to assume a body, his body, which is like air, less pure than hers, but not impure, and then he, like air, will become her manner of revealing her perfection while she will guide him in her embrace as an angel guides the sphere of its domination. He never quite denies that she is purer than he, but, as he says in the closing lines, women will always love creatures less pure than themselves. The object of women's love—the male sex—will always, like air, be slightly less pure than the object of men's love—the female sex—which is angelic. As higher beings, women will always be forced to lower themselves in order to raise up those fallen creatures whom they love. To be sure, there is a glint in the eye of this lover as he sympathizes thus with his lady. The note of facetious gallantry is unmistakable, but it coexists with a serious compliment, and it is perfectly consistent with the tone of serious playfulness characterizing the entire poem.

Although the mood is different, the image of the embrace is strongly reminiscent of the same image evoked by the opening lines of the last stanza of "A Valediction: Of Weeping": "O more then Moone, / Draw not up seas to drowne me in thy sphaere, / Weep me not dead, in thine arms." Here the woman's embrace is the sphere of the moon embracing the earth, her lover. In "A Valediction: Of Weeping" the metaphor is cosmological; in "Aire and Angels" it is theological. Hence, the embrace of the woman in the former poem can be represented by a sphere of greater influence than her lover's sphere, while in the latter poem the woman's embrace must become the divine influence that lends harmony to the motion of a sphere. In "A Valediction: Of Weeping" the woman's influence appears ominous, but the woman in "Aire and Angels" is told that with her embrace she can bring about that peacefulness in love to which "The Canonization" refers in its final stanza. She can bring to an end, the lover tells her, the quest of his mortal love for union with its true object.

At this point, a final word is in order about the meaning of the angel metaphor. Although medieval theologians differed radically about *how* angels assumed bodies, they all agreed on the ultimate *meaning* of angelic apparitions. In a passage in the *Summa theologiae* (Ia, 51, 2) within one page of St. Thomas's speculation on the aerial bodies he believed angels to assume when they made their appearances to humans, Donne could have found an epitome of the faith of ten centuries concerning the significance of angelic apparitions:

> Angels do not need bodies for their own sake but for ours: coming into our human world and speaking with human beings, they give us a foretaste of the spiritual intercommunication which we look forward to having with them in a future life. Moreover, their assumption of bodies in the Old Testament had a symbolic character; it signified the future assumption of a human body by the Word of God. For all appearances narrated in the Old Testament were granted in view of the future appearance of God's Son in the flesh.[9]

Of course, St. Thomas accepts it on faith that angels appeared to the patriarchs and prophets of the Old Testament, and as a metaphysician he is chiefly concerned with angelic natures per se, inter se, and in relation to God, so it is only in rare passages such as this one that he discusses why angels make their appearances to humans, and what meaning is to be assigned to those appearances. He may also have felt that there was little to discuss since there was so much agreement. On the other hand, Donne's speaker in "Aire and Angels," as a lover comparing his beloved to an angel and her embrace to an angel's form of communication with a mortal, is bound to be chiefly concerned with the angelic motive for assuming a body and with the most important meaning of this corporeal apparition. For his success in bringing the woman to consent to a physical expression of her love will naturally depend on the motive and the meaning he assigns to that act, and as the quotation from St. Thomas suggests, the apparition of angels symbolizes for a Christian the highest mystery.

When we read "Aire and Angels," we are as deeply immersed in "the language of paradox" as Cleanth Brooks could ever have imagined. With the association of sexual union with the Incarnation, the paradoxical fusion of love and religion in this poem reaches such an intensity that one can almost speak of an Ovidian theology or angelology at work in Donne's mind. In fact, the difficulty of "Aire and Angels" may owe as much to the intensity, the audacity, the unexpectedness of this fusion, or catachresis, as to the exceptional provocation it offers the reader to engage in the courtly game of imaginative expansion. The lover tells his beloved that the physical expression of her love will be like Christ's assumption of a body for the purpose of redeeming fallen humanity, except that her act will be limited to redeeming him. Viewed in this light, the closing lines contain a note of triumphant irony. The woman, the higher being, and the speaker, the inferior being, will enter each other's embrace in a desire that will render them virtually indistinguishable from each other, just as indistinguishable as an angel is from its body of air, and this will be because that desire will be a desire on the part of the woman to imitate Christ's love of mankind and on the part of the speaker a desire to unite his will with God's will. Or to put if differently, their embrace will be analogous to the Incarnation of God's goodness, to the sanctification of human nature by divine nature, and hence any question of a difference in purity between them will be rendered nugatory. Then the lover might be saying to his beloved that although individually there is a disparity between them, they can obliterate it with an incarnation of their love, since their intentions are as pure as they are mutually capable of making them be. Their embrace will join spirit and matter in an indiscerptible unity.

At first glance it would seem that the shift of reference required of the word "love" in order to make this entire reading viable is suspiciously abrupt. However, it can be argued, apart from the cogent resolution it lends the poem, that it has been prepared for by everything up to line 25, where it enters. The whole poem up to the final six lines has been about the problems of love considered as a passion seeking union with its object, and progressive embodiments, or incarnations, have been required in order to solve these problems, in order to make love inhere in its object. The first sestet of the double inverted sonnet deals with the difficulty love undergoes when only vaguely aware of its object, and the first octave resolves the difficulty by shifting the reference of "thou," which in line 5 of the sestet had denoted imperfect manifestations of the beloved in other women, to make it denote the beloved herself. In line 11 she stands revealed to the lover. Just as the soul must assume a body, his love has assumed a body, and that body is hers. By the end of the first stanza, she *is* the speaker's love, with the possibility almost canceled that the word "love" might subsequently refer to a passion still seeking its object. However, the second sestet introduces a new problem. Contrary to the lover's expectations, his love has still not quite come to inhere in its object, and hence he still can "nothing doe"—the sexual connotation of "doe" very much alive and well. His love is aware of its object, but the beloved is so dazzling to the eye (as one would expect an angel to be) that she threatens to overwhelm mere "admiration." She is too much merely to be looked at or contemplated. Love would run the risk of sinking under the awe-inspiring study of her each and every charm, so, says the gallant lover, not dropping his nautical metaphor, "some fitter must be sought," some means of adjusting the "wares" to the dimensions of his mortal love. The second octave then discovers this adjustment in the woman's action of lending her love physical expression. With this final manifestation of herself, she will make him her love and make herself his love, canceling at last any possibility at all that the word "love," from line 25 to the end, can mean anything but the object of a passion. Love at last inheres in its object. The ship will sail securely and the sphere will move harmoniously. The movement of the entire poem is toward a cancellation of love's reference to a passion seeking its object. In the second octave, the sought-after union is achieved.

Another troublesome question that might be asked of this reading involves its equation of the aerial body assumed by the woman with the lover's body. This too, at first glance, seems abrupt. However, the question brings to light a difficulty that is more an integral feature of the poem than of the reading advanced here. The angelic lady of the poem undergoes several different kinds of apparition: initially, as a voice and as a "shapeless flame," and then as a human female, "extreme, and scatt'ring bright," and finally, by assuming a body of air. So we are left with a disturbing contradiction in the lover's request that she assume a body of air after she has already manifested herself in human female form. What conclusion are we to draw from this if not the obvious one, by process of elimination, that the aerial body must be the lover's body? This fits the movement of the poem as a whole, which has the angelic woman going through progressively concrete, physical manifestations of her purpose as an angel to redeem the lover from his fallen condition by means of her love. Furthermore, the analogy with which the poem concludes, equating air with the male sex in general, supports an interpretation of the aerial body as the lover's body. However, here it might be objected that this interpretation is seeking corroboration from itself and not the poem—to which the only reply available is that the solution of a notorious interpretative problem by shifting the reference of the word *love* may also help to solve another problem that has not received the attention it deserves. Whether this reply is acceptable will probably depend on the school of thought about the poem to which the reader subscribes. In the end, it may be true that readers of "Aire and Angels" will always either seek resolutions affirming the poem to be a dramatic lyric or else will wish to dwell on contradictions rendering it a poetic riddle whose key lies somewhere in its cultural context. Of course, this reading has planted itself squarely in the former camp, but it also holds that the poem's cultural context is what makes it an effective dramatic lyric. Its peculiar intensity derives from Donne's rearticulation of social codes specific to his culture.

I have made the same effort in my reading of "Aire and Angels" as I have in all the readings in this book, which is to let the poem itself—to the extent that a formalist approach allows this to happen—drive toward its own conclusions. In reading poems as controversial, as ornately wrought and polyphonic, and as central to the understanding of a poet's oeuvre as "Aire and Angels," interpreters gain by neutrality—by holding in abeyance presuppositions about the author's poetics and about the author's implication in discursive practices specific to the surrounding culture. The result, in this case, is a reading that places "Aire and Angels" in sharply conflicting poetic traditions. The detailed theologizing of love accomplished by the angel metaphor and also the seriousness of its compliment to the woman suggest an affinity with the lyrics of the dolce stil novo; however, the sophistry of the poem's argument, the illusion of dramatic immediacy, spontaneity, agon, and irony, and the insistence on the carnality of the love represented place the poem more within the Latin elegaic tradition. It is as if Donne were assuming the roles of Dante and Ovid simultaneously. However, this is the poet with whom we are familiar, and of whom Yeats could say,

> I notice that the more precise and learned the thought the greater the beauty, the passion; the intricacy and subtleties of his imagination are the length and depths of the furrow made by his passion. His pedantry and his obscenity—the rock and loam of his Eden—but make me more certain that one who is but a man like us all has seen God.[10]

This response to Donne—across three hundred years—of a poet esteemed as much in the twentieth century as Donne was by his contemporaries returns us paradoxically to Donne's era and describes the response that Donne's speaker in "Aire and Angels" wishes to evoke in the woman whom he addresses. Yeats is persuaded that Donne is a visionary, or a philosopher-king, by Donne's frank *acknowledgment* of obscenity, but this acknowledgment is generated by a cultural code described and practiced by Castiglione. This is not necessarily evidence for an essentialist view of human nature, but it does strongly suggest that certain codes of conduct persist in being effective over long periods of time.

The paradoxical fusion of learned argument with sexual passion has the credibility for Yeats of speculation grounded in reality, just as for the speaker's beloved in "Aire and Angels" his theologizing of love has the ring of sincerity because it is grounded in respect for the actual dangers of her position. Her hesitancy to believe that she is different from his previous lovers provokes a magnificent credo on the part of the speaker, who seeks to make her understand that she and his response to her are unique; that it was she to whom he was responding when, before he met her, he was temporarily attracted to other women who vaguely resembled her; that these women, though lovely and glorious through their resemblance to her, were nothing by comparison with her once he finally saw her; that any love he bestowed on them represented a movement, though unbalanced and feeble, toward her; that now upon seeing her, he

stands in so much awe of her beauty that his love threatens to be over-
whelmed instead of dissipated as before; that she can save him by loving
him despite the impurity of his past behavior and by lending her love
physical expression; that the mutual love of human beings—physical by
necessity—has redemptive power and tends to nullify disparities between lovers. This lover engages her sympathy, because his cause is as
much her own as if he were defending, not just himself, but all humanity
against a charge of being tainted. Certainly, she would be inclined to
recognize that he takes her reserve seriously, and she would, therefore,
also be inclined to regard his love as sincere. The pervasive and dissonant Ovidian elements in his discourse render the Dantesque convincing. Acknowledgment of the dissonant, as Castiglione knew, wins consent for representations of transcendence.

In closing any discussion of "Aire and Angels," the temptation to
speculate about the form of the poem is irresistible. Actually, if one cares
to give a very detailed description of it, more has to be said than that the
poem is a double sonnet, or that the rhyme scheme of both stanzas re-
verses the normal eight-and-six division of the Petrarchan sonnet, so
that the sestet poses the problem and the octave resolves it. The fact is
that actual resolutions occur in the last six lines of the octave where
"thou" in line 11 of the first stanza, as opposed to "thou" in line 5, comes
to designate the woman being addressed in the poem instead of an imperfect manifestation of her, and "love" in line 25 (the eleventh line of
the second stanza) comes for the first time in the poem to designate the
object of a passion instead of a passion in search of an object. The overall
effect of this is to obliterate the disparity between the eight-and-six
units of the conventional Petrarchan sonnet without, however, obliterating the impression that such a sonnet makes. Nor is this all, for the triplets closing each stanza suggest the couplet, exaggerated, of the Shakespearean sonnet with its sententious summation of all that precedes. So
"Aire and Angels," especially with its second triplet resolving everything, can be regarded either as a double Shakespearean sonnet or as a
double inverted Petrarchan sonnet with a Shakespearean close. Not only
are the units of one kind of sonnet blurred, but the two types of sonnet
themselves merge into each other, producing the effect of an elaborate
shell game. Now you see it and now you don't.

Why did Donne go to such extremes? If one takes the subject of the
poem to be a kind of mutual desire that obscures distinctions in purity
between lovers, an answer emerges. If perfect human love obliterates
sharp distinctions between the purity of lovers, just as the Incarnation
spiritualized and revalued matter, rendering the absolute Platonic distinction between body and soul no longer tenable, then the utterance of
this love must assume words and a form in which the conventional dis-

parities of sonnet structure and the conventional referential categories of words are transcended and a new unity is established. So "Aire and Angels," in form, may reflect its content. Its form may be a metaphor of its content. A sonnet in one instant and not in the next, and then neither exactly one kind of sonnet nor another, though probably both kinds at once, "Aire and Angels," with its octaves and sestets reversed, serving each other's purpose, but not quite, may attempt to reflect in its form the Incarnation of spirit in matter to which its speaker compares the physical union of his beloved and himself. Man and woman, matter and spirit, content and form, air and angels merge into a transcendent unity. On the other hand, if one's lover is really an angel, she deserves something more than an ordinary sonnet—so why not a double sonnet with triplets instead of mere couplets? Does the form of "Aire and Angels" represent hyperbole in the service of flattery, or wit paying tribute to ecstasy? This reading insists on both. The cultural code governing this courtly speaker's tribute to ecstasy demands, if he wishes to be persuasive, willingness on his part to concede that he and his lover inhabit for most of their day a world of contention and deceit.

"The Dreame" makes a good sequel to "Aire and Angels." Here, the woman has lent her love the physical manifestation sought for by the speaker of "Aire and Angels," and, in consequence, he has learned that she is much more than an angel. By waking him in the midst of an erotic dream of her so that they can continue the dream in reality, she proves herself to possess powers "beyond an Angels art," the powers of God Himself, who is alone able to read minds. The hyperbole of "Aire and Angels," so exactingly articulated as to seem almost a law of human nature, here becomes playful, the subject of an intimate joke whose implications the speaker explores for the sake of making verbal foreplay. In comparing her "coming and staying" to Christ's mission in the world and her rising to leave after lovemaking to the Resurrection, he is being purposely outrageous. However, he must be *purposely* outrageous—he must establish his sense of humor—if he is to carry off with conviction the statement, with which the poem closes, that life will seem to him nothing but a dream until the next time they make love—until, that is, the second coming. This ornate blasphemy, in all its amusing detail, attempts also to supply a nobler motive than "Feare, Shame, Honor" for the woman's departure from his bedroom, and in its manifest failure acknowledges the danger of her position. The speaker of "Aire and Angels" achieves the impression of sincerity by straining all the resources of language and logic to make hyperbole coexist with empirical fact, while the speaker of "The Dreame" makes the same impression by pushing his overwrought conceit to the point where it explodes in a pun. Both speakers are good courtiers in that they can see and appreciate the other person's risks and they approach with candor their own capacity for prevarication.

The Bad Courtier

In describing the diversity of men's desires, the Magnifico Giuliano gives a detailed picture of sexual skirmishing at court. It deserves quotation in full because of the background it provides to the poems of sincere courtship already discussed and to the more cynical poems which are their complement. The passage is of special interest because, though the Magnifico seeks to draw sharp lines between the kind of passion that the ideal court lady will inspire and the less pure passions of other lovers, he ends up with a more confusing picture than he intended. He begins with what he regards as a portrait of honest love, progresses through varieties of deluded desire, and returns (he thinks) to where he began. But does he?

> For if beautie, manners, wit, goodnesse, knowledge, sober moode, and so many other vertuous conditions which wee have given the woman, be the cause of the Courtiers love toward her, the end also of this love must needes be vertuous, and if noblenesse of birth, skilfulnesse in martiall feates, in letters, in musicke, gentlenesse, being both in speech and behaviour indowed with so many graces, be ye meanes wherewithall the Courtier compasseth ye womans love, the ende of that love must needes be of the same condition that the meanes are by the which hee commeth to it. Beside that, as there bee in the world sundrie kindes of beautie, so are there also sundrie desires of men: and therfore it is seene that many, perceiving a woman of so grave a beautie, that going, standing, jeasting, dallying, and doing what she lusteth, so tempreth all her gestures, that it driveth a certaine reverence into who so beholdeth her, are agast and afeard to serve her.
>
> And rather drawne with hope, love those garish and enticefull women, so delicate and tender, that in their wordes, gestures and countenance, declare a certaine passion somewhat feeble, that promiseth to be easily brought and turned into love.
>
> Some to be sure from deceites, love certaine other so lavish both of their eyes, wordes and gestures, that they doe what ever first commeth to minde, with a certaine plainenesse that hideth not their thoughts.
>
> There want not also many other noble courages, that seeming to them that vertue consisteth about hard matters (for its over sweet a victory to overcome that seemeth to another impregnable) are soone bent to love the beauties of those women, that in their eyes, wordes and

gestures, declare a more churlish gravitie than the rest, for a tryall that their prowesse can enforce an obstinate minde, and bend also stubborne willes and rebels against love, to love.

Therefore such as have so great affiance in themselves because they reckon themselves sure from deceite, love also willingly certaine women, that with a sharpenesse of wit, and with arte it seemeth in their beautie that they hide a thousand craftes. Or els some other, that have accompanied with beautie a certaine scornefull fashion, in few wordes, litle laughing, after a sort as though (in a manner) they smally regarded who so ever beholdeth or serveth them.

Againe ther are found certaine other, that vouchsafe not to love but women that in their countenance, in their speach and in all their gestures have about them all hansomnesse, all faire conditions, all knowledge, and all graces heaped together like one floure made of all the excellencies in the world.

Therefore in case my woman of the Pallace have scarcitie of their loves proceeding of an ill hope, she shal not for this be without a lover: because she shall not want them that shall be provoked through hir desertes and through the affiaunce of the prowesse in themselves, whereby they shall knowe themselves worthie to be loved of her. (pp. 241–243)

What is the difference between the "affiance in themselves" that leads some courtiers to savor a difficult conquest and that which leads others to recognize the best in a woman and consider themselves worthy of it? How is the court lady to know the difference? The Magnifico has no answer. Furthermore, the rhetorical balance (admirably preserved in Hoby's translation) of the opening period only thinly veils its illogic. Certainly, if the courtier's love is inspired by a woman's best qualities, his love is apt to be sincere and genuine; however, it does not follow that his love is genuine if his means of winning a woman are his noble birth, his martial prowess, and his verbal skill. Few passages serve as a better warning that the dialogue of *The Courtier* is dramatic and that the reader must be cautious about regarding a speaker's words as having Castiglione's endorsement. In this case, the Magnifico's speech dramatizes—does not solve—the dilemma central to Book III of the impossibility, and yet the necessity, of discerning the invisible in the visible, of gauging words and deeds by the motives generating them. The speech exemplifies the problem that makes necessary much more subtle and complex utterances of the kind represented in "Aire and Angels" or "The Exstasie."

Those "loves" which the Magnifico speaks of as "proceeding of an ill hope" have in common the substitution of a power struggle for the mutual exchange which would be experienced by the good courtier and his ideal lady—the mutual exchange foretold by the speaker of "Aire and Angels." Fear of losing face and pride in conquest direct the desires of inferior courtiers to women whose fears and ambitions are similar to their own. The women are not reluctant to yield because they value integrity, but because they fear loss of reputation, or they see better prospects elsewhere, or they enjoy the prestige of having many suitors and playing them off against each other. The men pursue, not because they value the women, but because they enjoy winning, and especially if they can win where other men have lost. Of course, the game is played as if the players had only the most unimpeachable of motives. This is the squalid reality which the speaker of "Aire and Angels" labors to demonstrate was not his own experience before meeting the woman whom he declares an angel. Certainly, it is the reality that she fears in dealing with him and will have nothing to do with. It is the reality, however, in which many of Donne's speakers—bad courtiers—find themselves so at home that they can imagine nothing else. For them, eliciting an admission from the objects of their desire that they too are hypocrites is the essence of seduction. While the good courtier struggles against hypocrisy and gains the confidence of his beloved by acknowledging that the struggle can never be fully successful, the bad courtier adopts the opinion that, wherever there is an admixture of hypocrisy, all is dishonest except for the abjuration of any pretense to the contrary. He seeks to make the object of his desire an accomplice in his cynicism, not a partner in transcendence.

"The Prohibition," despite its airy tone, is a notable example of the quest for an accomplice. Its premise is that the woman wishes to show off her powers of attraction by keeping a man on the hook. To do this, the speaker advises her, she must avoid loving him, not because he would retaliate with the same scorn that she has used on him, but because love is more than he desires, too great a joy. It would exhaust him. On the other hand, she will lose even him if she continues her scorn, and then she will no longer have a devoted slave to place on exhibit. His not being there will lessen her. The answer, of course, is the golden mean—a lukewarm arrangement enabling him to "die the gentler way" and her to use him for as long as she likes as the stage for displaying her fatal charms. The speaker invites this woman to drop all pretenses and become his accomplice in the courtly game of one-upmanship. However, he does not mention that his interest in her might be the same as hers in him. She might serve as *his* stage.

"The Dampe" is too similar to "The Prohibition" to make any discussion of it necessary here, but one of the grimmest of these darker poems does deserve special attention. The speaker of Elegy VI ("Recusancy" in Gardner's nomenclature) prescribes capitulation to that court world which the lovers in "The Exstasie" attempt to transcend. The weary, disillusioned partnership that this speaker offers is the opposite of that mutual love which mends "defects of loneliness" and makes an "abler soule" where separate people were before. When in kissing he breathed his soul into his lover ("my Purgatory, faithlesse thee"), it did not, like a transplanted violet, redouble and multiply its strength, but, "like carelesse flowers strow'd on the waters face," it sank in a vortex. "The curled whirlepooles suck, smack, and embrace, / Yet drowne . . . " the souls of incautious lovers. The stream conceit, elaborated in lines 21–33, tells a sordid story of anxious maneuvering on the woman's part. While she carries on her affair with the speaker, calmly riding her "wedded channels bosome" (though with "doubtful melodious murmuring"), she entertains suitors some of whom she treats with disdain, swelling like the stream when it is touched by an overhanging tree branch. Others, who look like better prospects than the speaker, she labors to seduce just as the stream gnaws its banks. If she succeeds, she "rores, and braves it, and in gallant scorne, / In flattering eddies promising retorne, / She flouts the channel, who thenceforth is drie." Instead of breaking with the speaker, she tantalizes him in order to keep him available for doses of the same disdain which she had used on inferior suitors when she was his. Her conduct is sadistic, and he warns her not to let her "deepe bitternesse" get out of control, or she will drive him to scorn her in return, and her deceit will no longer hurt him. If she wishes to keep her idolater and to keep on tormenting him, she must moderate the sadism. The phrase "deepe bitternesse" suggests, in context, acrimony and anguish feeding on each other and arising, not from specific hatred of the speaker on the woman's part, but from a general malaise over the scramble to serve and be served in the court world so vividly depicted in the poem. Instead of the transcendence of this "deepe bitternesse" offered by the speaker of "The Exstasie," the speaker of "Recusancy" invites his court lady to recognize the depth of her cynicism and to collude with him in whatever poor excuse for gratification it affords.

If "Recusancy" exactly balances "The Exstasie" and gives a sharp taste of the reality from which the lovers of "The Exstasie" are in flight, "The Flea" offers a debased version of "Aire and Angels." "The Flea" resembles "Aire and Angels" as a dramatic lyric, with its concentration on a specific "I" and a specific "thou" and with its demand that we grasp the unstated circumstances prompting the speaker to engage in his formidably complex argument. Like "Aire and Angels," "The Flea" represents the turning point in a private drama which we are compelled to reconstruct. From the standpoint of that aesthetic play described in chapter 3, the major difference between the two poems is that "Aire and

Angels" insists on the reconstruction of an inciting moment while "The Flea" makes us wonder about its denouement. How much reason does the speaker have for his triumphant posturing at the end of the poem? As for the court lady trying to judge her suitor's sincerity, the poem attempts to convince by demonstrating that her concern with honor is hypocritical—that she is the insincere one and her pretenses are spoiling the fun. "The Flea" advocates a disillusioned love, while "Aire and Angels" invites the court lady to share a love that could be said to be disabused, in the same sense that the religious convictions of the speaker of Satyre III are disabused. The precision and learnedness of his argument bear witness that the speaker of "Aire and Angels" is not untroubled by the possibility of being a hypocrite himself, but he believes (and seeks to convince the object of his desire) that frank acknowledgment of this possibility insures a congruence between his avowals and his actual emotional engagement. For the speaker of "The Flea," all is hypocrisy—all, that is, except for recognition of that depressing fact.

"The Flea" is a miniature three-act drama in which the protagonist-speaker-lover's mind moves with the agility of that little animal upon which it loads its heavy burden of weighty arguments. In line with an argument that Donne's poetry exhibits a Mannerist tendency toward "the dematerialization of the physical universe and the tormented striving towards a more satisfying spiritual reality beyond the empirically verifiable world," Murray Roston notes "the implicit parodying of the empirical process" in the speaker's concentration on the flea as if it were evidence in support of his persuasion. Then oddly Roston goes on to wonder how, "within the context of the poem itself, we are led even momentarily to accept the argument."[11] It is alarming to contemplate whom Roston means by "we." Many readers would lean toward accepting the argument of "Aire and Angels," but who (except possibly the young woman recently bitten by Donne's immortal flea) would accept the argument of "The Flea"—"even momentarily"? Not Donne's contemporary readers, who could scarcely have considered it anything but an example of urbanely fallacious logic. The drama of "The Flea" lies in the impact of its speaker's overheated argument upon a silent young woman reclining in the spaces between its stanzas. Any momentary persuasiveness of this argument for the reader probably reveals more about her (or him) than about the poem.[12]

"The Flea" represents a burlesque of logic in a low-comic situation. The atmosphere is intimate, of course, or else the speaker would be unable to address the young woman on the subject of her virginity in quite the terms he uses. When he says that "use" has made her "apt" to kill him, he is suggesting that their often having been close to consummation and yet not performed the deed has given her to understand that she can deny him indefinitely and get away with it; while his earlier complaint that the flea "enjoyes before it wooe, / And pamper'd swells with one blood made of two" seems intended to remind her that he at least has had the decency to woo her when he might, like the flea, have taken her by surprise. Furthermore, the mingling of blood accomplished by the flea is more than they would do, because they would take care to avoid pregnancy. According to Renaissance medical belief, a mingling of the purest blood of the male and female resulted in conception; however, there is no indication of a belief that every act of coition, as Gardner and Roston suggest, resulted in a mingling of the blood.[13] So, says the speaker, alas, the flea has done much "more than wee would doe," because it has committed a rape and caused a pregnancy, but it is such a tiny, insignificant creature that we scarcely give it a thought. Why then, he continues, are you making such a fuss over the loss of your maidenhead? The flea has committed no sin in doing what comes naturally, so then in doing the same how could we be said to be committing a sin when we would be doing much less? This is where matters stand at the conclusion of the first stanza.

The second stanza could be said to begin before the print on the page begins, because it is a response to the young woman's having lifted her finger and poised it ominously over the flea. In threatening to crush the flea, she has decided to try to defeat the speaker at his own witty game; she has mutely declared that this is what she will do to any flea that dares to do to her all the things that her lover has suggested. She is still denying him, but she is doing so in a way that tacitly accepts his analogy of flea bite with sexual intercourse. So, before she is able to kill the flea, he quickly capitalizes on this minuscule advantage. In the second stanza, he confronts her, on the one hand, with a crazy syllogism: if life depends on the vital spirits carried in the bloodstream, and if the flea, a very small creature, mingles our two bloods with its bite, ergo our two lives depend on the flea. You will not only be killing the flea, he warns, but committing suicide and murder if you crush him. He carries the idea of a mingling of the blood through flea bite and sexual intercourse resulting in conception one step further into the absurd, but he is free to do so because the young woman has tacitly accepted the analogy. However, on the other hand, he presents her at the same time with a sneaky equivocation: therefore, and furthermore, he says, the flea, with its bite, has accomplished something far more drastic and even more solemn than our marriage would be if you consented to that. The flea has so thoroughly made of us one blood that our very lives depend on it. Hence, the flea is to be honored above marriage even. This is the state of the case by the end of the second stanza.

The third stanza, like its predecessor, begins before the words do.

Of course, the young woman can refute the fallacious syllogism ("blood" is the undistributed middle term) by crushing the flea, which is precisely what she does, but this only plays into the speaker's gambit, for it enables him, with mock surprise at her acuity as a debater, to agree with her that neither of them is the weaker now, and also to take advantage of his equivocation (which she has failed to notice) on marriage and loss of maidenhead, two very different kinds of union, the one honored by society and the other merely physical. On the one hand, he had said, in the first stanza, before she threatened to kill the flea, that its bite was like sexual intercourse, only more brutal and fraught with consequences than anything they would do. Then, on the other hand, as soon as he saw her fingernail poised for the kill, he said, in the second stanza, that the flea bite had accomplished something to be more solemnly revered than marriage itself. So, when she kills the flea, he is able to say in the third stanza, you are right, the flea contained only a small quantity of blood, no more than your hymen, which does not contain enough blood to kill you if you spilled it. However, you cannot think that the loss of this blood would cost you any honor, because you would not have killed the flea, our "marriage temple," if honor had been on your mind. He has maneuvered her into admitting that neither her life nor her honor, in her own opinion, depends on her virginity.

To continue with the chess metaphor: the young woman might have eluded his trap by letting his pawn survive, that is, by pretending to consent to the validity of his illogical syllogism. Then she might have restrained herself from killing the flea, and she might have said, yes, *you* are right, so let us cherish this flea because our lives depend on it, and cherish also my virginity, because my life might be at stake if I lost that much blood. Or else, she might, with greater seriousness, have turned his equivocation to her own advantage by telling him that if she had known how little her virginity and even a hypothetical marriage between them meant to him (less than a flea!), she would never have permitted herself to get on such intimate terms with him in the first place. That neither of these alternatives occurs to her strongly suggests that she prefers his game to any game of her own, and we are left with the impression that he will soon be purpling *his* nail in a different species of flea. With his allusions to the Trinity and the Crucifixion, the speaker is rubbing his victory in by inflating that side of his equivocation unnoticed by the young woman to proportions greater than which there can be none. He might also, out of the corner of his mouth, be suggesting that it is rather hypocritical of her to treat his sexual advances as if he were proposing to crucify her. Of course, there will always be readers who wish to regard the silent woman of this poem as the victorious one, and for them the speculation of Pierre Légouis as to the thoughts of a silent woman in another of Donne's poems may suffice: "Perhaps, we may add, she thinks the man rather tame, and laughs in her sleeve at his too intellectual method of seduction."[14] After all, the flea is dead.

As a courtly entertainment, "The Flea" engages its readers in a debate over the success of the speaker's persuasion. One the one hand, he defeats his purpose, because he pushes the cavalier advocacy of Nature's ways over Society's conventions into the domain of parody with his insistence that sexual intercourse between humans is as natural as a flea bite. He makes a fool of himself. On the other hand, the young woman, with her undistributed middle, hopelessly implicates herself in a melodrama of his creation by amusing herself with the outrageous comparison, and this when there are obvious alternatives. She too is a fool. In "The Flea," all is rhetoric, and appropriately, since the speaker is convinced that the woman's concern with honor is nothing but talk. His allusion to the Crucifixion calls attention to her lack of principle, her hypocrisy, her materialism, while the allusion to the Incarnation in "Aire and Angels" supports a belief on the speaker's part that a spiritualization of matter can be achieved by physical union of human beings. The speaker of "The Flea" has no difficulty contemplating his world as a stifling place contained inside those "living walls of Jet," while the imagination of the speaker of "Aire and Angels" ranges over the ocean and through the spheres of the Ptolemaic universe. The bad courtier writes the nauseating story of his life as a bloodsucking flea, while the good courtier goes in search of an angel. To the one all spirit collapses into matter; to the other matter stands poised at any moment for transfiguration into spirit.

Sincerity Then and Now

In arguing that "sincerity rests on something far more complex than an actual experience and the mere recording or transposing of autobiographical data," Henri Peyre claims that Donne is much closer to us than Sir Philip Sidney, because Donne was "a nexus of contradictions and . . . truer than most men in juxtaposing them." According to Peyre, "conflicting moods coexisted in him,"[15] and his treatment of them as *coexisting*—not as succeeding each other, but as inhabiting the same psyche at the same time—makes him resemble us. Peyre, as a modern, would sound less self-congratulatory without his assertion that Donne was "truer than most men." For many reasons (Eliot's advocacy not the least of them), Donne may *appear* so to us, and Peyre may be correct in citing the coexistence of opposites as lending Donne's poetry an air of sincerity. (This has, after all, been the argument of the present chapter.)

However, the sincerity with which we are impressed when we read a Donne poem is not quite the same thing that we call authentic (a word more in tune with our times), and perhaps the difference accounts for the puzzlement of modern critics who must deal with poems like "The Exstasie" and "Air and Angels."

Glancing at Peyre, Lionel Trilling wonders if sincerity may not be subject to national differences. He distinguishes between a French and an English mode.

> In French literature sincerity consists in telling the truth about oneself to oneself and to others; by truth is meant a recognition of such of one's own traits or actions as are morally or socially discreditable and, in conventional course, concealed. English sincerity does not demand this confrontation of what is base or shameful in oneself. The English ask of the sincere man that he communicate without deceiving or misleading. Beyond this what is required is only a single-minded commitment to whatever dutiful enterprise he may have in hand. Not to know oneself in the French fashion and make public what one knows, but to be oneself, in action, in deeds, what Matthew Arnold called "tasks"— this is what the English sincerity consists in.[16]

With minor adjustment of these categories, it is possible to speak of Donne's sincerity as English—not, of course, because Donne was English, but because it is the aim of the speaker (whether good courtier or bad) of every poem discussed so far in this study to give the impression that he is neither deceiving nor misleading and is capable of commitment. The French mode of sincerity actually corresponds to what moderns call authenticity. For all their acknowledgment of a share in the evils and paradoxes of court life, Donne's speakers never come close to the degree of disclosure found in Rousseau. If *The Confessions* determine one's standard of sincerity (and Trilling suggests that this is another way of saying "if one is modern"), Donne's poetry, despite its intensity and its other modern qualities, will always seem to fall short of the mark. It will always seem, not exactly sincere, but to be trying to sound sincere.

Comparison of the poem that has struck moderns as the most sincere of all Donne's poems, "A Nocturnall upon S. Lucies Day," with a modern counterpart—and a poem thought to have been written before its author entered his full confessional mode—should illustrate the point. To the best of my knowledge, it has never been noted that in "The Ghost" Robert Lowell adopted the stanza form invented by Donne for "A Nocturnall" alone among his poems. Hence, Donne, and probably Eliot, have to be added to the list of literary ghosts, including Propertius, Petrarch, and Ezra Pound, conjured by this intriguing poem. Both "A Nocturnall" and "The Ghost" reflect on literary endeavors, Donne's poem to repudiate them and Lowell's to stigmatize their infidelities. Although the death of a lover occasions the reflection in both cases, Lowell dwells on the details of physical death, as Donne does not, and even overgoes Propertius:

> But she no longer sparkles off in smoke:
> It is the body carted off to the gate
>   Last Friday, when the sizzling grate
>   Left its charred furrows on her smock
>   And ate into her hip.
> A black nail dangles from a finger-tip
> And Lethe oozes from her nether lip.
> Her thumb-bones rattle on her brittle hands
> As Cynthia stamps and hisses and demands . . . [17]

By comparison with this, Donne's disquisition on degrees of nullity seems abstract and rather cold. Furthermore, Cynthia hissing and stamping at the poet's bedside, "love's stale and public playground," suggests an intimate disclosure, on the poet's part, of the shameful, of the squalid and dissipated, in his life. The poet-speaker of "A Nocturnall" may confess an idolatrous love, but, by virtue of the poems to which he refers in the third stanza, his love was never a dark secret, nor would his repudiation of those poems have been unexpected by his Elizabethan readers, most of whom regarded poetry as the work of one's prodigal youth. Not even does the speaker of "Recusancy," despite his cynicism, reveal truths which were not public before he uttered them. Donne's speakers acknowledge truths which their world well knows but would prefer to forget. Lowell's speaker discloses information about himself that only he could know and that could not be brought to light other than by confession. Having visited the foul rag and bone shop of his heart and faced repulsive truths about himself, he—much sooner than Donne—will be credited by modern readers with authenticity.

In the absence of the confessional mode, modern scholars who admire "A Nocturnall" have sought in vain to connect the poem with its author's life through Ann More's death or Lady Bedford's illness. Historical criticism of Donne's poems searching anachronistically for a sign of authenticity where it does not exist provides—sad to say—some of the best evidence in Renaissance scholarship for the poststructuralist claim that all appeals to an extratextual reality are products of exegetic self-deception and screens for projection of whichever pieties appeal at the moment in academic circles. The positivist trend in biographical criticism of Donne's texts makes historical criticism look bad. Fortunately, a moral criticism—of the type described by Wayne Booth—will always have the integrity to question its literary likes and dislikes and, in doing so, insist that what it likes be sincere, at least by standards know-able to the authors in question. The modern reader who is concerned with the morality of literature and who likes John Donne has a bitter pill to swallow. For authenticity as a moral category was not only not re-quired by Donne's contemporary readers, but would have defeated the purpose of a poem like "A Nocturnall." "A Nocturnall," and the rest of Donne's secular poetry, was designed to present the author in the best possible light, not in the worst. Donne's poetry must not be thought of as recording a retreat and alienation from society, as Lowell's does, but as evidence of the author's right to membership in a social elite and of his eligibility to take office and assume political power. This is the harsh lesson of studies like John Carey's and Arthur Marotti's. The present study proposes that Donne sincerely respected the cultural codes which he discovered in Castiglione's text and that he strove to articulate them in the context of a social reality where their relevancy was becoming increasingly tenuous. As a producer of ideology Donne was deeply con-servative, idealistic, and as conscious of what he was doing as any human being can be expected to be. He was, like Plato's philosopher-king, dis-abused.

Trilling reminds his readers that the abrupt increase in upward mo-bility during the Renaissance, coupled with "the paucity of honorable professions which could serve the ambitious as avenues of social ad-vancement," made the plot or the scheme of the dissembling villain seem less alien then than it does now as the embodiment of pure evil.[18] Im-mense power concentrated in the hands of a very few led to a system of social deference that encouraged flattery and self-interested dissimula-tion. "Sole Priapus," as John Marston put it, "by plaine dealing mounts."[19] While Edmund and Iago using fraud to rise above the station to which they were born represented to the Elizabethans the canker at the heart of their social system, the case is different now. Trilling spells out the difference:

> The hypocrite-villain, the conscious dissembler, has become marginal, even alien, to the modern imagination of the moral life. The situation in which a person systematically misrepresents himself in order to practice upon the good faith of another does not readily command our interest, scarcely our credence. The deception we best understand and most willingly give our attention to is that which a person works upon himself. Iago's avowed purpose of base duplicity does not hold for us the fascination that nineteenth-century audiences found in it; our live-liest curiosity is likely to be directed to the moral condition of Othello, to what lies hidden under his superbness, to what in him is masked by the heroic *persona*.[20]

Lowell's speakers seem more convincing than Donne's because their gruesome disclosures suggest that they have seen beneath their masks. To the patricians whose attention Donne wished to attract with his poems (whether in the 1590s or much later), Donne's station in life, which was very nearly that of an Iago or a Bosola, would have constituted enough of a stigma to render supererogatory gruesome disclosures of any other sort. Donne's whole effort had to be concentrated on overcoming the disadvantage of his membership in a dangerous class of ambitious office seekers out to disturb the social order.

Poems like "Aire and Angels" and "The Exstasie" demonstrate that Donne could argue convincingly for the existence of noble, altruistic sentiments where only the most self-interested motives were to be expected. Poems like "The Flea" and "Recusancy" demonstrate that he knew the worst that was to be expected of his class. The coexistence of both types of poem in Donne's oeuvre is evidence that Donne had both the insight of an Emilia Pia and the powers of persuasion to disarm her skepticism. As a courtier, Donne learned from Castiglione—among others—that idealistic claims could be persuasive in his court milieu only if accompanied by an implicit, intellectually honest acknowledgment of real conditions.

Conclusion

Splitting the ideal from the real, adopting either/or readings of Donne's secular poetry, and giving the impression that they are not looking at the same texts, Donne's critics of the alienation and conformist schools make urgent the need for a synthesis. Rosamund Tuve and William Empson offer a classic example of the way that readings of Donne's poems become divided against each other to a point beyond controversy. Their interpretations of "A Valediction: Of Weeping" have had a profound influence on the way that we read Donne. Where Tuve sees in the poem a logical argument which is "persuasive with a great sweetness," Empson sees "a bright, argumentative, hearty quaintness" of the kind with which Dickens's good characters "make the orphan girl smile through her tears."[1] Tuve, stressing the logic of metaphysical imagery, captures the ideal addressed in the poem, while Empson, focusing on situational nuances, discovers the sordid, disconcerting reality which Donne dramatizes. Where Tuve sees a lover-speaker using logic to discover a sorrow that he can share with the young woman whom he consoles, Empson sees him grabbing for his hat. Examples of this polemic (for it can hardly be called a controversy when the parties share no common ground) are rife in Donne criticism. Robert Ellrodt's and Murray Roston's stress on religious mannerism (treated in chapter 5 of this study) could be contrasted with John Carey's insistence on the aggressive, self-interested, this-worldly dimension of Donne's writing. The Tuve-Empson difference over "A Valediction: Of Weeping" merely illustrates the problem in condensed form. One does not wish to be forced to choose between Tuve and Empson, or, for that matter, between Ellrodt and Carey. Too much is to be learned from both sides.

One purpose of the preceding chapters has been to find a way not to choose. It is tempting to think of the Tuve-Empson dichotomy as a displaced reenactment (as Jonathan Culler and others term it) of issues contained within "A Valediction: Of Weeping," but it would be unfair to Tuve and Empson (and presumptuous as well) to describe their insights as "displaced" or merely "reenactments." Their readings are more detailed, circumstantial, and to the point than most others and their approaches have been found useful beyond Donne's poetry for more than half a century. Seeing Donne as a very original poet of courtliness influenced by social codes contained in *The Courtier* has the advantage of bringing Tuve and Empson together. It accommodates the logical and the situational, the ideal and the real, and also situates the poem in its historical period. In terms of the preceding chapter's thesis, Tuve could be said to dwell on the good courtier's effort to achieve an interpretation of parting that transcends its brutal facticity by denying it emotional significance, while Empson focuses on the good courtier's implicit concession that any such interpretation may be self-deceiving and self-serving because partings do not happen unless at least one person has interests for which he is willing to risk private happiness. Together, Tuve and Empson's readings find in "A Valediction: Of Weeping" the elements of a courtly persuasion of sincerity. The ideal and real do not merely coexist in such an integral reading, they fuse with each other as they do in *The Courtier,* where the real creates desire for transcendence of its strictures and the ideal is never uncontaminated by a this-worldly rhetorical purpose.

Fragmentation is the curse of all analysis, however, and this study is more than moderately cursed. Since its purpose has not been to be exhaustive but to offer a new approach to Donne's poems as social performances, there has been no attempt to achieve coverage of the entire oeuvre, which would have been tedious in any case, with one poem after another marching into the examining room. Beyond tedious, such an attempt would be self-defeating since no interpretive paradigm works in every case of an author's writings unless the author is very uninteresting. The contention of this study is merely that its approach works in enough specific instances to make it useful. Moreover, the analytical categories advanced in the central chapters make no claim to be anything more than necessary fictions, like Dante's concentric heavens. Every poem mentioned in this study embodies all four codes of courtliness, not just the one that it was exemplifying at the moment. The codes themselves flow into each other, constantly imply or require each other, always add up to a whole greater than the sum of its separate parts. There could be no aesthetic of provocation without *sprezzatura*, without calculated self-effacement. Nor would it make much sense, in the courtly context, to develop a disabused awareness of impasse and not use it as a rhetorical instrument. Donne's *Satyres* might have served as the text for chapter 5 and "Aire and Angels" for chapter 2, Elegy VII for chapter 4 and Elegy XIX for chapter 3, and so on. Hence, in concluding, I shall take the luxury—and hope it is earned—of briefly discussing one poem in light of all four codes.

"A Valediction: of the Booke" (apart from its title's appropriateness to concluding chapters) has two great advantages for this purpose. As a valediction, it belongs to the subgenre with which we identify Donne more than any other English poet of his era, and yet it has not acquired a committed readership and may, therefore, be less resistant to a fresh approach. This elegant poem opens with the poise and self-assurance, the jauntiness, of a Fred Astaire dance number and shades off at its ending into a consideration of oblivion worthy of Sir Thomas Browne. The ease alone with which Donne carries the difficult form (unique to this poem, but close to the form of "A Nocturnall upon S. Lucies Day") through seven stanzas of dramatic dialogue with an implied young woman qualifies the poem to be considered an example of *sprezzatura* unsurpassed in *The Songs and Sonnets* or anywhere else in Renaissance poetry. However, the exhibition of *sprezzatura* here is peculiarly Donnean and relates the poem to "A Nocturnall upon S. Lucies Day" in a more than formal way.

If "A Nocturnall" is Donne's palinode, surely "A Valediction: of the Booke" represents a step in the direction of that dark renunciation. For it is not only a valediction *concerning* a book, it is also a farewell *to* a specific book and *to* the idea of writing a book. By the end of the poem, the speaker repudiates his own inflated claims, made in the opening stanzas, for the durability and beneficial effect of written productions. One feels even before reaching the end that one is in the presence of a travesty of the many Renaissance affirmations of literary power and longevity. Placed next to any of Shakespeare's meditations on the same subject, the poem displays an irreverence bordering on the impudent. The speaker has scarcely urged his lover to make herself famous by making a book of their love letters than he proceeds to give example after example of the futility of literature. If theologians, lawyers, and statesmen were able to recapture their learning after an invasion of Vandals by reading this book, it would be due only to their self-absorbed misreadings—"as in the Bible some can finde out Alchimy." Even the opening stanza contains a strong ironic suggestion that great poetry by Pindar, Lucan, and Homer, is, like Sibylline prophecy, considered great only because of its great capacity to be misread. The speaker concludes, in any case, by repudiating the book of love letters and acknowledging that time and experience, not books, are the true tests of love's endurance. Moreover, he not only repudiates his own pervasive metaphor of the book, but invents a new metaphor—of latitudes and longitudes—that is patently insubstantial, based on nothing but obvious wordplay (the "long" in "longitudes"), as if to acknowledge the impropriety of all verbal consolation in the face of those unavoidable "dark eclipses." As in "A Nocturnall upon S. Lucies Day," words, with their limited authority and their protean commodiousness—their promiscuity—only call attention to the final, inarticulate void which is real death and parting.

The speaker of "A Valediction: of the Booke" is in language but refuses to be of it, he means his consolation at the same time that he knows it to be meaningless, he practices a contempt of words with his self-destructing metaphors and precious wordplay, just as the courtly adept shows himself to be in the court world but not of it, disdaining the court in order to reap its greatest benefits. The acknowledgment of linguistic frailty, this speaker knows, is his best hope of duration in desire—and especially since the young woman whom he addresses is at least as skeptical as he that a book contains a presence. She shares his knowledge that it can only record absences. She is as disabused about books as he is. As a "flickering provocation," as an example of courtly aesthetic play, "A Valediction: of the Booke" equals any of Donne's lyrics for its effectiveness. The opening phrase of its last stanza ("thus vent thy thoughts") sends the reader back to the preceding three stanzas about theologians, lawyers, and statesmen to reread them as the thoughts of the young woman addressed, and each of these stanzas is marked off at its opening by an ironic "here," as if the young woman were pointing her finger at a flea before crushing it. Each stanza represents her thoughts as the speaker imagines them to be, and he gives her credit for insight into his character. The poem (we are informed by these hints of the sort defined by Légouis) responds—owes its existence—to her temperament, her intelligence, her skepticism, and she closely resembles Castiglione's Emilia Pia. She has the same perspicacity combined with the same ironic sense of humor.

The young woman's choice of theologians, lawyers, and statesmen as future readers of this book of love letters marks a dramatic turn, for these are not the schools, spheres, and angels to whom the speaker was just referring. Like the voice that we must imagine filling the space between Satyre I and Satyre II (the voice of the grave man who tugs Donne's sleeve and forces him to examine himself), the young woman's voice has cut into the tongue-in-cheek rhapsody of the first three stanzas of "A Valediction: of the Booke" and thickened the discourse with circumstances closer to home. Her voice has quietly asked what indeed someone would think while reading these letters—not an angel, but someone recognizable like Donne himself or any other ambitious person on the London scene at the turn of the seventeenth century. Students of theology (and one thinks of Donne absorbing all the issues controverted between the Churches of Rome and England) will be led, in reading the book of love letters, to a consideration of "faiths infirmitie." Lawyers (and again one thinks of Donne at Lincoln's Inn and later in Egerton's service) will reduce matters of honor and conscience to a sordid, exasperating quid pro quo. Statesman (and yet again one thinks of Donne, this time as soldier, secretary, parliamentarian, and aspiring diplomat) will be reminded by this book that absence is for them the same as nothingness. The young woman residing in the spaces between the stanzas of "A Valediction: of the Booke" wonders if her lover himself (not a man to credit books with much authority) would find this book a consolation. She has grounds to believe that his absorption in the matters which take him away from her will diminish his memory of her and his sense of the importance of their bond. As theologian, he may come to regard it as a "convenient type" of something better (just as the speaker of "Aire and Angels" does in contemplating his past erotic experience). She reminds him that "oblivion shares with memory, a great part even of our living beings,"[2] and, to his credit, he delivers the only sane response, which is to acknowledge in the final stanza those "dark eclipses" by which duration is measured.

Of course, his acknowledgment of the dark and dissonant, his capacity to read her misgivings, his respect for her vulnerability and his sense that he shares it, is a much greater consolation to her and a much more persuasive argument for the sincerity of his feelings than she could ever find in reading over and over a florilegium of old love letters. One could almost say that she teaches him how to read. She presses him to see the denial in his affirmations, the absence implied by his strained attempt to substitute a book for a living presence. She rejects his facile humanism of the word and demands a discourse more grounded in the divisive court world they both move in. The result is a poem whose great formal elegance asserts the power of language to prevail over destiny, while at the same time its stanzas are invaded by disruptive nuances, its speaker distracted by second thoughts to the point where he yields to the free play of adverse associations and allows them to usurp the place of his original discourse. Far from resigning herself to the compilation of a book of manuscripts to anger destiny, the skeptical young woman provokes her lover to voice a music angered *by* destiny, and the formal elegance of the voice comes to seem expropriated at the last minute from a universe of poetic discourse whose authority has collapsed for both of them. In the last stanza of "A Valediction: of the Booke," the only mean-

ing that stars and planets can have for them is conferred by the historical
moment conditioning their perception of each other. Their heaven has
been untuned but its old music is still audible.

All the codes of courtliness discussed in the preceding chapters
are active in the poem of this disabused couple. "A Valediction: of the
Booke" looks into the text as vortex signifying absence; the voice of
its speaker gains force only with acknowledgment of the impasse; his
words, provoked by a vulnerable—therefore skeptical—young woman,
provoke the reader to see him as she does; in the end, he registers the
futility of his brilliant performance, leaving the reader to wonder what
other talents he must have who can so gracefully renounce what he does
so well. Set to music, translated into Italian, and sent back in time, this
poem and others like it could as easily have filled out an evening's entertainment at Urbino as the dialogues of Castiglione by which Urbino is
remembered. What, however, was the effect of poems like this on their
actual audiences (at the Inns of Court, at York House, at the residences
of Donne's many friends and admirers) almost a century later in late
Elizabethan and early Stuart London? In closing, I should like to haz-
ard a guess based on the conviction that Donne valued his art, not as
art in a category by itself, but for its social function—that he regarded
his poetry as inseparable from a whole cultural system. In this, he—
sophisticated, urbane London wit—resembles certain primitive artists
who value their creations only to the extent that they are indispensable
for social ceremony and religious ritual.

In the early pages of *The Political Unconscious*, Fredric Jameson finds
in Lévi-Strauss's observations of a Brazilian Indian tribe a "defense," as
he puts it, "of the proposition of a political unconscious" expressing itself in indirect ways in a culture's art forms.[3] The text under consideration is chapter 17 of *Tristes tropiques*, in which Lévi-Strauss gives an
account of a tribe whose everyday relations of power emerge from a hi-
erarchical caste system, rigidly endogamous, hereditary, asymmetrical,
and potentially a source of dangerous conflict.[4] This tribe, however, also
divides itself into symmetrical moieties not having to do with caste,
though all the castes are represented within each moiety. While the keynote of intercaste relations is domination and submission, the keynote of
relations among the moieties is reciprocity. One moiety helps the other
perform its ritual duties, one moiety marries into another, but always
along caste lines. Lévi-Strauss refers to this moiety system as a "deceptive prosopopeia," in which the whole society participates, to the extent
of organizing the ground plan of its villages according to division into
moieties. The whole society gives itself the illusion that its political relations are egalitarian, its social relations mutual and symmetrically
balanced, when in fact they are asymmetrical, unstable, coercive. The

moieties then are symbolic products by which the social contradictions of hierarchy are resolved in the aesthetic realm, literally at the level of urban planning.

For the majority of his readers, Donne's secular poems must have been symbolic products of a similar nature in that they gave symbolic life to a higher style of social intercourse than could have existed for the average place seeker at the late Elizabethan court, where cutthroat competition for a diminishing number of posts fostered corruption and disillusionment on a large scale. Donne's poems gave the impression that these place seekers—or in MacCaffrey's phrase "daring aspirants"—could achieve a style of conduct possible only in more prosperous, less competitive times. The courtly codes by which he shaped his poems imply reciprocity, mutuality, self-awareness, disinterested and disabused, rather than disillusioned, exchanges in a spirit of cooperation. One thinks of the religion of friendship formulated in Donne's verse letters. However, most members of the coterie for which he wrote (the "pitiful no-accounts" in Kerrigan's cruel phrase) moved in an atmosphere of rampant self-interest, of fierce and cynical competition, which left little room for an uncoerced, private subjectivity to develop. For them and for their unreflecting superiors, Donne's poems probably operated in a way very similar to the functioning of that "deceptive prosopopeia" in the Brazilian society described by Lévi-Strauss. Hence the popularity Donne achieved in elite circles.

For Donne himself and for readers like Henry Wotton, I think that the case was different, although they like the others did experience the poems as much more than mere containers of the social as inert content. They too—in Jameson's terms—experienced the very form of the poems as enactments of the social in the realm of the aesthetic. The difference was that Donne and his more alert readers were conscious of what the poems were doing. The implicit equation made by many—not all—of his poems between the Urbinese and Elizabethan social worlds gained him, on the one hand, acceptance among the likes of Egerton and were therefore tests of himself, just as translation of *The Courtier* was for Bartholomew Clerke. However, on the other hand, his poems were tests of that social world itself, measuring to a fine point whether a social ideal as supple and spacious as Castiglione's was still tenable there for himself or anyone else. If a few readers like Wotton whom he respected and who were socially successful understood his poems it was probably sufficient proof to him that he was not deluded in his intense desire to be successful too. Therefore he did not enter the print culture of his time, where his poems would be widely disseminated and widely subject to discouraging misinterpretation.[5] He understood too well the lesson of a young woman in his own "Valediction: of the Booke."

NOTES

Introduction

1. *Timber or Discoveries*, ed. Ralph S. Walker (Syracuse: Syracuse University Press, 1953), p. 51.

2. Earl Miner, *The Metaphysical Mode from Donne to Cowley* (Princeton: Princeton University Press, 1969); Arnold Stein, "Voices of the Satirist: John Donne," in *English Satire and the Satiric Tradition*, ed. Claude Rawson (Oxford: Blackwell, 1984); Anthony Low, "Donne and the Reinvention of Love," *ELR* 20 (Autumn 1990): 465–486; Richard Strier, "Radical Donne: 'Satire III,'" *ELH* 60 (1993): 283–322; Arthur F. Marotti, *John Donne: Coterie Poet* (Madison: University of Wisconsin Press, 1986); John Carey, *John Donne: Life, Mind, and Art* (Oxford: Blackwell, 1981); Jonathan Goldberg, *James I and the Politics of Literature: Jonson, Shakespeare, Donne, and Their Contemporaries* (Baltimore: Johns Hopkins University Press, 1983). Preeminent among Donne studies which stand above the polemic is David Norbrook's "The Monarchy of Wit and the Republic of Letters: Donne's Politics," in *Soliciting Interpretation: Literary Theory and Seventeenth-Century English Poetry*, ed. Elizabeth D. Harvey and Katharine Eisaman Maus (Chicago: University of Chicago Press, 1990). I find the following description intriguing: "The quest for a standpoint is a unifying motif of Donne's writings. He constantly seeks to put his feet down on the ground, to become a part of a society from which he feels alienated. And yet he desires also to maintain a critical distance, a standpoint outside the existing social order from which he can criticize it" (p. 6). Elision of the first "from which" clause and substitution of "inside" for "outside" in the final clause would produce my position on Donne exactly.

3. William Kerrigan, "What Was Donne Doing?" *SC Rev* 4 (Summer 1987): 2–15.

4. Norbrook, "Monarchy of Wit," p. 10.

5. Marotti, *John Donne: Coterie Poet*, p. 13.

6. Carey, *John Donne: Life, Mind, and Art*, p. 92.

7. See Ben Jonson, "Conversations with Drummond," in *Ben Jonson*, ed. C. H. Herford, and Percy and Evelyn Simpson, 11 vols. (Oxford: Clarendon Press, 1925–1952), 1:135. In John Donne, *The Elegies and The Songs and Sonnets*, ed. Helen Gardner (Oxford: Clarendon Press, 1965), p. 193, Helen Gardner argues that the only evidence for dating a poem in either group as having been composed after 1602 appears in "A Valediction: of the Booke," because there was no printed source before then of the tradition that the works of Homer were written by a woman. However, ask we must if Donne would have needed a printed source. Would not such a tradition have had a lively word-of-mouth transmission in Donne's time and especially among the wags with whom he consorted? Would not the Greek of Eustathius of Thessalonica, available early in the sixteenth century, have found its way into English translation by word of mouth and crossed the channel from Basle in time to provide Donne with one

line of his poem long before any printed source appeared in England? Gardner supports Jonson's view with her argument, but she proves nothing. The absence of evidence that the poems were written after 1602 would not in any case prove that they were written before then. The rules of evidence must be stretched very thin if any of the poems in either group are to be dated by anything but conjecture. Gardner's edition of *The Elegies and The Songs and Sonnets* furnishes the texts from which I draw quotations throughout this study.

8. This is Low's "Donne and the Reinvention of Love." Low notes that we do not know which poems Donne wrote before and which after his wife died, but this does not deter him from claiming that after she died Donne reinvented love by reaching for the communal (the holy and the ludic) and absolutely rejecting the social (the profane and the professional).

9. This is the subtitle of a section of chapter 3 of Marotti, *John Donne: Coterie Poet*, in which "The Canonization" is treated. Marotti's claim that there is an allusion to the "current plague" can be found on p. 161. Marotti's awareness that there is a strong argument against the plague reference as a means of dating the poem is expressed in his notes on p. 324.

10. J. G. A. Pocock, introduction ("The State of the Art") to *Virtue, Commerce, and History: Essays on Political Thought and History, Chiefly in the Eighteenth Century* (Cambridge: Cambridge University Press, 1985), p. 7. I have also found very useful by the same author "Languages and Their Implications: The Transformation of the Study of Political Thought," in *Politics, Language, and Time* (New York: Atheneum, 1971). I have been influenced as well by the following essays of Quentin Skinner: "Motives, Intentions and the Interpretation of Texts," *New Literary History* 3 (Winter 1972): 393–408; "'Social Meaning' and the Explanation of Social Action," in *Philosophy, Politics and Society, Fourth Series*, ed. Peter Laslett, W. G. Runciman, and Quentin Skinner (Oxford: Blackwell, 1972), pp. 136–157; "Hermeneutics and the Role of History," *New Literary History* 7 (Autumn 1975): 209–232.

11. Paul R. Sellin, *So Doth, So Is Religion: John Donne and Diplomatic Contexts in the Reformed Netherlands, 1619–1620* (Columbia: University of Missouri Press, 1988).

12. Baldassare Castiglione, *The Book of the Courtier*, trans. Sir Thomas Hoby (London: J. M. Dent and Sons, 1956), p. 3. All subsequent page references to *The Courtier* will be in parentheses within the text and will be to this readily available edition of the sixteenth-century translation. For evidence that Donne read Hoby's translation, see R. W. Hamilton, "Donne and Castiglione," *Notes and Queries* 26 (1979): 405–406.

13. I am referring of course to the following passage in *The Schoolmaster*, ed. Lawrence V. Ryan (Ithaca: Cornell University Press, 1967), p. 55: "To join learning with comely exercises, Conte Baldassare Castiglione in his book *Cortegiano* doth trimly teach; which book, advisedly read and diligently followed but one year at home in England, would do a young gentleman more good, iwis, than three years travel abroad spent in Italy. And I marvel this book is no more read in the court than it is, seeing it is so well translated into English by a worthy gentleman, Sir Thomas Hoby, who was many ways well furnished with learning and very expert in knowledge of divers tongues." *The Schoolmaster* was first published in 1570 and, in light of the subsequent publication history of Castiglione's book in England, it must have done much to remedy the lack of interest Ascham notes.

14. In *Ambition and Privilege: The Social Tropes of Elizabethan Courtesy Literature* (Berkeley: University of California Press, 1984), p. 18, Frank Whigham

argues that the "assheads" passage announces Castiglione's purpose of teaching an anxious aristocracy how to repress competition from below. As evidence that the English recognized this use of *The Courtier*, Whigham quotes the Earl of Oxford's prefatory letter to Clerke's Latin translation of Castiglione: "Oxford lauds Castiglione's 'delineations in the case of those persons who cannot be Courtiers, when he alludes to some notable defect, or to some ridiculous character, or to some deformity of appearance.'" Whigham continues, "Necessarily, of course, the complementary effect of those proscriptions was to teach the members of an endangered aristocracy how to reascribe to themselves the self-evident ascriptive status their forebears had enjoyed, by the personal affirmation of the signs that disgraced the assheads." Of course, Donne was as aware as the Earl of Oxford of this possible use of *The Courtier* and adopts the strategy in some of his secular lyrics—notably "The Canonization." In his case, it could be called a preemptive strategy, since he was himself, by virtue of his rather low standing among the gentry, in danger of falling into the asshead category. However, I shall argue that there is a more important use to which Donne put the Elizabethan regime's canonization of *The Courtier*. He recognized that the process of reascription to which Whigham refers made what was a "self-evident ascriptive status" before seem anything but self-evident.

15. Peter Burke, *The Fortunes of The Courtier* (University Park: Pennsylvania State University Press, 1995), p. 65, attests to the success of this version in its day and notes that Gabriel Harvey advised his pupil Arthur Capel to read it.

16. Balthasaris Castilionis Comitis, *de Curiali sive Aulico, libri quatuor* (Frankfurt: Zetzner, 1606), p. 10.

17. *de Curiali*, pp. 3–5; my translation. The original reads as follows: Egit mecum non ita pridem (Illustrissima Princeps) heros nobilissimus Dominus Buckhurstius, ut de Aula Regia tua, & quod multo difficilius est, de tua Maiestate historiolam scriberem. Cui ego etsi tantum debeam, quantum hominem homini fas est tribuere, tamen cum incredibiles tuas tum animi, tum corporis virtutes perspicerem, cum divinum illud ingenii lumen recordarer, cum te supra hunc sexum, supra istam mortalitatem sapere meminissem: denique; cum nulla vox, nullum, ut audio, verbum, ita casu tibi possit excidere, quin sempiternis literis monumentisque decorandum videatur: timebam vehementer, ne, dum tuae excellentiae inservire, clarissimo viro & de me optime merito satisfacere desiderarem, onus Aetna gravius temere & inconsulto subirem. Atque hic (quod in proverbio est) lupum auribus tenebam. Nam, & nimium diffidere, insulsi timidique putabam esse: & plus aequo in tam magnis rebus audere, hominis parum considerati. Ista me tam seria deliberatio, cum per aliquantum temporis spatium, anxium & sollicitum tenuisset, tandem mihi venit in mentem, Italum quendam Castilionem, persimili in re egregiam navasse operam. Quae si a me in Latinum sermonem non incinne transferri posset, & stilo meo tanquam coticulam aliquam fore putavi, & ex ea indicia atque argumenta certissima posse desumi, num tantis conatibus quoquomodo possem satisfacere? Nam, si ego minus Latine, quam ille Italice, scripserim (quod valde metuo ne fiat) inanis omnis noster labor, stultumque studium est futurum, cum nec Anglorum Aula Urbinatium ulla in re inferior fuerit, & tua serenitas omnibus Aemiliis & Gonzagis multis gradis antecellat. Atque hic vicissim in labyrinthum nescio quem incidi. E quo ut me honestius expediam, istuc qualecunque opusculum, divinae indoli tuae, acutissimoque iudicio subieci, ut vel satis in me nervorum ad tantam historiam non dubites, vel contra (si libet) decernas. . . . Quocirca si tuae maiestati (quo es candore & clementia) facultas nostra tantis inceptis non indigna videatur (quae mihi quidem multo indignissima videri solet) & ego me illis addicam laboribus,

qui omnium sunt difficilimmi, & tua amplitudo, utcunque res cecederit, sui semper similimma erit.

18. Louis Adrian Montrose, "Renaissance Literary Studies and the Subject of History," *ELR* 16 (Winter 1986): 8.

19. For this reason, Frank Whigham's *Ambition and Privilege* has been an indispensable guide as to what Donne was *not* doing during his period of poetic creativity and place seeking—as to what Donne actively sought to avoid or else to distinguish himself from.

20. Norbrook, "Monarchy of Wit," p. 19.

21. Daniel Javitch, *Poetry and Courtliness in Renaissance England* (Princeton: Princeton University Press, 1978). I am, of course, indebted to this book, as who is not whose interests cross its path. However, for reasons having to do with Donne's uniqueness, Javitch's study provides more an essential treatment of cultural background—as does Whigham's book in a different way—than a guide to specific ways of reading Donne's lyrics, although I would hasten to add that *Poetry and Courtliness* has been an inspiration to me at critical moments in my specific readings. I disagree with Javitch only in his assertion that the courtly ideal was on the wane in the 1590s. The publication history of Castiglione's book during this time suggests otherwise—or, at least, that some qualification is called for.

22. In "The 'Press and the Fire': Print and Manuscript Culture in Donne's Circle," *SEL* 33 (1993): 85–95, Richard B. Wollman cautions that Donne's reluctance to have his poems printed did not necessarily stem from an aristocratic disdain for professionalism. I use the word here in the sense that Donne and the others in his category did not "profess" their mission in life to be the writing of poetry—as did Spenser—and did not earn their living by it—as did Shakespeare and Jonson. For them it was a secondary activity.

23. Javitch, *Poetry and Courtliness,* p. 50.

24. Wallace T. MacCaffrey, "Place and Patronage in Elizabethan Politics," in *Elizabethan Government and Society: Essays Presented to Sir John Neale,* ed. S. T. Bindoff, J. Hurstfield, and C. H. Williams (London: Athlone Press, 1961), p. 102.

25. R. C. Bald, *John Donne: A Life* (Oxford: Oxford University Press, 1970), pp. 93–94.

26. MacCaffrey, "Place and Patronage," p. 126.

27. For a discussion of Egerton's relations with Samuel Daniel, Sir John Davies, and John Davies of Hereford, see Virgil B. Heltzel, "Sir Thomas Egerton as Patron," *Huntington Library Quarterly* 11 (1948): 116–120.

28. Mark A. Kishlansky, *Parliamentary Selection: Social and Political Choice in Early Modern England* (Cambridge: Cambridge University Press, 1986), pp. 15–16.

29. *de Curiali,* p. 10; my translation. The original reads as follows: "Tune literarios homunculos maledicere audere putas, cum Illustrissima Princeps, summo iudicio, summa literarum scientia, primum illum librum, quem ego eius Maiestate mense Ianuario detuleram, tam apertis testimoniis approbaverit?"

30. In Bald's judgment, Donne's service with Egerton caused him to become too sure of himself and hence led to his disastrous elopement with Ann More. Bald, *John Donne: A Life,* pp. 125–127. On Donne's membership in parliament and his clandestine marriage, R. A. Shapiro is even more explicit: "That Donne should have been blinded to the gravity of this act is puzzling, and can be explained only on the assumption that circumstances had recently induced in him a feeling of equality with the members of the family into which he was marrying. He was in the employ of his future wife's uncle, but Walton tells us that

Egerton treated him rather as a friend than a servant, 'appointing him a place at his own table,' where Donne would meet on equal terms, among others, John Egerton (Sir Thomas's heir and Donne's old friend), Francis Wolley (Egerton's stepson, another friend of Donne) and probably many members of the More family. Such treatment might well tend to make Donne forgetful of his very uncertain position in Elizabethan society. In the Commons he enjoyed the same status as his future wife's brother, Robert More, her brothers-in-law, Nicholas Throckmorton and Thomas Grymes, and her cousins, Francis Wolley and John Egerton; and he listened probably with growing contempt to the effusions of her father, Sir George More. Is it altogether fanciful to surmise that his membership of Parliament at the end of 1601 helped to dispel from Donne's mind any lingering doubts about his eligibility for the hand of Anne More?" (*TLS*, 10 March 1932, p. 172).

31. While I am not persuaded by many of the more extravagant claims made in his book, Dennis Flynn, *John Donne and the Ancient Catholic Nobility* (Bloomington: Indiana University Press, 1995), delivers a colorful portrait of Donne as Roman Catholic in his early years and as nephew of Jasper Heywood. For the purposes of my study, Flynn's book is useful for its reminder that his Catholic connections involved Donne from childhood onward with an aristocratic class keenly interested in the stylized conduct in fashion at European courts. It is also likely that the Erasmian strain of English Catholicism, to which Donne was early and long exposed and which Flynn describes excellently, contributed to Donne's taste for texts like Castiglione's.

32. Sir John Ferne, *The Blazon of Gentrie* (London: Printed by John Windet, for Andrew Maunsell, 1586), pp. 7, 11. To do Ferne justice, one must note that he wavers on the subject of a merchant's benefit to the state. In a less conservative passage, which is probably more characteristic of prevailing attitudes, he states a rule of thumb by which merchants may be judged: "The trade of merchandizing, hathe been iudged alwayes, the more honest and competent, to the state of a liberall, and honeste civill man, when as the practizers thereof, doe carry from us, thinges superfluous, and bring in those that be necessarye. But, if merchants transport thinges needefull, and in recompence therof, retourne full fraughted, with a burthen of superfluities, tending to the vaine delightes, of our unconstant Islanders, & to the increase of sinnes amongst us, they are rather to be banished, than tollerated" (p. 72). He wavers likewise when he declares the Genoese to be of "a most vile and base iudgment" for considering commerce an enhancement of a man's chances to enter the gentry and then reviles the Neapolitans for their scorn of commerce and hence their incapacity to maintain their patrimonies (p. 73). Donne probably found himself sometimes victim, sometimes beneficiary, of this wavering attitude, and hence in a precarious position.

33. For an account of possible black-market manipulations, on the part of the elder Donne, and violation of the last will and testament of Thomas Lewin, a fellow ironmonger, whose wife Donne, Senior, served as business manager, see Baird D. Whitlock, "The Heredity and Childhood of John Donne," *Notes and Queries* 6 (July-August 1959): 260–262.

34. Ferne, *Blazon of Gentrie*, pp. 93–94.

35. *The Three Parnassus Plays (1598–1601)*, ed. J. B. Leishman (London: Ivor Nicholson and Watson, 1949), pp. 199–204. Leishman's identification of the characters, Gullio and Ingenioso, with the Earl of Southampton and Thomas Nashe, while not exactly suiting my purpose here, presents no obstacle either.

36. The phrase is Frank Whigham's, *Ambition and Privilege*, p. 16.

1. The Satirical Art of the Disabused

1. Thomas M. Greene, "Il Cortegiano and the Choice of a Game," in *Castiglione: The Ideal and the Real in Renaissance Culture*, ed. Robert W. Hanning and David Rosand (New Haven: Yale University Press, 1983), pp. 13, 3.

2. Greene, "Il Cortegiano," pp. 12–13, 5.

3. John T. Shawcross, "All Attest His Writs Canonical: Texts, Meaning and Evaluation of Donne's Satires," in *Just So Much Honor*, ed. Peter Amadeus Fiore (University Park: Pennsylvania State University Press, 1972), pp. 250–252.

4. All quotations of Donne's *Satyres* are drawn from *The Satires, Epigrams and Verse Letters*, ed. Wesley Milgate (Oxford: Clarendon Press, 1967).

5. Arnold Stein, "Voices of the Satirist: John Donne," in *English Satire and the Satiric Tradition*, ed. Claude Rawson (Oxford: Blackwell, 1984), p. 75. Stein's work on the *Satyres* has often been inspiring to me, though, of course, I cannot agree with his characterization of Donne as "alienated."

6. Alvin Kernan, *The Cankered Muse* (New Haven: Yale University Press, 1959), pp. 117–118; N. J. C. Andreasen, "Theme and Structure in Donne's *Satyres*," *Studies in English Literature* 3 (1963): 59–75, bases her study of the unity of the satires on Kernan's observations. In an earlier study, *Complaint and Satire in Early English Poetry* (Folcroft, Pa.: Folcroft Library Editions, 1956), pp. 116–118, John Peter gives a vivid description of the rugged satyr's persona and declares Donne to be "the most notable modification of the tradition," conceding that for "artistic excellence" Donne is supreme even if he does not conform to the conventions of the genre. Peter provides an eloquent summary of the main features of the satyr's persona: "The interrelated tensions which are present in varying degrees in all satire are the very essence of the satyr. He is at once the simple, plain man who speaks plain truth, and the heroic Nemesis of vice who uses all the elaborate tools of the baroque rhetorician. He is the savage enemy of all evil, who is himself tainted with the same failings with which he charges others. He argues that he alone of the poets tells the truth about the world, and yet his obviously melodramatic tone, his mental sickness, and his sadism suggest that his is a totally perverted and twisted view of humanity. He attacks others for their lack of reason or Christianity, and no one could be more unreasonable or unChristian than he is in his viciousness, scurrility, and pessimism. He belabors others for pride and yet is proud as Satan and eaten up by envy. He attacks others for sins of the flesh, yet he is himself lascivious and wanton. In no other period have the innate tensions of satire been allowed such free play in the formation of the satirist" (pp. 139–140). However, in Peter's judgment, Donne did not engage in this free play, and, in fact, Peter's description reads like a list of everything Donne's satirist is not. Clearly, though Donne exhibits awareness of literary models, literary authority was not the major formative influence on his *Satyres*.

7. For an argument in favor of discarding the persona as a useful concept for understanding the *Holy Sonnets*, see Richard Strier, "John Donne Awry and Squint: The *Holy Sonnets*, 1608–1610," *Modern Philology* 86 (May 1989): 357–384. Roma Gill, "A Purchase of Glory: The Persona of Late Elizabethan Satire," *Studies in Philology* 72 (1975): 408–418, calls attention to the flexible nature of the satiric persona, which combines the satirist's historical self and literary convention.

8. Emory Elliot, "The Narrative and Allusive Unity of Donne's *Satyres*," *Journal of English and Germanic Philology* 75 (1976): 105–116, bases his reading

of the *Satyres* on the premise that they are a narrative of the author's own experience.

9. Of the literature on Donne's *Satyres* with which I am familiar, I find my views to be most in accord with those of John R. Lauritsen, "Donne's *Satyres:* The Drama of Self-Discovery," *Studies in English Literature* 16 (1976): 117–130. The following passage represents a brilliant summation of the development of Donne's "book" of *Satyres:* "The progress of the *Satyres* is from detachment to engagement, from that detachment which is born of a desperate need to believe that one is morally superior to the world of ordinary mortals to the moral engagement and commitment which can only come when one realizes that one is not only *in* the fallen world, but *of* it" (p. 120). I have also found very stimulating Ronald J. Corthell's "Style and Self in Donne's Satires," *Texas Studies in Literature and Language* 24 (1982): 155–184, and I agree with his view, in general, that "the great endeavor of wit throughout [Donne's] life was to accommodate himself to public circumstances that he recognized as corrupt because human, to fashion a witty self that could mediate the claims of individual conscience and external power rather than merely defend the conscience against external power" (p. 156), however greatly I differ with Corthell on specific readings.

10. Goldberg, *James I and the Politics of Literature*, pp. 210–219.

11. For the argument that Donne revised his *Satyres*, see Wesley Milgate's textual introduction to John Donne, *The Satires, Epigrams and Verse Letters*, pp. lvi–lxi. John T. Shawcross, in "All Attest His Writs Canonical," disagrees with Milgate's argument.

12. I am quoting from the Newberry Library's copy of the 1599 edition, p. 103.

13. Angel Day, *The English Secretary, or methode of writing of epistles. Divided into two books. Now newly revised.* (P. S[hort] for C. Burbie, 1599) p. 117.

14. Ibid., p. 116.

15. To the best of my knowledge, R. W. Hamilton in "Donne and Castiglione," *Notes and Queries* 26 (1979): 405–406, is the first to have made this observation.

16. Here I should note my departure from the view of M. Thomas Hester, *Kinde Pitty and Brave Scorn: John Donne's* Satyres (Durham: Duke University Press, 1982), that zeal characterizes the satirist's voice. Despite the erudition of his study and its general helpfulness, Hester does not give enough attention to the various ways in which the satirist learns to moderate his zeal, to see the danger of zealous views of complex issues.

17. Gill, "Purchase of Glory," p. 416.

18. See Heather Dubrow, " 'No Man Is an Island': Donne's Satires and Satiric Traditions," *Studies in English Literature* 19 (1979): 80, for some of the same observations, but a very different explanation: "Why does Donne, the spearhead of the revolt against Elizabethan lyricism, give only passing attention to its faults? One explanation is that he sensed that its day was past and did not wish to flog a dead horse; he knew that his own poetry was already providing an alternative. Like the other satirists, he was attempting to teach a new literary style both through precept and example, but he was more confident than they of the power of his examples and hence less concerned about his precepts." The more obvious explanation—the one that accords with Donne's attitudes toward poetry as he expresses them in Satyre II itself and in his correspondence of the same period—is that poetry per se was not an important enough subject, in his opinion, to warrant the attention given it by the other satirists. He never at-

tempted to establish himself as a poetic innovator, as Jonson did; instead, all the evidence points toward his desire to enter the ranks of the politically active and influential. That he was a great poetic innovator was accidental.

19. *The Satires, Epigrams and Verse Letters*, pp. 127–128.

20. David Riggs, *Ben Jonson: A Life* (Cambridge, Mass.: Harvard University Press, 1989), p. 80.

21. See Milgate in Donne, *Satires, Epigrams and Verse Letters*, p. 139, for instance, or Hester, *Kinde Pitty*, pp. 50–52.

22. Evelyn M. Simpson, *A Study of the Prose Works of John Donne* (Oxford: Clarendon Press, 1924), pp. 295–296.

23. Milgate in Donne, *Satires, Epigrams and Verse Letters*, p. 135.

24. I am indebted to Lucille S. Cobb, "Donne's Satyre II, 49–57," *Explicator* 15 (1956), item 8.

25. I am quoting from a passage in the *Journal* of S. d'Ewes selected by Claire Cross, *The Royal Supremacy in the Elizabethan Church* (London: George Allen and Unwin, 1969), p. 212.

26. For a parallel treatment of Satyre III as dramatizing the conflict between the individual conscience and civil law, see Camille Wells Slights, *The Casuistical Tradition in Shakespeare, Donne, Herbert, and Milton* (Princeton: Princeton University Press, 1981), pp. 160–167.

27. In "Theme and Structure in Donne's *Satyres*," Andreasen observes that "Donne was in his very early twenties when he wrote these satires; their protagonist is an older man who gives grey-bearded advice to young men about town. Although this protagonist seems to state Donne's own views, none of Donne's contemporaries would have identified him as John Donne." While this is so obviously wrong when applied to Satyres I, II, IV, and V that there is no point in arguing the matter, Andreasen has hit the nail on the head where Satyre III is concerned. Satyre III differs from the other satires precisely because the speaker seems suddenly to age by about thirty years. In "The Persona as Rhetor: An Interpretation of Donne's Satyre III," in *Essential Articles: John Donne's Poetry*, ed. John R. Roberts (Hamden, Conn.: Archon Books, 1975), p. 426, Thomas O. Sloan disagrees with Andreasen that Satyre III is a soliloquy. On p. 430, he observes that Satyre III is addressed as an oration to "a youthful audience, to whom courage and valor must be expressed in terms of action, battle, and dueling. The speaker, it would seem, has adapted his discourse to reach young courtiers and gentlemen, the young men about London who are so prominent in Donne's other satires. Considering the amplification, particularly the comparing terms, it seems far less likely that this is discourse used by a retiring scholar to reason with himself in isolation!" Sloan's observation that Satyre III has the structure of a deliberative oration is, I believe, correct. A review of the hortatory or persuasive letters in Angel Day's collection would reveal that they follow that structure more or less as Thomas Wilson (Sloan's authority) laid it down, and Donne was in Satyre III acting the secretary who speaks for the elder statesman speaking to young men like himself.

28. Since my reading is so at odds with another recent one, which I respect for its subtlety and learning, I should at this point say a word as to why I do not find it persuasive. In "Radical Donne: 'Satire III,'" Richard Strier holds that "Donne's aim (or fantasy) in these poems [his satires] is to stand clear of the religious, political and social pressures of his world." A passing glance (which Strier does not take) at Satyre V announcing Donne's entrance into Egerton's service reveals the opposite. Again at the opening of his essay, Strier states that

during the period in which Donne must have written Satyre III he was a "religious nothing." However, Donne would have had no prospect of entering the service of the highest law enforcement official in the regime unless he had demonstrated his conformity to the regime's religious settlement. Strier goes on to claim radicalism for Donne by privileging the lines of Satyre III describing the skeptic, Phrygius, and the philosophe, Graccus, as if the list in which they appear did not devote more space to others. I agree with Strier that Donne was original and independent, but I hold that he was so as a dedicated member of the establishment. In "John Donne and the Religious Politics of the Mean" in *John Donne's Religious Imagination*, ed. Raymond-Jean Frontain and Frances M. Malpezzi (Conway, Ark.: UCA Press, 1995) pp. 45–80, Joshua Scodel provides a learned reading of lines 69–70 which more effectively than Strier's situates Satyre III within the Elizabethan discourse on faith by statute. I have learned much from Scodel's argument that Donne, with his adoption of Pyrrhonism as a skeptical mean and his conflation of religion and philosophical inquiry, opened a space for an independent subjectivity within the political condition of faith by statute. The only particular in which I disagree with his argument has to do with his claim that Satyre III's line of reasoning does not use the concept of the mean to defend the settlement. What better defense could there be than to demonstrate that freedom of conscience was possible despite inducements to idolatry and legislative prescription? Scodel claims that Donne "eventually" chose the settlement, but he provides the best argument I have ever seen that Donne had *already* chosen it by the time he wrote Satyre III. Membership in an establishment does not mean that one's subjectivity has somehow to have been "decentered." But then Scodel insists on a date of 1596 for Satyre III.

29. Francis Peck, *Desiderata curiosa*, 2 vols. (London, 1779), 1:33, 8.

30. I borrow this phrase from the title of a study of the Elizabethan Settlement: Norman L. Jones, *Faith by Statute: Parliament and the Settlement of Religion, 1559* (London: Royal Historical Society, 1982).

31. *The Letters and Life of Francis Bacon*, ed. James Spedding, 2 vols. (London: Longman, Green, Longman, and Roberts, 1861), 1:98–99.

32. Carey, *John Donne: Life, Mind, and Art*, p. 15. Carey cites Charles Hoole, *A New Discovery of the Olde Art of Teaching Schoole*, ed. E. T. Campagnac (Liverpool: University Press, 1913), p. 213.

33. For a discussion, from the Catholic point of view (and possibly Donne's), of the meaning of reconciliation as it appears in the statutes enacted by the 1581 parliament, see Philip Hughes, *The Reformation in England*, 3 vols. (London: Hollis and Carter, 1954), 3:343–344.

34. *The Execution of Justice in England by William Cecil, Baron Burghley, and A True, Sincere, and Modest Defense of English Catholics by William Allen*, ed. Robert M. Kingdon (Ithaca: Cornell University Press, 1965), p. 67.

35. John Carey considers Satyre III an "operative part" of Donne's crisis of conversion. I am indebted to his discussion of the father image. *John Donne: Life, Mind and Art*, pp. 26–30.

36. Jones, *Faith by Statute*, p. 123. Jones quotes Raphael Holinshed, *Laste Volume of the Chronicles of England, Scotlande, and Irelande* (London, 1577), p. 1801, and he notes that the original government report of the disputation in question is in the PRO, SP 12, III, fol. 163ff.

37. Jones, *Faith by Statute*, p. 145. Jones quotes from BL, Cotton Vespasian D 18, fol. 115v. In this quotation, Scot is arguing against the Bill of Uniformity. His equally eloquent arguments against the Bill of Supremacy are printed by

Claire Cross in *Royal Supremacy in the Elizabethan Church*, pp. 122–123. Scot argued that legislating in parliament for the church introduced the changeable and uncertain practices of the secular domain into spiritual matters, which should not be subject to ratification and cancellation from year to year. His argument touches closely on the causes of the malaise dealt with in Satyre III, with its focus on laws and mistresses still new like fashions.

38. John Donne, *Essays in Divinity*, ed. Augustus Jessopp (London: J. Tupling, 1855), p. 125.

39. See Carey, *John Donne: Life, Mind, and Art*, pp. 15–59 ("Apostasy" and "The Art of Apostasy"); and Strier, "John Donne Awry and Squint."

40. William Goddard, *A Mastif Whelp with other ruff-Island-lik Currs fetcht from amongst the Antipedes* (Dort[?] 1599[?]). The poem quoted is "Satire 74."

41. See Dubrow, "'No Man Is an Island,'" p. 75.

42. For a sensitive reading of Satyre IV, which attempts to explain its hallucinatory quality by referring to the tradition linking *satyr* by false etymology with *Saturn* and hence melancholy, see Nancy Mason Bradbury, "Speaker and Structure in Donne's Satyre IV," *Studies in English Literature* 25 (1985): 91–94. To Bradbury's argument, I would only add that Donne's melancholy can be attributed to the impasse of court life addressed in Satyre IV.

43. Joseph Wybarne, *The New Age of Old Names* (London, 1609), p. 113. I am indebted to M. Thomas Hester, *Kinde Pitty and Brave Scorn*, p. 152, n. 22, for this information.

44. Milgate, in Donne, *Satires, Epigrams and Verse Letters*, p. 149, refers to a letter by John Carey, "Clement Paman," in *TLS* (27 March 1959), p. 177. Carey quotes Paman's poem "The Tavern": "Oh happy Donne & Horace, you h'd but one / Devill haunted you, but me a legion."

45. Simpson, *Prose Works of John Donne*, p. 297.

46. Ibid., p. 292.

47. Ibid., pp. 293–294.

48. Ibid., pp. 291–292.

49. Milgate, in Donne, *Satires, Epigrams and Verse Letters*, p. 165.

2. Aesthetic Play

1. Simpson, *Prose Works of John Donne*, p. 125.

2. George Puttenham, *The Arte of English Poesie*, ed. Gladys Doidge Willcock and Alice Walker (Cambridge: Cambridge University Press, 1936), p. 195.

3. Sir Philip Sidney, *An Apology for Poetry; or, The Defence of Poesy*, ed. Geoffrey Shepherd (London: Thomas Nelson and Sons, 1965), p. 124.

4. See the opening sections of *S/Z* (Paris: Editions du Seuil, 1970).

5. Pierre Légouis, *Donne the Craftsman: An Essay upon the Songs and Sonnets* (1928; trans. New York: Russell and Russell, 1962), p. 50.

6. See Wesley Milgate, "Dr. Donne's Art Gallery," *Notes and Queries*, 23 July 1949, pp. 318–319.

7. Johne Donne, "To Mr. R. W." ("If, as mine is, thy life"), "To Mr. T. W." ("At once, from hence"), and "The Storme," quoted below from *The Satires, Epigrams and Verse Letters*, ed. Wesley Milgate.

8. See Nicholas Hilliard, "The Marshall Engraving and the Lothian Portrait," in Donne, *The Elegies and The Songs and Sonnets*, ed. Helen Gardner, pp. 266–270.

9. The full title of Hilliard's own work—unpublished during Donne's lifetime—on the subject of miniature painting is enough to reveal his feelings

about Haydocke's translation: *A Treatise / Concerning the Arte of Limning / writ by N. Hilliard / at the request of R. Haydocke who publisht in English a translation of / Paolo Lomazzo on Painting 1598.* This was edited by Philip Norman and published in the *Walpole Society* (1911–1912), 1:15–50. For a thorough discussion of Hilliard's indebtedness to Haydocke's Lomazzo, the reader should consult John Pope-Hennessy, "Nicholas Hilliard and Mannerist Art Theory," *Journal of the Warburg and Courtauld Institutes* 6 (1943): 89–100.

10. Hilliard, *Arte of Limning,* p. 24.

11. Giovanni Paolo Lomazzo, *A Tracte Containing the Artes of Curious Paintinge, Carvinge, and Buildinge,* trans. Richard Haydocke (Oxford: Joseph Barnes for R. H., 1598) pp. 2–3 of the Second Booke.

12. Umberto Eco's discussion of the "open work" is to be found in *The Role of the Reader* (Bloomington: Indiana University Press, 1979) in the chapter entitled "The Poetics of the Open Work."

13. Some of the terminology I use in this chapter—especially the term "imaginative expansion"—I have borrowed from John Rupert Martin's chapter on space in *Baroque* (New York: Harper and Row, 1977). Of course, the concept of imaginative expansion has its origin in Heinrich Wolfflin's *Principles of Art History: The Problem of the Development of Style in Later Art* (New York: Dover, 1979), where it is called open form.

14. John Pope-Hennessy, *The Portrait in the Renaissance* (Princeton: Princeton University Press, 1966), p. 255.

15. Hilliard, *Arte of Limning,* p. 23.

16. Frank Kermode, *English Renaissance Literature: Introductory Lectures* (London: Gray-Mills, 1974), p. 57.

17. For a recent, stone-faced reading of these lines, one should consult Stanley Fish, "Masculine Persuasive Force: Donne and Verbal Power," in *Soliciting Interpretation: Literary Theory and Seventeenth-Century English Poetry,* ed. Elizabeth D. Harvey and Katherine Maus (Chicago: University of Chicago Press, 1990), pp. 231–235. In declining to make a speaker/author distinction and ignoring conventional features of elegy, Fish reduces the mistress to "the wax tablet on which he [Donne?] inscribes his will" and claims that her turning herself into a page would leave Donne in fear that he might "betray his masculinity" by entering into an "unnatural relationship" with "him/her." For similarly humorless and anachronistic readings which turn Donne's elegies into gender skirmishes in our modern culture wars, one may consult Achsah Guibbory, "'Oh, Let Mee Not Serve So': The Politics of Love in Donne's *Elegies,*" 57 *ELH* (1990): 81–833, and Catherine Gimelli Martin, "Pygmalion's Progress in the Garden of Love, or Wit's Work is Never Donne," in *The Wit of Seventeenth-Century Poetry,* ed. Claude J. Summers and Ted-Larry Pebworth (Columbia: University of Missouri Press, 1995). The former depicts Donne as "deeply disturbed" (829) that gender hierarchies are threatened by the presence of a female monarch; the latter sees him as "objectifying, shaming, and figuratively raping" his mistress in order to cheer up a "host of phallic allies" who receive the "gift" of his "exploitation of women" (p. 80). Such readings do not stop to consider that Donne's argumentative, often angry and insulting, speakers lend their implied, female interlocutors a much greater presence to the reader's imagination and a clearer and more specific shaping influence on their poetic discourse than the glib, all-purpose, self-absorbed gallantry of so much conventional love poetry of Donne's time and even the sincere platonic compliment of sonnets like Spenser's. Whether Donne's women are accomplices in a bad game or partners in a

good one, they are generally treated as equals and certainly credited with intelligence, and this is extraordinary in a time when the Aristotelian gender hierarchy was, as Guibbory notes, a matter of received opinion.

18. Virginia Woolf, *The Second Common Reader* (New York: Harcourt Brace, 1960) p. 22. Woolf is not referring specifically to the woman of "On his Mistris," but to the female addressed in Donne's poems generally. For this quotation, I am indebted to Ilona Bell, "The Role of the Lady in Donne's *Songs and Sonnets*," *SEL* 23 (Winter 1983): 129. I subscribe to Bell's "minority perspective" that a reader can never disregard the woman's point of view in a Donne lyric, just as I agree with her distinction between the role of the lady in Donne's poems and in those of Wyatt, Sidney, and Shakespeare, where the lady seems little more than a vehicle for the speaker's issues: "Once we begin to recognize the lady's influence, Donne's poems seem less like ego-centric displays and more like attentive conversations, more like complexly shifting dialogues between a man and a woman than any lyric poems I know . . . " (116).

19. Hilliard, *Arte of Limning*, p. 23.

20. Horace, *Ars poetica*, 102–103. "If you wish me to weep, you must experience grief first yourself."

21. Rensselaer Lee, *Ut Pictura Poesis: The Humanistic Theory of Painting* (New York: Norton, 1967), p. 24.

22. Marjorie D. Lewis, "The *Adversarius* Talks Back: 'The Canonization' and Satire I," in *New Essays on Donne*, ed. Gary A. Stringer (Salzburg: Institute für Englische Sprache und Literatur, University of Salzburg, 1977), p. 1.

23. Dwight Cathcart, *Doubting Conscience: Donne and the Poetry of Moral Argument* (Ann Arbor: University of Michigan Press, 1975), pp. 13–32.

24. N. J. C. Andreasen, *John Donne: Conservative Revolutionary* (Princeton: Princeton University Press, 1967), pp. 93–94.

25. Simpson, *Prose Works of John Donne*, p. 298.

26. David Novarr, *The Disinterred Muse: Donne's Texts and Contexts* (Ithaca: Cornell University Press, 1980), pp. 60–61.

27. *Tibullus: A Commentary*, ed. Michael C. J. Putnam (Norman: University of Oklahoma Press, 1973), p. 26.

28. Robert Burton, *The Anatomy of Melancholy*, ed. Holbrook Jackson (1932; rpt. New York: Random House, 1977), p. 272.

29. A. LaBranche, "*Blanda Elegeia*: The Background to Donne's Elegies," *Modern Language Review* 61 (1966): 359. LaBranche refers in passing to Elegy VII as an "adulterous drama," but does not elaborate. Presumably, he regarded the matter as obvious. In "Donne's Elegy VII," in *English Studies Presented to R. W. Zandvoort* (Amsterdam, 1964), pp. 190–196, Eric Jacobsen also appears to take adultery for granted, and he does not elaborate either, his main concern being with the word "Inlaid" in line 22 of the poem.

30. Donne, *Elegies and The Songs and Sonnets*, p. 126.

31. Ovid, *Ars amatoria*, I, 655–656.

32. Kermode, *English Renaissance Literature*, p. 57.

33. The reference to Burton (*Anatomy*, part 3, sect. 2, memb. 4, subs. 1), with which Gardner annotates these lines, has the disadvantage that "charmes," according to the *OED*, are not connected with divination, but with the casting of spells and with bewitchment and enchantment.

34. Gardner, in *Elegies and The Songs and Sonnets*, p. 126; Smith, in *John Donne: The Complete English Poems*, ed. A. J. Smith (Harmondsworth: Penguin, 1971), p. 420.

35. John Donne, in *The Overburian Characters*, ed. W. J. Paylor (Oxford: Clarendon Press, 1936), p. 57. Donne's italics.

3. *Sprezzatura* or Transcendence: From Travesty to Palinode

1. I am particularly indebted for their discussions of this passage and others in *The Courtier* to Daniel Javitch (*Poetry and Courtliness in Renaissance England*) and Wayne A. Rebhorn (*Courtly Performances: Masking and Festivity in Castiglione's* Book of the Courtier [Detroit: Wayne State University Press, 1978]).

2. Eduardo Saccone, "*Grazia, Affettazione*, and *Sprezzatura* in *The Courtier*," in *Castiglione: The Ideal and the Real in Renaissance Culture*, ed. Robert W. Hanning and David Rosand (New Haven: Yale University Press, 1983), p. 60.

3. In "Painting and Poetry of the Cult of Elizabeth I: The Ditchley Portrait and Donne's 'Elegy: Going to Bed,'" *Studies in Philology* 93 (Winter 1996): 42–63, Albert C. Labriola makes an intriguing case that this poem satirizes the cult of Elizabeth, was written for a coterie of young men who were "iconoclastic toward endeavors that sublimated them," and contains enough fulsome praise to protect the author in case it got into the wrong hands. If, however, Labriola is correct about the object of the satire, the more fulsome the praise the more outrageous and dangerous it would be. Also a main characteristic of elegy is to turn its satire on the speaker (as in Elegy VII), and this accords well with the excited comparison this speaker makes between himself and explorers like Ralegh and Drake. His comparison makes *him* seem absurd, not the captain of the Golden Hind. Labriola's reading (like Strier's in "Radical Donne") contributes to the alienation school of Donne criticism, which this study opposes.

4. Kermode, *English Renaissance Literature*, p. 59.

5. Carey, *John Donne: Life, Mind, and Art*, p. 106.

6. Carey, for instance, sees Donne carrying on "like a disappointed careerist who has flung the world away for love, as he did when he married, and is maddened by the thought of what he has lost" (ibid., p. 43).

7. Murray Roston, *The Soul of Wit: A Study of John Donne* (Oxford: Clarendon Press, 1974), p. 160.

8. Ibid., p. 69.

9. Robert Ellrodt, "Présence et permanence de John Donne," in *John Donne*, ed. Jean-Marie Benoist (Evreux: L'Age d'Homme/Herissey, 1983), p 22. This article was written originally for Donne's tercentennial celebration in 1973.

10. Basil Willey, *The Seventeenth Century Background* (London: Chatto and Windus, 1933), p. 43.

11. With its perception that Donne may have been imitating the musical canon with his strategic repetition of the word *love*, an article by Louis I. Middleman—"Another Canon in Donne's 'Canonization,'" *English Language Notes* 22 (June 1985): 37–39—attests to the harmonious effect that Donne sought to achieve in this poem.

12. Donald Guss, *John Donne, Petrarchist* (Detroit: Wayne State University Press, 1966), p. 164.

13. Clay Hunt, *Donne's Poetry: Essays in Literary Analysis* (New Haven: Yale University Press, 1954), pp. 72–93.

14. Leone Ebreo, *Dialoghi d'amore* (Bari: Laterza, 1929), p. 57.

15. Guss, *John Donne, Petrarchist*, p. 160, and for the original, Ebreo, *Dialoghi d'amore*, p. 56.

16. Particularly helpful to me have been Albert C. Labriola, "Donne's 'The

Canonization': Its Theological Context and Its Religious Imagery," *Huntington Library Quarterly* 36 (1970–1973): 327–339; A. R. Cirillo, "The Fair Hermaphrodite: Love-Union in the Poetry of Donne and Spenser," *Studies in English Literature* 9 (1969): 61–95; Guss, *John Donne, Petrarchist*, especially the chapter "Donne's Neoplatonic Posture."

17. Andreasen, *John Donne: Conservative Revolutionary*, p. 159.

18. Richard Sleight, "John Donne: 'A Nocturnall upon S. Lucies Day, Being the Shortest Day,'" in *Interpretations: Essays on Twelve English Poems*, ed. John Wain (London: Routledge and Kegan Paul, 1955), p. 39.

19. Clarence H. Miller, "Donne's 'A Nocturnall upon S. Lucies Day' and the Nocturns of Matins," in *Essential Articles for the Study of John Donne's Poetry*, ed. John R. Roberts (Sussex: Harvester Press, 1975), p. 308.

20. Donne, *Elegies and The Songs and Sonnets*, pp. 244–251.

21. Donald L. Guss, in *John Donne, Petrarchist*, provides an ample bibliography of anthologies of Italian poetry available in England at the close of the sixteenth century. The theme of the beloved's death figures prominently in those which I have had the opportunity to inspect. Although there is nothing surprising about this, it is noteworthy that the theme is so difficult to find in English poetry of the time.

22. John A. Clair, "Donne's 'The Canonization,'" *PMLA* 80 (June 1965): 300–302.

23. G. W. H. Lampe, "Martyrdom and Inspiration," in *Suffering and Martyrdom in the New Testament*, ed. William Horbury and Brian McNeil (Cambridge: Cambridge University Press, 1981), pp. 122–123.

24. Jacobus de Voragine, *Jacobi a Voragine Legenda aurea vulgo historia lombardica dicta*, ed. J. G. Theodor Graesse (Osnabruck: Otto Zeller Verlag, 1969; rpt. of 1890 edition), p. 31.

25. Quoted from Bald, *John Donne: A Life*, p. 232.

26. Edgar Hill Duncan, "Donne's Alchemical Figures," *ELH* 9 (1942): 282, gives a lucid explanation of the alchemical metaphor: "Before looking at these steps of descent to quintessential nothingness, we need to consider the question of how *love* can be blamed with the poet's sad state. Here the crux of the subtlety of the poem seems to lie. The answer is, I believe, something like this: By his surrender to the power of love, the lover (i.e., the poet) has put himself into the position of being affected by the accidents of love. It is only because he loved that absence from his mistress, quarrels with her, even her death, could affect him. Because he loved, these things affected him very much; they became the determiners of his existence as a happy, loving being. It is poetically just, therefore, that he attribute these accidents, which love did not cause but which the fact of his love had endowed with meaning and tragedy for him, to love itself. And it is also poetically just for the lover to identify himself with the creature, subject to the effect of these accidents, he has been made by love. So, love is the alchemist, and the accidents (to which the poet's submission to love had given the power of determining his happiness, his very being) are materials from which and by which he (the poet) has been made the quintessence of nothingness" (italics in original). I differ from Duncan only in that the speaker, in my reading, is blaming, not love, but his own imagination under the influence of love, for making the various "accidents" of his erotic relationship "the determiners of his existence."

27. *The Sermons of John Donne*, ed. George R. Potter and Evelyn M. Simpson, 10 vols. (Berkeley: University of California Press, 1962), 3:360.

28. Ibid., 3:354.

29. Ibid., 3:365.

30. Ibid., 4:109.

31. *St. Chrysostom: Homilies on the Gospel of St. Matthew*, trans. Rev. Sir George Prevost (Grand Rapids: Wm. B. Erdmans, 1956), p. 223.

4. Discerning Insincerity

1. Joan Kelly, "Did Women Have a Renaissance?" in *Becoming Visible: Women in European History*, ed. Renate Bridenthal and Claudia Koontz (Boston: Houghton Mifflin, 1977), p. 159.

2. In Julia Cartwright, *Baldassare Castiglione, the Perfect Courtier, His Life and Letters, 1478–1529*, 2 vols. (New York: Dutton, 1908) 1: 308–309.

3. Dwight Cathcart's *Doubting Conscience: Donne and the Poetry of Moral Argument* (Ann Arbor: University of Michigan Press, 1975) is one of the most useful and informative books ever written about Donne's poetry because it focuses so sharply on the issue of casuistry, on the eagerness of the poems' speakers to prove that they are the exception to the rule. The only addition I would make to Cathcart's thesis is that the court environment—from what we know of it in Castiglione—made the mastery of casuistical argument a matter of self-preservation for courtiers.

4. I believe that it is precisely this crosscutting, which is so much at the heart of the poem, that causes Gardner to waver about the sincerity of Donne's belief in ecstasy. She finds it necessary to argue, despite a good deal of external and internal evidence (of which she is quite aware), that Donne is serious, when it is precisely the indeterminacy of this question of the speaker's sincerity and the speaker's awareness of its indeterminacy that lends the poem its peculiar energy. Helen Gardner, "The Argument of 'The Ecstasy,'" in *Elizabethan and Jacobean Studies: Presented to Frank Percy Wilson in Honour of His Seventieth Birthday*, ed. Herbert Davis and Helen Gardner (Oxford: Clarendon Press, 1959), pp. 279–306.

5. As indebted as I am to David Novarr ("'The Exstasie': Donne's Address on the States of the Union," in *The Disinterred Muse*, pp. 17–39), I think that it is far from begging the question to ask if someone is being led up the garden path by the speaker's lecture on love. The speaker's very determination to prove the unprovable derives from his own disconcerting awareness that his sincerity can rightly be questioned by his beloved and cannot be safely vouched for even, or perhaps especially, by himself.

6. C. S. Lewis's "Donne and Love Poetry in the Seventeenth Century" and Joan Bennett's "The Love Poetry of John Donne, A Reply to Mr. C. S. Lewis" are printed in *Seventeenth Century Studies Presented to Sir Herbert Grierson* (Oxford: Clarendon Press, 1938). Helen Gardner's discussion of "Aire and Angels" is to be found in Gardner, *The Business of Criticism* (Oxford: Clarendon Press, 1959), pp. 65–75. A. J. Smith's "New Bearings in Donne: 'Aire and Angels'" is to be found *John Donne: A Collection of Critical Essays*, ed. Helen Gardner (Englewood Cliffs, N.J.: Prentice-Hall, 1962), and Wesley Milgate's "'Aire and Angels' and the Discrimination of Experience" in *Just So Much Honor: Essays Commemorating the Four-Hundredth Anniversary of the Birth of John Donne*, ed. P. A. Fiore (University Park: Pennsylvania State University Press, 1972). Roughly speaking, Lewis and Bennett read the poem as a dramatic lyric, while Gardner, Smith, and Milgate regard it as a meditation or a lecture on love. One notable essay occupies both camps: Katherine Maus, "Angel Imagery and Neoplatonic Love in Donne's 'Aire and Angels,'" *Seventeenth Century News* 35 (Winter 1977): 106–111. My own conviction is, of course, that the poem is a dramatic

lyric, but I have tried to benefit from the findings of the opposing camp, especially from Milgate's. I have also relied heavily on the annotations of Theodore Redpath in *The Songs and Sonets of John Donne* (London: Methuen, 1956).

7. Richard Hooker, *The Laws of Ecclesiastical Polity, Books I–IV,* ed. Henry Morley (London: G. Routledge, 1888), p. 70.

8. F. R. Leavis, *Revaluation: Tradition and Development in English Poetry* (London: Chatto and Windus, 1936), p. 12.

9. St. Thomas Aquinas, *Summa theologiae,* vol. 9: *Angels* (Ia, 50–64), a bilingual text, trans. and ed. Kenelm Foster, O.P. (Cambridge: Blackfriars, 1968), p. 37.

10. Yeats to Sir Herbert Grierson; letter reprinted in *Discussions of John Donne,* ed. Frank Kermode (Boston: Heath, 1962), p. 41.

11. Murray Roston, *The Soul of Wit* (Oxford: Clarendon Press, 1974), pp. 69, 109–110.

12. It would be a bad day for literary criticism if a disgruntled undergraduate ever took it into her or his head to edit an anthology of "flea" criticism. In *John Donne and the Rhetorics of Renaissance Discourse* (Columbia: University of Missouri Press, 1991), James S. Baumlin claims that the speaker's "arguments resist a reader's resistance, refusing to deconstruct" (p. 244). It is difficult, however, to understand what this means unless Baumlin regards the reader as literally having assumed the posture of the *puella* in bed with the speaker and lost, as if it were virginity, any sense of the ironic. Readers of "The Flea" may regard the young woman as seduced by the speaker's arguments without being seduced themselves. The young woman of this poem is not a mental giant. In "Receiving a Sexual Sacrament: 'The Flea' as Profane Eucharist," in *John Donne's Religious Imagination,* ed. Raymond-Jean Frontain and Frances M. Malpezzi (Conway, Ark.: UCA Press, 1995), pp. 81–95, Theresa M. DiPasquale offers, based on biographical conjecture, the theory that "The Flea" parallels the type of seduction to which Ann More was subjected. DiPasquale's reading is ingenious, but loses sight—with its absorption in eucharistic symbolism—of the poem's central image—a squalid flea and a rumpled bed. The eucharistic symbolism (if it actually exists and is not a figment of the exegetic imagination) works best if the speaker is taken to be saying that the young woman's reification of the sign (the flea) is papist hypocrisy grounded in fear and superstition, not faith or honor. Then the speaker has exposed her for the frightened sensualist that she is and urges her to become along with himself a courageous libertine. If faith and honor had ever been much on her mind, she would not have taken his argument—that the flea represents a precontract between them—seriously enough even to take the moment that she does to crush the flea. She would have walked out of the room. Poems like "Air and Angels" and "The Ecstasy" probably offer better examples of the type of persuasions to which Ann More responded with ardor.

13. Gardner in her notes to this poem, and Roston, *Soul of Wit,* p. 110. My source for medical theory of the time is the same as Roston's: D. C. Allen, "John Donne's Knowledge of Renaissance Medicine," *JEGP* 42 (1943): 334.

14. Légouis, *Donne the Craftsman,* p. 76.

15. Henri Peyre, *Literature and Sincerity* (New Haven: Yale University Press, 1963), pp. 32–33.

16. Lionel Trilling, *Sincerity and Authenticity* (Cambridge, Mass.: Harvard University Press, 1972), p. 58.

17. *Lord Weary's Castle* (New York: Harcourt Brace, 1946), p. 50.

18. Ibid., pp. 13–16.

19. John Marston, *The Scourge of Villanie*, ed. G. B. Harrison (New York: Dutton, 1925), p. 57.

20. Trilling, *Sincerity and Authenticity*, p. 16.

Conclusion

1. William Empson's comments on "A Valediction: of Weeping" are to be found in *Seven Types of Ambiguity*, rev. ed. (London: Chatto and Windus, 1947). Rosemond Tuve addresses the poem in "Imagery and Logic: Ramus and Metaphysical Poetics," *Journal of the History of Ideas* 3 (October 1942): 388–391.

2. Sir Thomas Browne, *Religio Medici and Other Works*, ed. L. C. Martin (Oxford: Clarendon Press, 1964), p. 122. The quotation is, of course, from *Hydriotaphia*.

3. Fredric Jameson, *The Political Unconscious: Narrative as a Socially Symbolic Act* (Ithaca: Cornell University Press, 1981), pp. 77–80.

4. Claude Lévi-Strauss, *Tristes tropiques*, trans. John Russell (New York: Atheneum, 1971), pp. 60–80.

5. See Wollman, "'Press and the Fire,'" for an excellent account of Donne's concern over being misinterpreted.

INDEX

Peter DeSa Wiggins
is Professor of English at
The College of William and Mary.
He is the author of
*Figures in Ariosto's Tapestry: Character and
Design in the "Orlando Furioso."*